Interpreting the Qur'ān

Debates among Muslims over the conception of the authority of the Qur'ān underlie much of what is read about Islam in the popular media these days. This book by Abdullah Saeed will add a new voice to those debates and, as its impact is felt, broaden the popular conception of what Islam is all about today.

Andrew Rippin, University of Victoria, Canada

How is the Qur'ān – central to all Muslim societies – to be understood today in order to meet the needs of these societies? Abdullah Saeed, a distinguished Muslim scholar, explores the interpretation of the ethico-legal content of the Qur'ān, whilst taking into consideration the changing nature of the modern world.

Saeed explores the current debates surrounding the interpretation of the Qur'ān, and their impact on contemporary understanding of this sacred text. As he attempts to determine the text's relevance to modern issues without compromising the overall framework of the Qur'ān and its core beliefs and practices, he proposes a fresh approach, which takes into account the historical and contemporary contexts of interpretation.

This book is likely to inspire healthy debate and appeal to a generation of students and scholars seeking a contemporary approach to the interpretation of the Qur'ānic text.

Abdullah Saeed is the Sultan of Oman Professor of Arab and Islamic Studies and the Director of the Centre for the Study of Contemporary Islam at the University of Melbourne, Australia. He has written widely on Islam and is the author and editor of a number of books, including *Approaches to Qur'ān in Contemporary Indonesia* (2005), *Freedom of Religion, Apostasy and Islam* (co-author, 2004), *Islam and Political Legitimacy* (2003), *Islam in Australia* (2003) and *Islamic Banking and Interest* (1996).

Interpreting the Qurʾān

Towards a contemporary approach

Abdullah Saeed

Routledge
Taylor & Francis Group
LONDON AND NEW YORK

First published 2006
by Routledge
2 Park Square, Milton Park, Abingdon, Oxon OX14 4RN

Simultaneously published in the USA and Canada
by Routledge
270 Madison Ave, New York NY 10016

Routledge is an imprint of the Taylor & Francis Group

Typeset in Sabon by
Florence Production Ltd, Stoodleigh, Devon
Printed and bound in Great Britain by
Antony Rowe Ltd, Chippenham, Wiltshire

British Library Cataloguing in Publication Data
A catalogue record for this book is available from the British Library

Library of Congress Cataloging in Publication Data
Saeed, Abdullah.
Interpreting the Qur'an: towards a contemporary approach/Abdullah Saeed. – 1st ed.
p. cm.
Includes bibliographical references and index.
1. Koran – Hermeneutics. 2. Koran – Criticism, interpretation, etc.
I. Title
BP130.2.S193 2005
2997.1'226'01 – dc22 2004029204

ISBN 0–415–36537–6 (hbk)
ISBN 0–415–36538–4 (pbk)

For Rasheeda and Isaam

Contents

Acknowledgements

Many people have contributed to the research, writing and publication of this book. In particular I would like to express my gratitude to Andrew Rippin, who read the manuscript and provided critical comments for revising it and strongly encouraged me to publish it; to Lesley Riddle of Routledge for her encouragement and support for the publication of the book; to Gemma Dunn and Diana Chambers for editorial support; to my colleagues and friends, Jacky Angus, Redha Ameur, Abdul Ghafoor Abdul Raheem, Riyad Asvat and Rachel Woodlock, for their comments and feedback; to Donna Williams for her reading and contribution to the polishing of the manuscript; to Andy Fuller for his critical look at the manuscript and his comments as well as his research assistance and help in the final preparation of the manuscript; to the *Journal of Qur'anic Studies* for permission to publish a revised version of the article 'Rethinking "Revelation"' (1999) which forms Chapter 3 of this book; and finally to my wife Rasheeda and son Isaam who have supported me without any complaints, as usual.

Foreword

The challenges that face the modern religious thinker are both daunting and profound. Two assumptions are generally made: that the fundamental truths of religion itself (however they are defined) are of value to humanity and that the relevance of religion to human concerns of today must at all costs be demonstrated. The stumbling block for many people seems to be the structures of traditional religious authority that are so closely tied to the text of scripture in Judaism, Christianity and Islam; questions that the twenty-first century poses so frequently thus appear to strike at the heart of religion itself as it has conventionally been conceived. This is true whether the discussion is about gay ministers in Christian churches, definitions of Jewish descent, or Muslim marriage to multiple wives. How are the deeply felt moral principles of today to be reconciled with a text of scripture that has always been understood in ways that challenge those emerging and evolving contemporary positions?

When Muslims deal with the text of the Qur'ān, understood to be literally the 'Word of God', the issue arises in many ways, some of which certainly prove to be more pressing morally than others. Within the Muslim world, the matter first arose in recent times when the question of the relationship between the text and history was discussed. How was the text of the Qur'ān to be reconciled with older historical sources (e.g. the Bible) that recount the 'facts' differently? Such discussions invoked the principles of the historical-critical method and were, for many people, reasonably well accommodated within the strictures of Muslim faith. That is, the authority of the text was relocated through a process of interpretation so that it resided, for example, in the moral vision of Islam as a whole where the details of history do not matter, but only the moral aims of the story remain relevant. These discussions raised the difficult issue of how to reconcile modern intellectual attitudes to the text of scripture and did so by dealing with concerns that, certainly by the measure of more contemporary debates, could not be said to raise the more pressing and practical issues of law and morality.

It is the problem of how to deal with the explicit moral commands of the Qur'ān that has undoubtedly created the greatest controversy and difficulty for the modern Muslim community. These discussions have become a place where academics play a significant role in pushing the community to face the issues and undertake open debate. Approaches to these questions, using methods that were first tried out in biblical studies especially, show how the age-old binary of 'Western' scholarship versus 'Muslim' views is rapidly breaking down. The work of Fazlur Rahman, especially his *Major Themes of the Qur'ān* (1980), was fundamental in both shaping the discussion and bridging that gap. The current state of that process may be seen today in a collected work such as the *Encyclopaedia of the Qur'ān* (2001–2005) in which the many voices of scholarship come together in one catholic framework (whether such exists within a unified and well-enunciated epistemological vision is another matter).

The book that is presented here, written by Abdullah Saeed, is another manifestation of this tendency, and is a particularly striking one. Using the tools of historical-critical scholarship to analyse the resources of the Muslim tradition, Saeed sets forth a model of Qur'ānic interpretation that is solidly scholarly and, at the same time, relevant to the central concerns of the Muslim community. The knowledge of the past provided by scholarly tools allows for interpretations to be put forth that have a solid grounding in a firmly understood and well-documented Muslim world view. This respect for that past and the willingness to learn from it are the central marks of the approach and are what put it at such a distance from studies that are often termed Salafī or 'fundamentalist' with their rhetorical denial of the value of the cumulative development of the community through history. Gone, too, is the customary alibi of scholarship that pretends that the work undertaken by academics is just 'there', to be accepted or rejected by the Muslim community with no value judgement or even concern attached to the impact of the study.

Debates among Muslims over the conception of the authority of the Qur'ān underlie much of what is read about Islam in the popular media these days. This book by Abdullah Saeed will add a new voice to those debates and, as its impact is felt, will broaden the popular conception of what Islam is all about today. In addition, as a result of this work, the relevance of scholarly investigations into Muslim heritage will become evident, given the way both the potential creativity and the realized constraints (and subsequent restraints) of classical thought become clearer. These are conversations in which the more of us who participate – as women and men interested in and concerned with the human condition – the better for broadening the basis of our common understanding and shared goals for the future of human existence.

Andrew Rippin, University of Victoria, Canada

Chapter 1

Introduction

This book is about the interpretation of one particular type of Qur'ānic texts: the texts that are considered ethico-legal in nature and are represented in the Qur'ān's beliefs, rulings, laws, commandments, prohibitions and instructions.[1] Examples of such ethico-legal content include belief in God, prophets and life after death; regulations related to marriage, divorce and inheritance; what is permitted and prohibited; commandments relating to fasting, spending, jihad and *ḥudūd*; prohibitions related to theft, dealing with non-Muslims; instructions relating to etiquette, inter-faith relations and governance. The book is not intended as a manual providing a step-by-step guide to interpreting such texts, even though it contains useful ideas for their interpretation. Rather, it is an argument for releasing the ethico-legal verses from the legalistic-literalistic approach[2] that has been the hallmark of their interpretation from the post-formative period of Islamic law[3] to the modern period in both exegesis (*tafsīr*) and law (*fiqh*). The book is, first and foremost, a justification for using a different approach to the interpretation of the ethico-legal texts. I will refer to this approach as 'Contextualist'.[4] The thrust of my argument, therefore, is towards a more flexible approach to interpretation of these texts by taking into consideration both the socio-historical context of the Qur'ān at the time of revelation in the first/seventh century and the contemporary concerns and needs of Muslims today. My main interest is how the meaning of the Qur'ān can be related to the life of the Muslim, in a sense its application to day-to-day practicalities in different times, circumstances and places, particularly as it relates to the concerns and needs of the modern period.

Historically, Muslim exegetes and jurists often relied on linguistic criteria only to interpret the ethico-legal content and to determine whether a particular ruling in the Qur'ān is to be universally applicable or not. In this, the question of social and historical context in which the ruling was given at the time of the revelation of the Qur'ān was seen as irrelevant or unimportant, except in rare cases. In writing this book, I am emphasizing that this social and historical context of the Qur'ān needs to be taken into account with the linguistic criteria to provide a fuller meaning of the Qur'ān that is relevant to changing needs and circumstances of Muslims.

A question that arises is, 'What are these concerns and needs that justify embarking on the approach to the Qur'ān I am suggesting?'. One could, of course, argue that such concerns and needs are transient and subjective, and that Qur'ānic interpretation should not be linked to such concerns and needs. However, my position is that the epoch making changes in the world over the past 150 years have affected Muslims as well as non-Muslims and altered significantly how we see the world. These changes are enormous: globalization, migration, scientific and technological revolutions, space exploration, archaeological discoveries, evolution and genetics, public education and literacy, to name a few. We must add to this an increased understanding of the dignity of the human person, greater inter-faith interaction, the emergence of nation-states (and the concept of equal citizenship) and gender equality. These changed perceptions and institutional structures have had repercussions for law and governance. Moreover, today the destiny of individuals and communities is bound with that of other people who may or may not share their beliefs, values, norms and understandings. In short, the contemporary world is vastly changed from the one our forefathers knew. This requires effort from people of all faiths to look at how their world views, traditions, teachings and rules should guide believers today.

One of the clearest illustrations of the need to rethink the interpretation of the ethico-legal content of the Qur'ān can be found in the predicament of 'Islamic law' represented in *fiqh* (which essentially is the result of the interpretation of the ethico-legal content of the Qur'ān and other sources such as sunnah). The reality is that many of the interpretations that functioned as law in the pre-modern period are no longer considered viable, except by a relatively small number of Muslims. Only in essential beliefs, certain ethical and moral norms, clearly spelt-out *ḥalāl* (permissible) and *ḥarām* (prohibited) guidelines and limited areas of family law is there consistent practice and tradition. Even in the stricter, more conservative Muslim countries, such as Saudi Arabia, their legal systems are significantly different from pre-modern legal regimes that were based on *fiqh* rules. Their laws and legal systems incorporate many features that would be alien to pre-modern Islamic legal systems, such as institutional structures that are prefaced on European court structures. More broadly, the nation-state exists without reference to Islamic sources or notions. Much of the rest of Islamic law as it exists in standard *fiqh* works is now generally ignored in most of today's Muslim societies. In the area of prescribed punishments *ḥudūd*, Islamic law is not implemented fully anywhere in the Muslim world and those who call for it are increasingly opposed by an apparent majority of Muslims. Even in the area of family law, the emphasis on gender equality means that new statutes are being developed by almost all Muslim majority countries to protect women's rights more adequately. Those who seek to retain gender *inequality* as part of their social and political systems are adhering to pre-modern interpretations in the face of inexorable change. This demonstrates that much of the earlier interpretations of the ethico-legal content of the Qur'ān that exist in *fiqh* are no longer serving the needs of Muslims today. Therefore, unless the issue of refocusing the interpretation of the Qur'ān on contemporary circumstances is addressed, the risk is that the ethico-legal content of the Qur'ān will gradually become ignored, or simply irrelevant, and Muslims will lose their connection to the Qur'ān in a significant way.

Among Muslims, three broad approaches may be identified in relation to the interpretation of ethico-legal content of the Qur'ān in the modern period: Textualist, Semi-textualist and Contextualist. This classification is based on the degree to which the interpreters (1) rely on just the linguistic criteria to determine the meaning of the text, and (2) take into account the socio-historical context of the Qur'ān as well as the contemporary context of today.

Textualists argue for a strict following of the text and adopt a literalistic approach to the text. For Textualists, it is the Qur'ān that should guide Muslims, rather than any so-called modern 'needs'. They consider the meaning of the Qur'ān to be fixed and universal in its application. For instance, if the Qur'ān says that a man may marry four wives, then this should apply forever, without any need to consider the socio-historical context in which this text was 'revealed'. For them, why the Qur'ān allowed a man to marry four wives in the first/seventh-century Hijaz is not important. The clearest examples of Textualists are found today among those referred to as Traditionalists and Salafīs.

Semi-textualists essentially follow the Textualists as far as linguistic emphasis and ignoring of the socio-historical context are concerned, but they package the ethico-legal content in a somewhat 'modern' idiom, often within an apologetic discourse. Usually they are involved with various offshoots of modern neo-revivalist movements, such as the Muslim Brotherhood (Egypt) and Jamā'at Islamī (Indian subcontinent), as well as a significant section of the modernists.[5]

Those I refer to as Contextualists emphasize the socio-historical context of the ethico-legal content of the Qur'ān and of its subsequent interpretations. They argue for understanding the ethico-legal content in the light of the political, social, historical, cultural and economic contexts in which this content was revealed, interpreted and applied. Thus they argue for a high degree of freedom for the modern Muslim scholar in determining what is mutable (changeable) and immutable (unchangeable) in the area of ethico-legal content. Contextualists are found among those Fazlur Rahman called neo-modernists as well as Ijtihādīs, the so-called 'progressive' Muslims and more generally 'liberal' Muslim thinkers today.[6]

The methodological innovations introduced by thinkers such as Fazlur Rahman to resolve the problem of interpretation of ethico-legal texts are pertinent to this debate.[7] They represent an important step in relating the Qur'ānic text to the contemporary concerns and needs of Muslim societies. Rahman relies heavily on understanding the socio-historical context of the revelation, at a macro level, and then relating it to a particular need of the modern period. In this, he draws on the idea of the 'prophetic spirit' or, in other words, seeks to imagine how the Prophet might act were he living in these times. In doing so, Rahman does not adopt an analogical model, so common in *fiqh*, in which the interpreter looks at the superficial aspects of two different situations, one being the precedent and the other being the contemporary situation. Then, based on any similarities between the two situations, the interpreter attempts to project the ruling or value associated with the precedent on to the modern one. Rahman is arguing for something more substantial – one that has not, so far, been generally accepted in the interpretation of the Qur'ān or in *fiqh*.

In line with the ideas advocated by Rahman and other Contextualists, I argue that the interpretation of the ethico-legal content of the Qur'ān needs to take social change into account in order to sustain the close relationship between the Qur'ān and the Muslim today. The Qur'ānic interpretation up to now, which has been to a large extent philological, needs to give way to a more sociological, axiological and anthropological exegesis in order to relate it to the contemporary needs of Muslims today.[8] However, a search for acceptable methods in the modern period should not neglect the classical Islamic exegetical tradition entirely. On the contrary, we should benefit from the tradition and be guided by it where possible without necessarily being bound by all its detail. Contemporary scholars must be informed about the ways in which the texts have been interpreted throughout history. That understanding can be helpful in our formulation of new interpretations in the light of new circumstances and challenges.

Interpretation – unlike revelation – is a human endeavour. Thus, one could argue that there is nothing sacred about the personal interpretation given to a verse even by a Companion of the Prophet, or by a Successor or by early imams. Their understandings, like ours, are limited by context and culture and may or may not be relevant outside *their* culture, *their* context. Muslim scholars today need to explore the tradition in the light of contemporary experience, including modern knowledge and methods of research. They should benefit from rational methods, historical research and critical scholarship as developed in a range of fields of scholarly research. The methodologies, terminologies and concepts provided by the classical scholars of Qur'ānic exegesis are not permanently relevant or invariably applicable as the sole source of understanding the Qur'ān.

I am writing this as a Muslim – as a person who believes that the

Qur'ān is the revelation of the will of God to the Prophet Muḥammad. I also take the view that the Qur'ān we have today is a historically authentic text that contains the revelations that Prophet Muḥammad received over a 22-year period, collected by Muslims who were witnesses to these revelations in the immediate aftermath of the Prophet Muḥammad's death in 11/632. My argument in this book should not be taken to mean that I am rejecting the heritage of *tafsīr* or *fiqh*. I believe that we need to respect that heritage, learn from it and use what is relevant and beneficial to our contemporary concerns. I do not accept the idea that somehow Muslims in the past reached the zenith of intellectual achievement in the area of *tafsīr* or *fiqh*. In my view, Muslims are engaged in a continuous process of refinement, improvement, change and addition to the existing body of knowledge. This also means that new approaches will be continuously developed as time passes and as the needs of the community change. Our era is one of major upheaval and technological and social change that requires significant intellectual contributions to relate the meaning of the Qur'ān to the needs and concerns of Muslims today. In this book I hope readers will find some useful ideas that they will in turn challenge, refine and question.

One reason why this project is important is that there is a strongly felt need among Muslims to make the Qur'ānic teachings, in particular their ethico-legal content, relevant to the needs of Muslims today, as these have greatly changed from those of the past. For many Muslims, some of the Qur'ānic teachings in this area, if taken literally, may appear ancient and archaic and not very relevant to contemporary concerns and situations. An appropriate methodological framework is therefore needed to translate this ethico-legal content in a meaningful manner for a Muslim today.

There are, of course, Muslims who strongly believe that all of the Qur'ānic instructions should be taken literally and put into practice and who therefore find it difficult to acknowledge the historical nature of the Qur'ānic revelation. They accept the view that, because the Qur'ān is the Word of God, whatever it contains (even if taken literally) cannot fail to be relevant to the needs of *all* societies for *all* times and *all* places. They do not see any reason for rereading any part of the Qur'ānic text. They argue that Muslims must follow it to the letter, whatever the circumstances. Even though this superficially attractive and simplistic option is highly problematic, there are large numbers of Muslims who argue for it.

In order to relate the ethico-legal content of the Qur'ān to the concerns and needs of the modern period, Muslim scholars and thinkers who believe that such a project is needed and necessary have adopted several approaches. All of these appear to bypass the literalistic and legalistic bent of the classical *tafsīr* tradition as far as ethico-legal texts are concerned. This includes the 'back to the principles' approach advocated by Ghulam Ahmad Parvez,[9] rationalist interpretations of modernist scholars, and 'spirit of the Qur'ān'-based approaches advocated by Fazlur Rahman.[10] Many more ideas have been advanced by Mohammed Arkoun,[11] Farid Esack[12] and Khaled Abou El Fadl.[13] All these are part of a promising trend in the interpretation of the ethico-legal content of the Qur'ān in the modern period, that could be referred to as 'Contextualist'. Though they may not use this label, specific features of the approach are observable in the undertakings of these and an increasing number of other Muslim scholars and thinkers today.

This book comprises 12 chapters. The first is the Introduction. Chapter 2 explores the context in which rethinking of the interpretation of the ethico-legal content of the Qur'ān is taking place today. It presents a brief overview of the development of interpretation of the Qur'ān from the earliest to the modern period. It then highlights a range of issues that are helpful to understand the context of the debates on the interpretation of the ethico-legal content today.

Chapter 3 explores the traditional understanding of 'revelation' and emphasizes that accepting this understanding does not necessarily preclude a Contextualist reading of the revelation. It also presents an alternative model of revelation.

Chapter 4 deals with interpretation based on tradition and highlights interpretation of the Qur'ān by the Qur'ān as well as by the Prophet, the Companions and the Successors. It then examines the development of what I call 'Textualist' interpretation, which adopted a strictly literalistic and legalistic approach.

Chapter 5 explores the question of interpretation based on reason, the views of the opponents of this approach and their arguments, as well as the views of the proponents and their reasoning. The chapter highlights the Contextualists' view that interpretation based on reason is essential.

Chapter 6 shows the flexibility in *reading* the Qur'ānic text, which the tradition maintains was given in the prophetic period. It suggests that, if this flexibility is provided in reading the actual text, the very Word of God, one could argue that the same flexibility should be available in the case of understanding and interpreting the Word of God.

Chapter 7 addresses the topic of abrogation (*naskh*) and argues that *naskh* provides a justification for reinterpreting some of the ethico-legal texts in line with the changing needs of Muslims. By changing ethico-legal rulings of the Qur'ān to suit different situations of Muslims during the Prophet's time, which the theory of abrogation suggests, God appears to be providing the community with an important tool with which it can make the Qur'ān relevant to people's needs and circumstances.

Chapter 8 provides examples of three types of text in the Qur'ān. It argues that, if it can be shown that a substantial part of the Qur'ānic text is interpreted and explained in an 'approximate' fashion, applying this notion to the ethico-legal content is not such a strange argument after all.

Chapter 9 deals with the question of 'meaning'. It focuses on a number of issues that are important for a meaningful and relevant interpretation of the ethico-legal content in the modern period. It highlights that complete objectivity in understanding and interpreting the text is impossible and that meaning is highly complex.

Chapter 10 explores the notion of 'socio-historical context' of the Qur'ān and argues that this context must be taken into account to arrive at a meaningful interpretation of the ethico-legal content.

Chapter 11 provides a framework for thinking about the ethico-legal content of the Qur'ān – in particular, how one can classify the ethico-legal rulings and texts, the importance of each category, and the degree of obligation on the Muslim. The chapter identifies five levels of Qur'ānic values: obligatory, fundamental, protectional, implementational and instructional. The chapter addresses each level, with particular focus on the instructional values, which seem the most problematic as far as mutability and immutability are concerned.

In Chapter 12, the Epilogue, I present the key aspects of the argument presented in the book and suggest a basic model for interpretation of the ethico-legal texts based on the discussions in the book.

In summary, this book attempts to provide a foundation and argument for the validity of a Contextualist approach and to outline a range of methodological principles. In this, it relies on existing interpretations of the ethico-legal content by a variety of Muslim scholars today and derives from those interpretations the necessary principles and ideas relevant to a Contextualist approach. Its aim is to propose ideas and stimulate discussion. It is the prerogative of the Muslim community to explore, accept, modify or even reject the ideas.

Note on dates and transliteration

Some conventions may be noted here. Where double dates are given in the form of 1/622, the first figure refers to the Muslim calendar and the second to the Christian. When only one date is given, it usually refers to the Christian calendar. With regard to Arabic terms, on the whole the full transliteration has been used, including diacritics and macrons. With a few exceptions, this transliteration follows the system adopted by the *Encyclopaedia of Islam*.

Chapter 2

The context of the debate on interpretation

Muslims can be divided into three broad categories as far as their responses to the challenges posed to Islam by modern ideas, institutions and values are concerned. The first category sees no need to change 14 centuries of tradition and regards any 'modernization' of the understanding of religion as tantamount to a mortal blow against Islam. The second feels that opposition to change is unwise and counterproductive if Muslims are to be active participants in the modern world. They present Islam in a way that suits people living in the modern period, but do not go as far as significantly altering traditionally held Islamic ideas, institutions and values. The third category wants to re-present Islam by questioning key aspects of the tradition, ignoring what is not relevant to the modern period, while emphasizing what *is* relevant and attempting to remain faithful to the immutable Qur'ānic ethos, objectives and values.[1]

Perhaps the most important issue for Muslims is how a Muslim of the twenty-first century should relate to the Qur'ān – the Holy Scripture of Muslims and the most important text on which Islam is based. Since the Qur'ān, for Muslims, is the Word of God and remains the prime source of authority for Islam's ethical and legal systems, Muslims make consistent efforts to relate it to their contemporary concerns and needs. In the process, many questions are asked that are as challenging as their answers. Such questioning should be considered an essential part of modern Islamic thought and an important positive contribution that may bear fruit in time. The fact that difficult questions are being asked now provides a strong basis for further work in this area. This chapter explores first the development of the *tafsīr* tradition and then the context in which rethinking of the interpretation of the ethico-legal content of the Qur'ān is taking place today. It is a stepping stone to a more detailed discussion in the rest of the book.

Overview of the classical *tafsīr* tradition[2]

A rudimentary *tafsīr* tradition began to emerge during the Prophet Muḥammad's time. The Qur'ān says that one of the functions of the Prophet was to explain the Qur'ān (16:44). However, there is debate as to whether the Prophet ever provided explanations for the entire Qur'ān. Little of the Prophet's own interpretation of the Qur'ān was recorded, and much of this exists only in a form that we might call 'practical exegesis'.[3] After his death, the Companions played their role in explaining and interpreting the Qur'ān. Even though the number of Companions was large, only a few reportedly contributed directly to Qur'ānic exegesis. They included the first four Rāshidūn caliphs (11–40/632–660) (Abū Bakr, 'Umar, 'Uthmān and 'Alī) as well as 'Abd Allah b. Mas'ūd, who settled in Iraq, Ubay b. Ka'b in Medina, 'Abd Allah b. 'Abbās in Mecca and Zayd b. Thābit in Medina.[4]

The Companions who engaged in exegesis had several sources for understanding and interpreting the Qur'ān: parts of the Qur'ānic text that explained other parts; information received from the Prophet, both oral and praxis; and their own understanding of what the Qur'ānic text meant. They were also familiar with the language of the Qur'ān, the overall social context of the revelation, the Prophet's ways of thinking, and the norms, values and customs of the Arabs, all of which provided them with a unique basis for making sense of the Qur'ānic text within the overall framework of the emerging 'established practice' of the Muslim community.

The need for interpretation of the Qur'ān increased with the second generation of Muslims, known as 'Successors'[5] (*tābi'ūn*), who were a more heterogeneous group. They included children of the Companions brought up within the new religious (Islamic) environment, and Arabic-speaking and non-Arabic-speaking converts to Islam. Also, the wider the gap between their era and the time of the Prophet, the stronger the need to address questions of exegesis of the Qur'ān. With the Successors based in locations such as Medina, Mecca and the area now known as Iraq, these locations began to develop proto-traditions of local exegesis around the teachings of the respective Companions residing there.

Other events led to the further development of exegesis: the political conflicts and their associated theological debates that raged after the death of the Prophet and in the wake of the assassination of 'Uthmān, the third caliph, in 35/656; the interest of popular preachers and storytellers in the Qur'ānic narratives; and the development of ḥadīth and Arabic linguistics and literature as new disciplines. A number of other disciplines also began to emerge during the late Umayyad and early Abbasid periods (second/eighth century) and provided further support to the emerging tradition of *tafsīr*. These included *qirā'āt* (reading and recitation of the Qur'ān), which explored the ways in which the Qur'ān could be recited, and its legitimate recitations, their sources, and chains of transmission.

The earliest forms of *tafsīr* are represented by (a) brief explanations of words or phrases in the Qur'ān that were unclear, uncommon or ambiguous; (b) explanation of legal texts;[6] and (c) Qur'ānic narratives.[7] The early developments of *tafsīr* continued into the third/ninth century, by the end of which exegetical works that covered the entire Qur'ān were produced. By this time, *tafsīr* had become a fully established discipline. After this period, the body of work becomes extensive and varied and includes theological, legal, religio-political and mystical exegetical works.[8]

The third/ninth century saw the maturing of distinct schools, legal, theological or religio-political, within Islam. While we cannot speak about Sunnī, Shi'ī or Khārijī *tafsīr* in the first/seventh century, we can certainly use those terms in the third/ninth century. Since then, all three groups continued to produce *tafsīr* works that project their legal, theological and religio-political views. In addition to these, *tafsīr* works that focused on law, theology or spirituality also emerged. The range of works in *tafsīr* is wide and the approaches are diverse.

Despite the existence of a range of approaches to *tafsīr*, it is noticeable that Muslim exegetes, on the whole, did not consider the changing needs of Muslims in their interpretation of the ethico-legal material in the Qur'ān, especially after the establishment of the disciplines of *fiqh* and *tafsīr*. Much of the *tafsīr* tradition remained steadfastly *literal* and *legal* in relation to the interpretation of ethico-legal texts. A legalistic-literalistic approach was considered to be the least error-prone.

Tafsīr in the modern period

Modern trends in the interpretation of the Qur'ān may be traced to Shāḥ Waliullāh of India (d. 1176/1762). While he was still a child, the stable and powerful leadership of the Mughal ruler Aurengzeb (r. 1658–1707CE) ended. In the course of Shāh Waliullāh's life, several monarchs occupied the throne in Delhi. As internal and external forces pressed on the Mughal Empire, its power declined. From within, the Mughals lost territory to the Sikhs and the Hindus. Externally, the Mughal rulers faced challenges from the King of Persia and the Afghan Rohillas.[9] The Mughal Empire continued to decline and break up until it was replaced by a Western power in the form of the British Raj in the course of the eighteenth and nineteenth centuries. As Baljon indicates, Shāh Waliullāh reacted to this changed situation for Muslims in India by initiating his reform movement.[10] He rejected *taqlīd* (blind imitation of early scholars) and advocated *ijtihād* (independent judgement) and the application of fresh ideas in interpreting the Qur'ān.[11] In emphasizing a move away from the blind following of tradition, Shāh Waliullāh rejected some accepted views related to the principles of exegesis (*uṣūl al-tafsīr*). An area of the Qur'ān where he saw this as especially possible was *naskh* (abrogation of one ruling by another).[12] He said, for instance, that, if a Companion (*ṣaḥābī*) or a Successor (*tābi'ī*) said that a certain verse was revealed on a certain occasion or following an incident, this did not always mean that the verse was revealed as a result of that occasion. For him, the Companions and Successors were merely illustrating what the verse was saying.[13]

Though Shāh Waliullāh's reformist ideas about interpretation are not radical from the perspective of the twenty-first century, they seemed so at the time. They became quite influential, particularly in the late nineteenth and early twentieth centuries. According to Baljon, from the end of the nineteenth century:

> Shāh Waliullāh was loudly acclaimed in the Indo-Pakistan subcontinent as the man who discerned the signs of his times. And when at present an Urdu-writing modernist is looking for arguments from Muslim lore, he weighs in with opinions of the Shah.[14]

Perhaps one of the most radical attempts to reinterpret the Qur'ān in the modern period was by Sir Sayyid Ahmad Khan of India (d. 1316/1898), who published a six-volume work on the Qur'ān from 1879.[15] Khan believed that Muslims needed to reassess their tradition, heritage and ways of thought in line with newly emerging, dynamic and all-too-powerful knowledge, values and institutions.[16] In his view, the gulf between Western and Islamic modes of thought was vast, and Muslims who had been educated in the West or influenced by Western education were no longer able to comprehend the religious discourse of the ulama of the time. This widening gap threatened the very relevance of Islam as a religion for many Muslims.

In the Middle East, in particular in Egypt, contact with Western civilization was rudely brought about by Napoleon's short-lived invasion (1798–1801). Debate emerged and continued on the relevance of certain institutions of Islam and the need for a degree of change. Advocates of reform and change faced fierce resistance from the ulama and scholars at influential traditionalist institutions, such as the Azhar seminary (later converted to a university) in Cairo, who suspected in the views of reformists a hidden 'colonial' agenda to subvert Islam. Despite this resistance, in the late nineteenth century, Muḥammad ʿAbduh (d. 1323/1905) began expounding his views on the interpretation of the Qur'ān. He gave a series of lectures on interpretation and dictated a partial commentary, which was later published by his pupil Muḥammad Rashīd Riḍā (d. 1354/1935). This commentary, *Tafsīr al-Manār*, though not as radical as Ahmad Khan's works, was nevertheless new in its approach. ʿAbduh criticized some of the approaches and techniques employed in traditional *tafsīr*. He dismissed the emphasis on philological and rhetorical features, saying that such an exercise is 'dry and distances [one] from God and His Book'.[17] Similarly, he was critical of the focus given to the legal content of the Qur'ān by the jurists (for whom the main function of the Qur'ān had become a legal one), saying that legal topics were the least-discussed themes (*aqallu mā jā'a fī al-Qurān*).[18] Going beyond the grammatical, linguistic and legal approaches in the *tafsīr* tradition, 'Abduh attempted to relate his commentary to contemporary problems in the lives of Muslims. For him, Qur'ānic *tafsīr* should aim at clarifying the intended meaning – the underlying reasons in the legislation, belief system and rulings – in such a way as to attract people to the Qur'ān.[19] 'Abduh insisted on the relevance of a new interpretation:

> It is possible for some people today to argue that there is no need for a [new] examination and explanation of the Qur'ān. For the scholars of the past had already examined the Qur'ān and the sunnah and had derived the laws from them. Thus we only need to look at their books and be satisfied with them. . . . [No doubt] God addressed the Qur'ān to those who were living during [its] revelation. However God did not address them because of some special personal qualities they had. . . . Thus, would it stand to reason that God will be satisfied with us if we were content with looking at someone who had examined it, and do not [try to] understand this word of His. No revelation from God has come to us obliging [us] to believe in such a person. It is a must for every person to understand the verses of the Book according to their capacity. There is no difference [in this regard] between a learned and a lay person.[20]

Following this line of thinking, a number of twentieth-century Muslim scholars argued for a rethinking of the interpretation of the ethico-legal texts. The literature on the interpretation (both theoretical and applied) of ethico-legal texts in the modern period indicates that there is a strong desire on the part of many Muslims, scholars and laity alike, to find the relevance of the Qur'ānic text to contemporary issues without compromising the overall message of the Qur'ān, its value system or its essential beliefs and practices. In the twentieth century, Muslim scholars made many attempts to demonstrate the relevance of the Qur'ān to contemporary life. Reformist thinkers, such as Muḥammad 'Abduh (d. 1905), Muhammad Iqbal (d. 1938), Ḥasan al-Bannā (d. 1949), Abu'l Ala Mawdudi (d. 1979), Murtaza Mutahhari (d. 1979), Fazlur Rahman (d. 1988) and Ayatollah Khomeini (d. 1989), argued that the Qur'ānic text is relevant to the modern period and is the basis on which any reform project must be attempted.

Challenges to traditionalist assumptions

During the twentieth century, several Muslim scholars and thinkers attempted to put forward new ideas for the interpretation of the Qur'ān and relate its ethico-legal content to the needs of Muslims. These ideas were viewed with hostility by the traditionalist ulama, who often labelled such ideas as anti-Islam. Despite this, the voices of those who wanted to go beyond the traditionally accepted *tafsīr* methods remained relatively strong, including scholars such as Muḥammad ʿAbduh, Maḥmūd Shaltūt (d. 1963) and Muḥammad al-Ghazālī (d. 1996), even though their influence on the wider Muslim population remained somewhat limited.

The traditionalist ulama regarded with particular hostility challenges to traditionally held assumptions about Islam, its early history and its primary sources (the Qurʾān and ḥadīth). A series of studies undertaken by Western scholars of Islam, such as Ignaz Goldziher[21] (d. 1921) and Joseph Schacht (d. 1969),[22] questioned assumptions Muslims held about the authenticity and historical reliability of ḥadīth. One of the sources of Islamic law was suddenly claimed to be baseless, therefore lacking the authority it had enjoyed for centuries. Several other studies also challenged the historicity of narratives related to the *sīrah* (biography of the Prophet) and, indeed, to the documentation of the Qurʾān. Such critical-historical studies undertaken not only by non-Muslim Western scholars but also by Muslims influenced by those scholars, came to be seen in traditionalist circles as threatening the very essence of Islam.

The critique of Islam by a number of Western scholars nevertheless provided an impetus towards a more critical outlook on the part of a significant number of twentieth-century Muslim intellectuals, who made a powerful argument for a re-examination of a range of assumptions in Islamic disciplines, including ḥadīth, law, exegesis and even theology. But more traditionalist scholars were not prepared to engage with such ideas. Instead, they summarily dismissed such studies as irrelevant, nonsensical or 'Orientalist'.

Emphasis on reason

An offshoot of this critical spirit was the emphasis on reason in the interpretation of the ethico-legal content of the Qurʾān. For many scholars, reason should be seen as an important medium through which God's word is made intelligible to the human mind. For Ghulam Ahmad Parvez (d. 1985), a modernist Muslim thinker, the Qurʾān contained all the necessary principles for practising the Islamic conception of right belief and action. The task of explaining those principles was to be assigned to both reason and divinely sanctioned political authorities.[23] Irrational or mythological views previously ascribed to the text by early Muslims were to be discarded.

An aspect of the emphasis on reason adopted in some modern interpretations of the Qurʾān, though not necessarily related to its ethico-legal content, is the negation of miraculous or supernatural elements of narratives found therein. Several modernist scholars attempted to 'strip the text of legendary traits and primitive notions'.[24] For instance, ʿAbduh, in his explanation of Q.2:63 in which the Qur'ān refers to the 'suspension' of Mount Sinai (*wa rafaʿnā fawqakum al-ṭūr*), interprets this as referring to an earthquake (*wa qad yakūn dhālika fi al-āyah bi ḍarb min al-zilzāl*).[25] Similarly, Sayyid Quṭb (d. 1966), in his commentary, *Ẓilāl*, also seems to draw back from the literal understanding of 'suspension'. He states that the important point in Q.2:63 is that it alludes to the image of the mountain above the people's heads.[26] Other 'mythical' references, such as to the people of *kahf* (cave)[27] and the talking of birds and ants,[28] were given more 'rational' interpretations by modernist Muslim scholars, such as Ghulam Ahmad Parvez and Khalifa Abdul Hakim (d. 1959).[29] In emphasizing his rational approach, Ahmad Khan believed that what the Qur'ān contained was not contrary to nature. Miracles were not to be seen as miracles, but as phenomena that followed laws of nature but which people of the time were unable to see as acting according to those laws.[30] Muḥammad Iqbal of the Indian subcontinent stated that the Qur'ān contained what he called 'legends'; an example of this is his reference to the Qur'ānic 'legend' of the fall.[31] Ṭanṭāwī Jawharī (d. 1940) of Egypt argued that some ideas in the Qur'ān were related to an outdated worldview; for instance, the concept of seven heavens and seven earths (to which the Qur'ān refers a number of times) is, according to Ṭanṭāwī Jawharī, part of an antiquated worldview held by the Sabians, for whom the number seven was important.[32]

The need for new ways of looking at the Qur'ān

Despite the views and arguments of scholars who adopted a more rationalist approach to the interpretation of the Qur'ān, there was little interest or even awareness among most Muslims of the importance of rethinking interpretation, particularly of the ethico-legal content, until as recently as the 1960s. Highlighting this problem while writing in the 1960s, Ismail al-Faruqi, the chief architect of what later came to be known as the 'Islamization of Knowledge' movement, argued that Muslims had made alarmingly little progress in reconstructing their methods of thinking in relation to the interpretation of the ethico-legal content:

> True, our salvation lies in the capacity to make the Qur'ānic content the ultimate determinant of personal and social action. But this presupposes a clear grasp of that sublime content; and it is precisely here that Muslim efforts have, at least during the last half-century, been laggardly groping towards their goal.[33]

Faruqi is also critical of what he calls 'self-styled defenders of Islam' for taking too simplistic an approach to the interpretation of the ethico-legal content. He goes so far as to accuse what he calls the 'apologists' of not even acknowledging there is a problem:

> The problem the modern Muslim faces is not one of whether or not he ought to observe 'that which God sent down,' but of finding out and understanding 'that which God sent down;' of ascertaining and securely grasping 'that which is in the Book.' There is no denial that the good is God's will and command, or that the Holy Qur'ān contains that Divine will and hence, that its content ought to be the determinant of action. The whole problem is one of determining what precisely that content is. The question which troubles the mind of the contemporary Muslim is, 'What is the moral imperative which the Holy Qur'ān had brought from God? How does it read when translated into the language of obligation pertinent to the concrete situations of real life?'[34]

Faruqi questions the assumption that 'that which is in the Book' is clearly spelt out and obvious to believers:

> 'That which is in the Book' is a futile answer to such a question. It presupposes that the Holy Qur'ān is a catechism of questions and answers covering every possible situation of life and containing an unequivocal, simple and straightforward imperative which assigns precisely and exactly the real act which the moral agent is supposed to do in every one of those situations. Indeed, our greatest exegetes, theologians and saints of history were far more disturbed by the difficulty of finding out 'that which is in the Book' and 'that which has been sent down' than our modernist apologists. The latter wallow in a self-complacent assurance of their knowledge of the word and will of God whereas the former had made the quest of that knowledge the agonizing turbulence of their whole lives. Nonetheless, the Holy Qur'ān is relevant to every situation of life in all times and places; but this comprehensiveness is not what the apologists have meant. What, then, is its meaning?[35]

The views of Faruqi and others who argued in the 1960s for new approaches to interpreting the Qur'ān's ethico-legal content had an undoubted impact during the latter half of the twentieth century. They gave the lead to a significant amount of activity by several scholars and thinkers whose work has gained a degree of acceptability and respectability in the wider Muslim world, despite the continued hostility from more traditionalist Muslims.

Critique of the reduction of the Qur'ān to its legal content

After the second/eighth and third/ninth centuries, particularly after Shāfiʿī (d. 204/820), there was a marked change in the way the jurists (*fuqahā'*) approached the Qur'ān and ḥadīth. Any Qur'ānic texts (or for that matter ḥadīth) with possible relevance to ethico-legal matters were used to construct laws. In their quest to develop a comprehensive system of law, the jurists effectively made the Qur'ān a legal 'manual'. If the Qur'ān could not supply a ruling, the ḥadīth were used to supply one. The developments that occurred in jurisprudential methodology (*uṣūl al-fiqh*) in the post-Shāfiʿī period emphasized that the law should be based strictly on the text; that is, the Qur'ān and ḥadīth. Observing this the Pakistani scholar Ahmad Hasan stated:

> The concept of *naṣṣ* [text] was not dominating in the pre-Shāfiʿī period. As a result of al-Shāfiʿī's emphasis on textual evidence [as argued in his *Risālah*], it acquired a dominant position in legal reasoning and became a substitute for the *ra'y-ijmāʿ* [individual judgment-consensus] phenomenon. Unrestricted *ra'y* was violently attacked by al-Shāfiʿī, and, therefore, *Qiyās* [analogy] was naturally narrowed down to *naṣṣ*.[36]

This focus on the legal texts became so entrenched that, in all subsequent developments, non-legal aspects of the Qur'ān were in practice relegated by the jurists to secondary importance. The Qur'ānic emphasis on nature and the creation of the natural environment as signs of God was overshadowed, as were the historical references to peoples and tribes, and the descriptions of the creation and development of human beings. This emphasis on the legal content ignores the fact that the Qur'ān gives little space to strictly legal matters. At a statistical level, the number of verses with *strictly legal* connotations is very small, numbering only 80 to 100 instances.[37] Even in the most generous assessment of their quantity, they cover only a relatively small portion of the Qur'ān.

Once the Qur'ān came to be seen as law or as a legal text, developments in the area of *fiqh* determined how the Qur'ān came to be viewed by subsequent generations. The law and legal schools were well established by the end of the fourth/tenth to the fifth/eleventh centuries, by which time the idea that Muslims were merely to follow what the great founders of the different legal schools had taught in the area of law was taking root in Muslim culture and practice. As the enormous creativity that accompanied the developments in law in the first three centuries of Islam gradually subsided, the creativity associated with the rather 'liberal' manner in which the earliest Muslims had approached the Qur'ān also began to disappear. The fate of the *tafsīr* tradition was bound to that of the legal tradition in relation to creativity (or the lack of it). By the time we reach the modern period, *tafsīr* has been reduced to storytelling, mystical speculation or dry philological analysis.

Making the Qur'ān accessible to contemporary Muslims

Several reformist thinkers of the modern period perceived the gap between the Qur'ān and the everyday life of Muslims that had been caused by the reduction of the Qur'ān to a legal code. One of their main concerns was the distance between the Qur'ān and young Muslims who were deeply impressed by the achievements of Western civilization, and were keen to embrace what is 'Western'. In the twentieth century, these Muslims often studied at Western universities, learnt European languages, such as French, English and German, and read widely in European literature and thought or at least were influenced by them. The Qur'ān and traditional Islamic scholarship, including its discourse, language and vocabulary, became increasingly foreign to them. Sensing this, Muslim scholars of a 'modern mindset' wanted to recapture this increasingly alienated, but highly influential, generation. Abu'l Ala Mawdudi (d. 1979), a well-known Pakistani scholar and founder of the neo-revivalist Jamā'at Islamī, explained in the preface to his famous *tafsīr* that his principal aim in writing was the explanation of the Qur'ān to the young educated Muslim, not to the academics:

> The present work is neither directed at scholars and researchers, nor is it aimed at assisting those who, having mastered the Arabic language and the Islamic religious sciences, now wish to embark upon a thorough and elaborate study of the Qur'ān. Such people already have plenty of material at their disposal. Instead it is intended for the lay reader, the average educated person, who is not well-versed in Arabic and so is unable to make full use of the vast treasures to be found in classical works on the Qur'ān.[38]

In a similar vein, Muhammad 'Izzat Darwaza (d. 1984) concludes the introduction to his *tafsīr*:

> We sense a strong desire among the majority of the Muslim youth to have an understanding of the Qur'ān, its meaning, and the circumstances [surrounding its revelation], through a modern *tafsīr* which is in keeping with the spirit of the times, [and is written] in simple style, easy to comprehend, and without digressions and embellishments of technical sciences. Especially, this desire is growing among the Muslims in order to surmount [the barrier of] long centuries in which ignorance

> and indifference prevailed. During all those years the Muslims have stagnated and [confined themselves] to blind imitation and repetition. [They have also lagged behind] in understanding the goals of Islamic mission, its vicissitudes, and its directives [enshrined] in its timeless miracle, the noble Qur'ān.[39]

Sayyid Quṭb wrote his commentary (*Fī Ẓilāl al-Qur'ān*) also to provide a fresh perspective on the relevance of the Qur'ān to the Muslim of today. Quṭb's particular style of writing, his uncompromising commitment to his view of Islam, and his portrayal of many of the institutions of modern society as *jāhiliyyah* (akin to pre-Islamic institutions, that is, non-Islamic), ensure for his commentary an important place among those whose primary aim is to establish Islam as the dominant socio-political force in Muslim societies. Quṭb's work, a good example of a *tafsīr* of a personal reflective nature, is somewhat divorced from standard exegetical tradition in its more free-flowing ideas around the text; it draws in the modern world and its challenges, and refuses to follow any early approach to *tafsīr*. It is, as the title suggests, 'in the shade' of the Qur'ān, and attempts to find relevance and meaning at a personal and collective level for Muslims of the modern period. It is perhaps this feature of the *tafsīr* that has provided the basis for the wide acceptability of *Ẓilāl* among many Muslim youth, particularly those committed to the ideological orientation of the Muslim Brotherhood and similar movements.

Limiting the concept of revelation

According to classical principles of jurisprudence (*uṣūl al-fiqh*), revelation consists of both 'recited' (*waḥy matluw*) and 'unrecited' revelation (*waḥy ghayr matluw*). The recited revelation is the Qur'ān, the speech of God, whereas the unrecited revelation is the ḥadīth, the sayings and deeds of the Prophet, considered as inspiration from God. 'Recited' refers to the fact that during prayer Muslims recite verses of the Qur'ān as an act of worship as they consider reciting the Word of God to be a form of worship. However, the ḥadīth are not 'recited' as such, as ḥadīth are not considered the Word of God but sayings attributed to the Prophet Muḥammad. Both are, in theory, 'revelation', but (according to the principles of Islamic jurisprudence) the recited revelation, that is the Qur'ān, is superior. In Islamic law both, however, enjoy *almost* equal authority in ethico-legal matters. Emphasizing this, Ghazālī (d. 505/1111) indicates that the origin of both the Qur'ān and the ḥadīth (sunnah) is the 'Word of God'. According to him, 'God has but one word which differs in the mode of its expression. On occasions God indicates his Word by the Qur'ān, on others, by words in another style, not publicly recited, and called ḥadīth.'[40] Ḥadīth were considered *waḥy*, based on one interpretation of the Qur'ānic verse, 'Nor does he say [aught] of [his own] desire. It is no less than inspiration sent to him.'[41] Such a view implies that, in theory, every word of both the Qur'ān and ḥadīth has to be followed, regardless of time, place and circumstances, since both are God's revelation and hence eternally valid. The implication of this is less flexibility for Muslims to develop laws based on changing circumstances and needs. Unlike the Qur'ān, which tends to be less intent on detailed and specific regulations and laws, the ḥadīth are full of specific rulings. If both were accepted as revelation – and immutable – the ḥadīth would restrict the freedom of Muslim thinkers and scholars to a crippling extent in many areas, not to mention the chaos that would result, since ḥadīth are, at times, contradictory.

To counter the equation between Qur'ān and ḥadīth, a number of Muslims in the modern period rejected the view that ḥadīth were part of the revelation, or even an interpretation of the Qur'ān.[42] They argued that if ḥadīth were to be considered revelation, there would be no sense in the Qur'ān's admonition of the Prophet in cases such as (a) that of the prisoners of the Battle of Badr,[43] when the Prophet apparently made a mistake by accepting ransoms from these prisoners, and (b) the case of the blind man (Ibn Umm Maktūm), who came to learn from the Prophet while the Prophet was busy preaching to some of the leading figures of the Quraysh, but the Prophet 'frowned upon him'.[44] These Muslims also rejected the interpretation by early scholars, such as Shāfi'ī[45], of certain terms in the Qur'ān as referring to ḥadīth – *ḥikmah* (literally 'wisdom') being an example.[46] Muḥammad 'Abduh, for instance, rejected the interpretation of *ḥikmah* in Q.2:129 as sunnah.[47] 'Abduh explained *ḥikmah* as 'understanding the objectives of the Qur'ān, its underlying reasoning, its congruence to human nature, the laws of human society and the interests of people in all places and times'.[48]

Ahmad Khan, taking a more radical line, argued that *tafsīr* should rely on the principles of reason and 'nature', free even from sunnah.[49] His principles of interpretation 'make no mention of sunnah, focusing instead on the use of philological and rational principles to interpret the text'.[50] According to Brown:

> For Sayyid Ahmad the great miracle of the Qur'ān is its universality. He was struck by the fact that each generation continues to find the Qur'ān relevant despite the constant increase in human knowledge. Too heavy a reliance on ḥadīth for the interpretation of the Qur'ān puts at risk this eternal and universal quality. Ḥadīth-based *tafsīr* tends to limit the meaning of the Qur'ān to a particular historical situation, thus obstructing its universality.[51]

Some, such as members of the Ahl-i-Qur'ān (Followers of the Qur'ān) movement, which emerged in the Indian subcontinent, were radical enough to suggest that the ḥadīth be discarded in favour of reliance solely on the Qur'ān as the only authoritative text.[52] The Ahl-i-Qur'ān movement arose as a reaction to the Ahl-i-Ḥadīth (Followers of Ḥadīth), who emphasized the importance of ḥadīth and wanted to reject the 'accretions' of the medieval period, be they law or theology. Unlike the Ahl-i-Qur'ān, for whom ḥadīth were not that important, the Ahl-i-Ḥadīth believed in the primacy of both the Qur'ān and the ḥadīth. For the Ahl-i-Ḥadīth, the Qur'ān and ḥadīth were the sources that would provide the guidelines needed in religion. All else (including classical *fiqh*) was, by implication, 'accretions' that would hinder a Muslim's access to Islam in its pristine form. The Ahl-i-Qur'ān went a step further and wanted to reject even the ḥadīth, reliance on which they saw as too constraining. As the Ahl-i-Qur'ān saw it, the Ahl-i-Ḥadīth were allowing their reliance on ḥadīth to bar the way to the purest form of Islam. Brown expresses their point thus:

> The Ahl-i-Qur'ān . . . movement was, in essence, an extension and a more extreme manifestation of Ahl-i-Ḥadīth scripturalism. The basic impulse – returning to Islam in its original and pure form – was the same for both groups. The Ahl-i-Qur'ān simply substituted different criteria by which this 'pure' Islam was to be defined.[53]

For the Ahl-i-Qur'ān, 'the elevation of the Qur'ān and the explicit rejection of all aids to its interpretation, including sunnah, became central tenets of dogma. Their doctrine implied, first of all, that the Qur'ān needed nothing external for its interpretation'[54] except a sufficient command of Arabic.[55] This approach gave a free hand to the interpretation of the ethico-legal content, which was the most difficult challenge at the time. Despite the apparent strength of this movement, its ideas have not achieved lasting influence, and the movement is now virtually unknown outside the Indian subcontinent.

Adaptation of the ethico-legal content of the Qur'ān

An important idea advanced in the modern period has been that a number of Qur'ānic ethico-legal instructions were *primarily* intended for a specific people in specific circumstances; that is, the Muslims of Hijaz of the early first/seventh century. Thus, when these ethico-legal instructions are applied to subsequent generations of Muslims whose social and historical context and experience differ widely from that of the seventh-century Hijaz, some consideration has to be given to the relevance of ethico-legal instructions in the new environment. If this is the case, one can argue that each generation may reach understandings of the Qur'ān's ethico-legal instructions that may differ from the understandings of previous generations.

Thus, fresh understandings of the ethico-legal content of the Qur'ān are a necessary product of a new age, and should not be excluded in favour of a simple, single, permanent and immutable understanding received in the tradition.

Two ideas have been advanced in the modern period in support of the need for fresh understandings of the Qur'ān in different times and contexts. First, for Ghulam Ahmad Parvez, a proponent of the self-sufficiency of the Qur'ān, Islam has an unchanging core, but in application is adaptable and fluid. This implies that the 'texts of revelation do not have a single, fixed meaning. Rather, each new generation can expect to find in the Qur'ān new treasures as their own capacity to understand its teaching grows.'[56] Second is the idea that the ethico-legal instructions of the Qur'ān can be approached at two levels: a surface one related to putting into practice a specific ethico-legal instruction, and a deeper one related to underlying reasons for such an instruction. The argument is that the underlying reasons should determine whether the surface level practice has to be followed to the letter strictly in all times, places and contexts. If the underlying reasons for an ethico-legal instruction are associated with specific social, historical, economic, political or other circumstances, and if these circumstances no longer exist, then the practice of that ethico-legal instruction may be left 'suspended' or 'idle'. If circumstances change again, the ethico-legal instruction may be reinstated. This gives a prominent place to the underlying reason, an approach familiar to classical Muslim jurists, as the debates on *ḥikmah* amply demonstrate. However, although earlier interpreters of the ethico-legal content of the Qur'ān were somewhat interested in the historical context of the revelation through the medium of *asbāb al-nuzūl* (occasions of revelation) literature, they did not emphasize this context in the same way that modern-day Contextualists do, who highlight the contextual nature of the Qur'ān in their argument for rethinking Qur'ānic rulings, where such rulings are seen to be inappropriate in the modern period.

Democratization of understanding

A relatively new phenomenon today is that many Muslims who are not trained in traditional religious disciplines are attempting to read and understand the Qur'ān on their own. In the past, such attempts would have been frowned upon and highly discouraged. The belief was that, unless one was fully trained and qualified, one should not attempt to read and understand the Qur'ān lest one came to an erroneous understanding and attributed that understanding to God. In the *tafsīr* tradition, conditions were placed on anyone who sought to interpret the Qur'ān. These conditions included 'correct' belief; not allowing interpretation to be led by personal desires; relying on *tafsīr* by the Qur'ān first, followed by *tafsīr* by sunnah and then by the statements of the Companions and the Successors; knowledge of the Arabic language; knowledge of the Qur'ānic disciplines; and excellent understanding of the Qur'ān.[57] Such conditions were considered a precautionary measure by which faithful following of the tradition and pious ancestors (*salaf*) could be maintained. In line with this, many of today's Textualists maintain that the Qur'ān is to be 'explained' only by an *'ālim* (person learned in Islamic religious disciplines). The fear that one may even think wrongly about a text of the Qur'ān is very strong among Textualists.

Despite the Textualists' position, Muslims who were not ulama continued to approach the Qur'ān, and the trend towards this is growing. The many reasons for this include a huge growth in public education, the spread of literacy, the emergence of Muslim movements the leaders or members of which do not necessarily come from the ulama class, and, more recently, the availability of the internet. Moreover, people attempting to read and understand the Qur'ān may not even be familiar with Arabic. In such cases, they rely on the translation of meanings of the Qur'ān available in a range of languages today and, with the help of the internet, attempt to read commentaries to enrich their understanding.

Some Contextualists are sympathetic to this phenomenon. While not recommending that the Qur'ān be approached in an uninformed manner, they seem to see the growth of individual reflective study of the Qur'ān as a positive development. They see it as the right of all Muslims to approach the Qur'ān at a personal level and to try to make sense of it according to each person's ability. These are personal and individual efforts, not necessarily attempts at interpreting the Qur'ān in a formal sense. These Contextualists argue that the emphasis on individual and personal interpretation and on reflective study is not foreign to the Qur'ān, and that, in many verses, the Qur'ān calls on individuals to contemplate and think over its verses.[58]

The argument, therefore, is that people do not have to rely on an *'ālim* to have a basic understanding of the Qur'ān: all Muslims have an equal right to understand the Scripture according to their ability and skills. Whether the text is read in Arabic or in translation, aiming at some understanding of God's word is not a sin; on the contrary, it reflects obedience to the Qur'ānic command to think and reflect on its meanings.[59] This view seems to have had a profound impact on the thinking of Muslims today, with translations of the Qur'ān and simple, accessible commentaries produced to meet this need.

Experimenting with new approaches to the interpretation of ethico-legal content

More recently, interpretation of the Qur'ān has been subjected to interrogation and evaluation from several perspectives. One is that of Muslim feminism, which is bringing cultural politics into exegetical scholarship.[60] An increasing number of Muslims who are taking up both structuralist and post-structuralist approaches are also having some impact on the debate. The 'reader theory' has disturbed the traditionalist understanding of how interpretation of the Qur'ān may be undertaken, by shifting the object of study from the author–text to the text–reader nexus.[61] The advocates of such perspectives, though recent, refuse to be peripheral, and see these perspectives as appropriate methods by which Muslims can relate the ethico-legal content of the Qur'ān to the needs of the time. Context-ualists who follow these perspectives question several assumptions made by classical Muslim interpreters of the Qur'ān about the text and the meaning of revelation, as well as about the relationship of revelation to the actual context in which the revelation took place. While Textualists of today see their methods as the only reliable and authoritative ways to understand the Qur'ān, Contextualists argue that the Muslim of today is entitled to question the assumptions of the Textualists. They also see the methods of the early Muslims as historically determined and thus not to be accorded sole authority in exegetical scholarship.

For instance, a number of Muslim feminists have recently argued that it is important for Muslims to reread the Qur'ān.[62] They criticize the 'male-oriented' readings of early and modern interpreters as being biased against women and as perpetuating historical injustices against women. They argue that, if Muslim society is to bring one-half of the Muslims to a respectable level of equality, the Qur'ānic rules and values concerning women must be understood and interpreted in the light of the socio-historical context of the time of revelation. Their argument continues that if such contexts can change, so can the interpretations and rulings derived from them. The belief is that, although the Qur'ān improved the lot of women in first/seventh-century Hijaz, many of its reforms were ignored or sidelined in its interpretation in succeeding generations, with the result that women's positions in most Muslim societies actually worsened over the course of Islamic history.

These Muslim feminists are not interested in casting religion and scripture aside in order to gain the rights they are seeking. Their most important tool is the Qur'ān itself and sustained arguments about how it should be read. Fatima Mernissi attempts to present the case for re-reading in a number of her works. She developed a critical approach to Islamic tradition over several years and ventured into hitherto 'taboo' areas. In a number of her works, she examines the Qur'ānic text in the light of ḥadīth, focusing on the biases of some of the Companions who narrated these ḥadīth, particularly those concerning women.[63] She claims that the Companions, at times, attributed their own views to the Prophet himself. These biased ḥadīth achieved dominance in the interpretation of the Qur'ān and provided justification for Muslim theologians to retain the status quo regarding women. Mernissi is at pains to 'humanize' the Companions and show them as fallible, well beyond the ideal images developed in Sunnī Islam and upheld to the present day. Emphasizing that the Qur'ānic message in relation to women was probably lost in the cultural beliefs and practices of the seventh century CE and beyond, Mernissi poses a rhetorical question:

> Is it possible that Islam's message had only a limited and superficial effect on deeply superstitious seventh century Arabs who failed to integrate its novel approaches to the world and to women?[64]

Amina Wadud, another Muslim feminist, also argues for a return to the message of the original text. She is interested in applying Fazlur Rahman's approach to the interpretation of the Qur'ān in order to argue for a more balanced approach regarding women:

> Thus, I attempt to use the method of Qur'ānic interpretation proposed by Fazlur Rahman [Pakistan/United States, 1919–1988]. He suggests that all Qur'ānic passages, revealed as they were in a specific time in history and within certain general and particular circumstances, were given expression relative to those circumstances. However, the message is not limited to that time or those circumstances historically. A reader must understand the implications of the Qur'ānic expressions during the time in which they were expressed in order to determine their proper meaning. That meaning gives the intention of the rulings or principles in the particular verse. Believers from another circumstance must make practical applications in accordance with how that original intention is reflected or manifested in the new environments. In modern times this is what is meant by the 'spirit' of the Qur'ān.[65]

Apart from Muslim feminists, several thinkers of the modern period have argued for fresh approaches to the interpretation of the Qur'ān. Fazlur Rahman, who is one of the most original thinkers in relation to the interpretation of its ethico-legal content, provides many useful ideas in dealing with the problem. The Qur'ān remains at the centre of Rahman's thought. He is critical of an ad hoc decontextualized approach that treats the Qur'ān as a series of isolated verses and fails to 'yield insight into the cohesive outlook on the universe and life'.[66] In his view, if different fields of intellectual endeavour in Islam are to cohere, one of the tasks is to formulate an Islamic metaphysics firmly based on the Qur'ān.[67] Only if the metaphysical part is clearly understood can a coherent rethinking of the moral, social and legal message of the Qur'ān be possible.

Rahman is, as a result, preoccupied with 'the correct method of interpreting the Qur'ān',[68] the most important religious document and most comprehensive guide for humankind.[69] In his view, despite the importance of method in interpretation, 'the basic questions of method and hermeneutics were not squarely addressed by Muslims'.[70] Rahman criticizes Muslims for their failure to 'understand the underlying unity of the Qur'ān' and for their adoption of an 'atomistic approach'.[71] He also says that, in the modern period, the piecemeal treatment of the Qur'ān has worsened,[72] and that the formulation of an 'adequate hermeneutical method' is 'imperative'.[73]

Though Rahman's interest in the Qur'ān is broader than its ethico-legal content, this area occupies an important place in his writing, because it is central to his concern with the need for rethinking the interpretation of the Qur'ān. In his view, the rigidity of the jurists' interpretations, and their denial of an historical context to the revelation, resulted in archaic laws that not only prevented Muslims from dealing with modern problems, but also undermined the vibrancy of Islam itself.

Other recent contributors to this area include Khaled Abou El Fadl. In his study of the use of legal authority in contemporary Islamic discourses, he criticizes what he calls 'authoritarian hermeneutics'.[74] For him, this type of hermeneutic 'involves equating between the authorial intent and the reader's intent, and renders the textual intent and autonomy, at best, marginal'.[75] He argues that authoritarian methodologies of interpretation 'corrupt the integrity of Islamic texts and mute their voice' and 'are bound to erode the effectiveness and dynamism of Islamic law'.[76] Abou El Fadl argues for a high degree of autonomy of the text:

> [Texts] need not only become independent of the domineering paternalism of their authors, but also of the suffocating authoritarianism of their readers. If there is going to be a dynamic and vigorous process of determination in which the text plays a central role, there must be a continuing state of indeterminacy.[77]

Abou El Fadl's contribution lies primarily in the area of the ethico-legal content and therefore has much commonality with the aims of my project. His ideas about authority, the interpretive community and its role in the production of meaning, and the balance between text, author and reader, as well as his critical but careful approach to ḥadīth, are major contributions to the debate on interpretation of the Qur'ān and law within an Islamic context today.

Chapter 3

Revelation and interpretation

This chapter outlines the traditional Muslim understanding of revelation,[1] and suggests a theory of revelation that could be useful in interpreting the ethico-legal content of the Qur'ān by taking into account both the socio-historical context and the context of Muslims today. In classical Muslim scholarship there is little debate about a necessary connection between the theory of revelation on the one hand and the ability of Muslims to interpret the Qur'ān on the other. But such a connection has been argued for in the writings of some Western scholars of Islam, an example being Kenneth Cragg. For him it is important to find out:

> the human element authentically within the act of God and conceive of the latter as moving with and by the former. For prophetic revelation is not the less divine for being also, instrumentally, human. And the instrumentality of Muḥammad in the Qur'ān deserves, and will no doubt eventually receive from Muslims far more adequate exploration and recognition than it has yet enjoyed.[2]

It is a connection, though not in the way Cragg puts it, in which some Muslims of the modern period are also taking some interest. The writings of Fazlur Rahman,[3] Nasr Hamid Abu Zayd,[4] Farid Esack[5] and Ebrahim Moosa[6] all deal with the concept of revelation and suggest that perhaps a more sophisticated understanding of the notion of revelation may indeed be helpful in the contemporary debate on interpretation. Such an understanding would require establishing a close connection between the revelation and the religious personality of the Prophet Muḥammad, something that most Muslim theologians in the past were not prepared to accept. Fazlur Rahman, for example, believes that early Muslim theologians did not have the intellectual tools to confront the issue of this close relationship between the Qur'ān and the Prophet Muḥammad:

> The Qur'ān itself certainly maintained the 'otherness', the 'objectivity' and the verbal character of the revelation, but had equally certainly

> rejected its externality vis-à-vis the Prophet. . . . But orthodoxy (indeed, all medieval thought) lacked the necessary intellectual tools to combine in its formulation of the dogma the otherness and verbal character of the revelation on the one hand, and its intimate connection with the work and religious personality of the Prophet on the other, i.e. it lacked the intellectual capacity to say both that the Qur'ān is entirely the Word of God and, in an ordinary sense, also entirely the word of Muhammad.[7]

For Rahman, it is important to emphasize the role of the Prophet in the genesis of revelation, although the role is a minor one. What Rahman emphasizes is the close connection between the Qur'ān as Word of God, the Prophet and his mission, and the socio-historical context in which the Qur'ān was revealed. It is this relationship that Rahman stresses, rather than arguing that the Qur'ān is the word of the Prophet. In Rahman's words, 'We see then, that the Qur'ān and the genesis of the Islamic community occurred in the light of history and against a social-historical background.'[8] He adds:

> For the Qur'ān itself, and consequently for the Muslims, the Qur'ān is the Word of God (*kalām allah*). . . . Not only does the word *Qur'ān*, meaning 'recitation', clearly indicate this, but the text of the Qur'ān itself states in several places that the Qur'ān is *verbally revealed* and not merely in its 'meaning' and ideas.[9]

While it may be useful to rethink certain aspects of traditional understanding of the nature of revelation, it is my view that accepting or rejecting this traditional understanding should not have a bearing on our ability to interpret the Qur'ān. The theory of revelation is one thing and interpretation is another; the two are not necessarily connected. The *tafsīr* tradition steadfastly holds the view that the Qur'ān is the speech and Word of God, but at the same time it also believes that the text is subject to interpretation. In fact, over the centuries many exegetes interpreted the Qur'ān rather liberally. Of course, some wanted to limit their interpretation to the guidance provided by the Prophet and the earliest Muslims while others were keen to go beyond that to explore further the meanings of the text. The fact that they believed the Qur'ān was the Word of God did not limit their interpretation.

While the traditional Muslim understanding of revelation holds the Qur'ān is the Word of God and not of Prophet Muḥammad, it also holds that the language of the Qur'ān, Arabic, is a human language, deeply embedded in human life. Despite the attempts of early Muslim theologians to separate the 'revelation' from the mundane by emphasizing its existence on the 'Preserved Tablet' (*al-lawḥ al-maḥfūẓ*), the understanding of revelation and the revelation itself are firmly grounded in human experience, in the time, place and circumstances of the seventh-century Hijaz in Arabia. The Qur'ān is in the language of Mecca and surrounding regions, and its concerns often were directly or indirectly connected to the Prophet and his community. In the Qur'ān, references are made to the Prophet's relationship to the people around him and the response of his people to his message. The indifference of the people of Mecca to the poor and needy is also highlighted. The revelation included instructions to the people to act upon or refrain from certain things. It provided stories of earlier prophets and their peoples as a lesson to the Prophet's contemporaries. The Qur'ān refers repeatedly to the places, times, customs, norms, beliefs, values, ideas, institutions, practices and attitudes of the people surrounding the Prophet.

Pre-Islamic understanding of 'revelation'

Pre-Islamic understandings of 'revelation' were grounded in contemporary experience and seem to have been based on people's familiarity with three literary genres: the scriptures of Judaism and Christianity; poetry and the Arabic poetic experience; and *saj*ᶜ *al-kuhhān* (soothsayer texts).

Pre-Islamic Arabs who were not Christian or Jewish were usually referred to as 'pagans'. They had no direct experience of a scripture or a revealed book from God. Those living in settled communities like Mecca and Medina (Yathrib) were nevertheless aware of the Jewish and Christian religions and their scriptures. There is some evidence to suggest that in Mecca itself there were some Christians from Quraysh stock.[10] The town of Medina, where the Prophet migrated in 1/622 after 13 years of preaching in Mecca, had a large Jewish community: three tribes of the town were Jewish. Considerable social interaction existed between the Jewish communities of Medina and the non-Jewish communities of Aws, Khazraj and surrounding tribes. Through the Jewish community, the non-Jewish people of the town would have known about notions of revelation, scripture and, in a rudimentary fashion, communication between God and His prophets.

Importantly, the pre-Islamic Arabs made a connection between poetry, the most important literary genre they possessed, and a higher spiritual source. They believed that the *jinn* (a type of spiritual being) regularly offered poets help to compose poetry.[11] The creative aspect of poetry was often attributed to *jinn* because such sophisticated and creative texts could not be produced by ordinary mortals, or so it was believed. Perhaps it is for this reason, when the Prophet began preaching and reciting the Qur'ān, his opponents accused him of being a 'poet possessed'.[12] The Qur'ān says: '"Nay", they say, "[these are] medleys of dreams! Nay, he forged it! Nay, he is [but] a poet."'[13]

Again, following their view of the relationship between creative literary texts and spiritual beings, pre-Islamic Arabs also made a connection between another important literary genre and *jinn*: the texts produced by soothsayers (*kāhin*).[14] Soothsayers held important positions in the community, foretelling the future, interpreting dreams and preparing the community and the individual for future catastrophic events through their 'advice'. They were believed to have access to *jinn*, relaying matters to the superior *jinn* and conveying the *jinn*'s information back to humans in a language familiar to them called *saj*ʿ *al-kuhhān*. This was a style of expression in which highly structured forms of language were used to convey the knowledge the soothsayer had acquired to human beings.

The initial Meccan reaction to the Qur'ān – the accusation that the Prophet was a soothsayer – indicates that the Meccans judged the Qur'ān on its linguistic character: they related it to *saj*ʿ *al-kuhhān*. Since many of its early verses were highly alliterative, abrupt or given in short sentences and phrases, some of these early texts of the Qur'ān were reminiscent of *saj*ʿ *al-kuhhān*. But the Qur'ān rejects the idea that it is the product of a soothsayer: 'It is not the word of a poet: little you believe! Nor is it the word of a soothsayer: little admonition it is you receive.'[15]

Revelation: God's speech in human language

The concept of 'God's speech' is not foreign to the Qur'ānic view of revelation. Nor is it difficult to demonstrate that, in the Qur'ān, it is taken for granted that God speaks and has spoken from the beginning of creation. The Qur'ān refers to a variety of contexts in which God has spoken. One of those most quoted is God's communication with Moses, in which God addressed Moses in his own language and a dialogue ensues. God also spoke to Noah,[16] Abraham,[17] Zachariah,[18] Jesus[19] and even Iblīs (Satan).[20] God's speech is referred to by terms such as *qaṣṣa* (telling or narrating) and its derivatives. There are 14 instances in which the verb *qaṣṣa* and its derivatives are used to indicate that God 'tells' or 'narrates' His 'words'.[21]

In understanding the problem of God's speaking in Arabic, a human language, one option is to emphasize the difference between the revelation as it relates to the 'speech' of God (at the level of the 'Unseen') and the revelation as it relates to a human language. Revelation at the Unseen (*ghayb*) level is 'a "theological mystery" incapable of being grasped by human analytic thought. The phenomenon of revelation, in this respect, is something essentially mysterious, which does not allow of analysis, it is something only to be believed in.'[22] Revelation in a human language, however, is capable of being analysed. According to Izutsu:

> It is difficult, then, to resist the conclusion that, although, in so far as it is *God's* speech, Revelation is something mysterious and has

> nothing in common with ordinary human linguistic behaviour, in so far as it is *speech*, it must have all the essential attributes of human speech. In fact, the Koran uses also other words in reference to Revelation, that are most commonly applied to ordinary, commonplace products of speech: *kalimah* meaning 'word' for example in Sūrat al-Shūrā.[23]

God's speech at the Unseen level is not accessible or comprehensible to humans. Hence it would be a futile exercise to explore the modality of God's speech at this level. Exploring this would be similar to attempting to describe what is in the Unseen world, such as Paradise (*jannah*) and Hell. Though there are many references to and descriptions of these in the Qur'ān, they all have to be understood in line with the reported prophetic saying about Paradise: 'What is in Paradise is what an eye has not seen, an ear has not heard, and which has not been imagined by the heart.'

When the Qur'ān describes Paradise, the language, ideas, meanings and descriptions used in that context are based on the experiences of human beings in this world. What is beyond human experience and imagination cannot be comprehended in anything but approximate terms and within the confines of our experience and via our language, which itself is extremely limited. Understanding of the references to the Unseen world are dependent on the experience of the world we live in, and such references are largely metaphorical. God's speech is beyond our experience unless it is somehow expressed in a human language form we can understand. As Ghazālī says:

> He [God] expressed that attribute [of speech] in human images and words to mankind. If the glory and excellence of the words of God could not have been made understandable in the garb of words, heaven and earth could not stand to hear His words and all things between them would have smashed to pieces.[24]

That God 'spoke in Arabic' certainly caused difficulties for many Muslims when they came into contact with Greek philosophy in the second/eighth and third/ninth centuries. Muslims generally have two standpoints on the speech of God in Arabic. These represent two extremes of a continuum: one is that God's speech in Arabic (in the Qur'ān) is 'uncreated' and the other is that it is 'created'. The first is the Ash'arī[25] position, which is commonly followed today in the Islamic world. The second is the Mu'tazilī[26] position, which, strictly speaking, has become a minority position. However, both groups believe that the Qur'ān is the speech of God. As the exegete Rāzī says, 'There is consensus of the *ummah* (community) on the issue that God speaks.'[27] For theological reasons, the Ash'arīs do not accept that the Qur'ān is 'created', whereas, for the Muʿtazilīs, also for theological reasons, the Qurʾān is 'created'. Even for Ashʿarīs, the 'uncreatedness' of the Qurʾān should not be taken too crudely. There are three levels of 'speech' in the Qurʾān: language and utterance (*lughah wa nuṭq*), letters and writing (*ḥurūf wa kitabāh*) and spirit and meaning (*rūḥ wa maʿnā*). It is only in the last sense that the Qurʾān, the speech of God, can be said to be 'uncreated'; that is, co-eternal with God. However, for our purposes here, the question of the 'createdness' of the Qurʾān and the controversy it generated among early Muslims is irrelevant. Neither party – the Muʿtazilīs or the Ashʿarīs – has argued that the Qurʾān is not the Word of God, or that the Prophet composed the Qurʾān, or that the Qurʾān in words, ideas and composition can be attributed to any being other than God.

God speaks to human beings in three ways

The Qurʾān provides detail as to how revelation, in the sense of communication, comes from God to human beings; that is, the types of communication that occur between God and people. One important verse explains this as follows:

> It is not fitting for a Man that God should speak to him except by inspiration, or from behind a veil, or by the sending of a messenger to reveal, with God's permission what God wills: for He is Most High, Most Wise.[28]

Many verses in the Qurʾān have a direct bearing on the issue of revelation. Often the terms associated with revelation are used in the sense of transmitting a message either from God to human beings or from God to non-human beings. These usages indicate that revelation or inspiration (*waḥy*) is not strictly limited to a relationship between God and His prophets. In fact, there are several forms of revelation or inspiration mentioned in the Qurʾān: to inanimate objects;[29] to animals;[30] to human beings in general, such as the mother of Moses;[31] to prophets in particular, such as Jesus;[32] and to angels.[33] The Qurʾān uses the word *waḥy* and its variants on a number of occasions that span both the Meccan and Medinan periods.

The first method of speech mentioned in the above verse, *waḥy*, is the most direct mode of communication; it comes directly from God to the person intended, without voice or messenger. The person who receives it 'understands' that it is from God.

The second method, 'from behind a veil', means that God speaks to a person without the hearer's seeing the one who speaks, since in His essence God is invisible.[34] A well-known example is that of the Prophet Moses, which the Qurʾān describes as follows:

> So when he [Moses] reached it [the fire], he was called from the right side of the valley, in the blessed place from the tree: 'O Moses! Verily! I am God, the Lord of the worlds [and all that exists]!'[35]

Here God addresses Moses directly but has placed a tree as a *ḥijāb* ('visual barrier'): Moses cannot 'see' God. In fact, when Moses expresses his desire to see God by saying 'O my Lord! Show me [Yourself], that I may look upon You,'[36] God replies:

> 'You cannot see Me, but look upon the mountain if it stands still in its place then you shall see Me.' So when his Lord appeared to the mountain, He made it collapse to dust, and [Moses] fell down unconscious. Then when he recovered his senses he said: 'Glory be to You, I turn to You in repentance and I am the first of the believers.' God said: 'O Moses I have chosen you above people by My messages, and by My speaking [to you]. So hold that which I have given you and be of the grateful.'[37]

According to several scholars, the third method, 'through a messenger', is the surest and clearest form of revelation. Muslims believe that it is through this method that the revelation of the Qur'ān to the Prophet occurred. This revelation comes to the Prophet through a messenger who brings the Word of God from God to the Prophet verbatim. Muslim theologians believe that the messengers are 'angels', and in the case of revelation to prophets 'sending a messenger' is the most common method of revelation. Usually this messenger is believed to be the angel Gabriel (Jibrīl). In the case of Prophet Muḥammad, Gabriel transmitted the revelation from God in a form the Prophet could understand – the Arabic language.[38]

Revelation in the Arabic language

That the revelation was given to the Prophet in Arabic is stated several times in the Qur'ān. Some verses indicate that the communication between the angel Gabriel and the Prophet Muḥammad was in the Prophet's own language:

> Verily this is a revelation from the Lord of the Worlds. With it came down the Spirit of Faith and Truth to your heart and mind, that you may admonish in the perspicuous Arabic language.[39]

Some verses indicate that, when the Prophet 'hears' the message, he understands it and tries to repeat the words in order to memorize them; in other words, he was receiving the revelation in a language he understood:

'Move not your tongue concerning the [Qur'ān] to make haste therewith.'[40] Furthermore, the Qur'ān tells the Prophet not to be overly concerned with memorizing, as God will enable him to preserve the revelation. It says, 'It is for Us to collect it and to promulgate it.'[41]

Many other references in the Qur'ān indicate that it was revealed in Arabic, not in a mysterious code or in a tongue unknown to the Prophet: 'We have sent it down as an Arabic Qur'ān.'[42] The exegete Bayḍāwī (d. *c.*685–716/1286–1316) explains why the Qur'ān was revealed in Arabic in his interpretation of Q.12:2:

> '*Perhaps you will understand*': This is the reason why God sent down the Book in this (Arabic) form. The meaning is (therefore): We have sent it down to you as something that is composed in your own language or can be recited in your own language, so that you will be able to understand it and grasp its meanings.[43]

According to Izutsu:

> And Revelation means in Islam that God 'spoke', that He revealed Himself through language, and that not in some mysterious non-human language but in a clear, humanly understandable language. This *is* the initial and most decisive fact. Without this act on the part of God, there would have been no true religion on earth according to Islamic understanding of the word religion.[44]

Several of the verses quoted above also indicate that the Prophet was fully aware of what he was receiving at the time of contact with the 'source'. In a ḥadīth reported in Bukhārī's *Ṣaḥīḥ*, the Prophet's wife 'Ā'ishah attempts to explain the revelatory experience:

> Al-Ḥārith b. Hishām asked the Prophet: 'O Allah's Messenger [Prophet Muḥammad]. How is the *waḥy* (revelation) revealed to you?' Allah's Messenger replied: 'Sometimes it is [revealed] like the ringing of a bell, this form of inspiration is the hardest of all and then this state passes off after I have grasped what is inspired. Sometimes the angel comes in the form of a man and addresses me and I grasp whatever he says.'[45]

The Qur'ān as divine revelation

The Qur'ān strongly denies that it is the speech or ideas of the Prophet or, indeed, of any other human.[46] It also asserts that the revelation came directly from God and in Arabic so that it could be without human-induced errors or inaccuracies. Several verses explain this:

> This Qur'ān is not such as can be produced by other than God; on the contrary it is a confirmation of [revelations] that went before it, and a fuller explanation of the Book – wherein there is no doubt – from the Lord of the Worlds. Or do they say, 'He forged it?' Say: 'Bring them a *sūrah* like unto it, and call [to your aid] anyone you can, besides God, if you are truthful!'[47]

This is repeated in another verse:

> Or they may say, 'He forged it.' Say, 'Bring you then ten *sūrahs* forged, like unto it, and call [to your aid] whomsoever you can, other than God! – if you speak the truth.'[48]

Again, in Q.2:23, the Qur'ān challenges those who believe it to be merely the words of Muḥammad to produce a book similar to it or even just one chapter like it. Ṭabaṭabā'ī says:

> The force of this challenge becomes clear when we realize that it is issued for someone whose life should resemble that of Muḥammad, namely, the life of an orphan, uneducated in any formal sense, not being able to read or write and [who] grew up in the unenlightened age of the *jāhiliyyah* period (the age of ignorance) before Islam.[49]

The Qur'ān argues that, if it were from any source other than God, there would be many inconsistencies and inaccuracies in the text: 'Do they not consider the Qur'ān [with care]? Had it been from other than God, they would surely have found therein much discrepancy.'[50] The angel was entrusted with a direct message in Arabic, not simply with meanings and ideas. It was intended to be immediately comprehensible to ordinary people.[51] Furthermore, any change to the revealed text is also attributed to God alone:

> When we substitute one revelation for another, and God knows best what He reveals [in stages], they say, 'You are but a forger': But most of them understand not.[52]

Farid Esack summarizes the point:

> For Muslims the Qur'ān as the compilation of the 'Speech of God' does not refer to a book inspired or influenced by Him or written under the guidance of His spirit. Rather, it is viewed as His direct speech.[53]

The spoken word and the written word

Many verses refer to the revelation as a *qawl*, which may be translated as 'saying', 'word' or 'words' that are 'said', 'communicated' and then 'heard'. These are referred to at times as ḥadīth,[54] meaning 'narrations' or 'stories'. In some instances, the Qur'ān is referred to as *kalimah*[55] or *kalimāt*,[56] meaning 'word' or 'words' of God. The root *qwl* and its derivatives, such as *qāla*, are also used many times in the Qur'ān to refer to God's 'speaking'.[57] These and similar verses indicate that the Qur'ān is primarily spoken word coming from God. These terms fall within the broad category of 'speech'. According to Izutsu:

> It is no wonder, then, that Islam should have been from the very beginning extremely language conscious. Islam arose when God spoke. The whole Islamic culture made its start with the historic fact that man was addressed by God in a language which he himself spoke. This was not a simple matter of God's having 'sent down' a sacred Book. It meant primarily that God 'spoke'. And this is precisely what 'Revelation' means. Revelation is essentially a linguistic concept.[58]

While there is much in the Qur'ān to suggest it is primarily spoken word, it also contains many verses indicating that it is also 'written' word. From the Qur'ānic point of view, spoken word and written word appear to be two sides of the same coin. Even though terms associated with speech are used more frequently to refer to the Qur'ān, the use of writing-related terms is also common. In fact, even in the first verses to be revealed to the Prophet, the connection of revelation to the 'pen' is established.

In referring to previous scriptures, the Qur'ān uses several terms that suggest that some of these at least were written. The Qur'ān uses the terms *ṣuḥuf* (scripture, pages)[59] and *alwāḥ* (tablets)[60] to refer to scriptures revealed by God. It also uses the term *asfār*[61] to indicate written scripture. Moreover, in many instances, the Qur'ān refers to Tawrāh (Torah) and Injīl (the Gospel) as 'scripture of God' (*kitāb allah*) or just *kitāb* (written scripture), or to earlier scriptures as written documents revealed to Moses,[62] to Jesus[63] and to descendants of Abraham.[64] These written scriptures are read by their respective followers.[65]

There are several verses that indicate that, during the time of the Prophet, the Qur'ān came to be conceived of as 'scripture', not just spoken word. It thus became a book or a scripture much like the earlier scriptures given to prophets before Muḥammad.[66] As the Qur'ān says: 'God has sent down to you the Book and Wisdom and taught you what you knew not before.'[67] Certainly the Qur'ān considered itself as scripture: 'And recite what has been revealed to you of the Book of your Lord: none can change His words.'[68] This is reiterated in the verse, 'We have revealed for you a book in which is a message for you.'[69] In fact, the Qur'ān uses *kitāb* to refer to itself more than 70 times in various contexts, indicating that the concept of the Qur'ān as a 'book' or scripture was well established before the Prophet's death in 11/632.[70]

Revelation and *muṣḥaf*

Muslim tradition holds that, immediately after the death of the Prophet, the Qur'ān was put together as a complete document. Since the codification and collection were completed very early and in the presence of those who had witnessed the reception of revelation by the Prophet, there was the opportunity to prepare an accurate copy of the Qur'ānic text. We may always wonder whether the collected material and that which now exists in the *muṣḥaf* (codex) is all of what was revealed to Prophet Muḥammad. Muslims generally believe it is so. However, the question could be asked whether parts of the revelation were omitted because they had been simply 'abrogated' or 'forgotten', as is indicated in Q.2:106, or whether such omission was part of an attempt by those who collected and codified the Qur'ān to unify Muslims on the basis of a single version of the text. The latter could have resulted in the omission of material not in line with the Qurayshī dialect, the remnants of which exist in the *qirā'āt* (traditions of recitation). Muslim scholars of the Qur'ān do not deny this omission; the *tafsīr* literature is full of reports on this. For example, on the interpretation of Q.2:106, Zamakhsharī expresses eloquently the extent of the acceptance of this omission by Muslims:

> To abrogate a verse means that God removes it (*azāla*) by putting another in its place. To cause a verse to be abrogated means that God gives the command that it be abrogated; that is, he commands Gabriel to set forth the verse as abrogated by announcing its cancellation. Deferring a verse means that God sets aside (with the proclamation) and causes it to disappear without a substitute. To cause a verse to be cast into oblivion means that it no longer is preserved in the heart. The following is the meaning [of the verse]: Every verse is made to vanish whenever the well-being (*maṣlaḥah*) (of the community) requires that it be eliminated – either on the basis of the wording or the virtue of what is right, or on the basis of both of these reasons together, either with or without a substitute.[71]

Regardless of any omission, for Muslims the *muṣḥaf* of 'Uthmān, as collected during the reign of Caliph 'Uthmān (d. 35/655), represents the historical and authentic codification of the revelation. Texts that 'God may have caused to be forgotten', or readings that were omitted in an attempt to unify Muslims on one version, are not considered essential to the codified text, and for the present purposes may be ignored. My interest here (in what might have been omitted) does not go beyond the historical. It is this codified text[72] that became the basis of Islam, and, for Muslims, its authenticity and reliability cannot be seriously questioned. It is this text that also became the basis for developments in its understanding and interpretation.

The nature of revelation

According to the Qur'ān, revelation is an initiative of God. It is God who intends to reveal His Will to the human prophet. The prophet is receptive to the revelation and a relationship between God and the human prophet is established. The Prophet Muḥammad, however, is not reduced to a passive bystander. He is a recipient, but an active one nonetheless. Being active does not mean that the Prophet Muḥammad composed the content of the revelation, but that he received the content (what was said) while being conscious of the event and witnessed in his heart the grandeur of the experience of the presence of the 'voice' of God. The importance of this experience lies in what was said, not in what was experienced by the Prophet at the time. It is probably for this reason that Muslim theologians were less concerned with the experience of revelation than with what was said in the experience. That experience could not be fully represented in human language as it is related to what the Qur'ān calls the 'Unseen'. What was said, however, can be transmitted and reported. It is this verbal message that is central.

Revelation does not mean that God makes His Being known; it is His Will, in an understandable human language, that is revealed. The Prophet does not 'see' God. This is emphatically denied throughout the Qur'ān. The only instance that could be considered to have a link to 'seeing' is problematic, as it refers to seeing 'with the heart', not with the eyes. Fazlur Rahman says:

> It is only in connection with certain special experiences (commonly connected with the Prophet's Ascension [known as *miʿrāj*]) that the Qur'ān speaks of the Prophet having seen a figure or a spirit, or some other object 'at the farthest end' or 'on the horizon'.[73]

For the Prophet, then, the revelation was real, even though the modality of both the revelation and the experience cannot be described except in metaphorical terms, such as the 'ringing of a bell' as mentioned in the ḥadīth cited on p. 33. Despite being unable to give a scientific description of the experience, the Prophet was firm in his view that the context of revelation was objective, not subjective, and that this objectivity was established by the fact that the message was given in his own language.

His experiences of 'seeing' the intermediary (the angel) and of 'hearing' the voice at times, and of comprehending what was said (as reported in ḥadīth) all indicate for the Prophet the objective reality of the content of the revelation.[74]

The most common Muslim view of revelation strongly affirms the language as an essential aspect of the content. The words of the Qur'ān are thus equivalent to the verbal revelation given to the Prophet. When the Qur'ān says that God 'says', 'speaks' or 'commands', these terms are taken literally. Via the intermediary (*rūḥ*), the Prophet 'receives' this Arabic communication and transmits it verbatim to his followers, who in turn do the same for the generations succeeding them. It is a faithful transmission of a verbally revealed message in the same format in which it was revealed. On the nature of revelation, the theologian Nasafī (d. 508/1114) says:

> The Quran is God's speaking, which is one of His attributes. Now God in all of His attributes is One, and with all His attributes is eternal and not contingent, (so His speaking is) without letters and without sounds, not broken up into syllables or paragraphs. It is not He nor is it other than He. He caused Gabriel to hear it as sound and letters, for He created sound and letters and caused him to hear it by that sound and those letters. Gabriel, upon whom be peace, memorized it, stored it (in his mind) and then transmitted to the Prophet, upon whom be God's blessing and peace, by bringing down a revelation and a message, which is not the same as bringing down a corporeal object and a form. He recited it to the Prophet, upon whom be God's blessing and peace, the Prophet memorized it, storing it up (in his mind), and then recited it to his Companions, who memorized it and recited to the Followers.[75]

Towards a broader understanding of revelation

In summary, the dominant Muslim view of revelation in Islam on the whole accommodates the following, notwithstanding differences among Muslims on specific elements: God revealed his Will (not his Being) to the Prophet Muḥammad; revelation occurred through an intermediary, known as 'the Spirit' or the Angel Gabriel; this revelation to the Prophet was in Arabic, the language of the Prophet, and came to be equated with the text of the Qur'ān; there is a clear distinction between God's 'word' and the Prophet's 'word'; while both are considered 'revelation', the former is 'recited' revelation and the latter 'un-recited' revelation (ḥadīth); revelation as God's word ceased to exist with the death of the Prophet

Muḥammad, and therefore no further revelation is to be accepted; revelation is eternal and independent of specific socio-historical context; and the total 'otherness' of revelation is to be maintained.

Muslim scholarship on the nature of revelation has focused heavily on revelation from God to the Preserved Tablet (*al-lawḥ al-maḥfūẓ*) and then from the Tablet to the Heavens and to the Prophet Muḥammad via the Angel Gabriel. Much of this debate is on the basis of several statements in the Qur'ān about revelation. Little emphasis is placed on the connection between the revelation once it is received by the Prophet and the socio-historical context of the revelation. In order to maintain the total 'otherness' of the revelation (which the Qur'ān also maintains on a number of occasions) and separate it from the personality and psyche of the Prophet (and to emphasize that the sole author of the Qur'ān is God), Muslim scholarship on the whole reduced the Prophet to a passive recipient of revelation. In this the Prophet is nothing but a receiver, a mere instrument through whom the revelation as text was transmitted to the human community. In theory, then, the revelation that the Prophet received has no direct connection to the 'situation on the ground' or the concerns and issues of the Prophet or his community. To emphasize this further, any suggestion of a continuing 'inspiration' (even if a non-linguistic, non-textual nature) was eliminated from any understanding of revelation, again notwithstanding views to the contrary (particularly among certain Sufīs).

Given that the revelation before it reached the Prophet is at the realm of Unseen (*ghayb*), we may only make conjecture about how revelation came to be (created or uncreated as Mu'tazilīs and Ash'arīs argued respectively), whether it was revealed all in one go to the Heavens directly from God or from the Preserved Tablet, and how the revelation then was conveyed to the Prophet, and whether it was always through the Angel Gabriel. All these issues may be interesting from a theological point of view, but they add very little when it comes to the authority of the revelation. Once God is identified as the source of revelation, however it may have come about, is not of particular concern to us. What matters is what happens in the physical world. Once the revelation reaches the Prophet, it becomes a reality in our physical world through the human instrument, the Prophet. In the following section, I propose an understanding of revelation that takes into consideration the socio-historical context, while adopting as much as possible from the standard Muslim view of revelation. In this, revelation can be thought of on four levels which can be summarized as follows.

Level 1: God-Preserved Tablet-Heavens-Gabriel

At this level, revelation is at the level of Unseen (*ghayb*) and is simply unknowable. The few references to revelation that are found in the Qur'ān that are associated with this level do not provide us with any definite understanding of how revelation came to be. Any perceptions we may have of these references will not go beyond a mere approximation. The sequence of revelation is generally understood to be: God-Preserved Tablet-Heavens-Gabriel. The method of transmission is simply unknowable as it is beyond human experience.

Level 2: Spirit-Prophet's mind-externalisation-socio-historical context

This is the stage at which a connection is made between the 'Spirit' *(rūḥ)*, known as Gabriel, and the Prophet. The Spirit brings the revelation to the Prophet's mind in a way known to God. This entry of revelation into the physical world means that the revelation occurs in a form that human beings could understand. Therefore, revelation in the mind of the Prophet is communicated in a human language – Arabic (the language of the Prophet and his community). It also becomes deeply embedded in the concerns, needs and issues of the Prophet and his community as evidenced in the constant references in the Qur'ān to that community's people, norms, customs, systems and institutions. Additionally, the Qur'ān addresses the people of the community giving them warnings and outlining Gods expectations of them. The revelation does not remain at an abstract level divorced from the concerns of the community; its message becomes *specific* to the Prophet and his community. Other communities on earth at the time which had no connection to that community were not a primary concern for the revelation. The universal message that other prophets received from God is doubtless present in the Qur'ān, but that message is also conveyed through the Prophet Muḥammad and his community.

Level 3: text-context-enlarged text

Once the revelation is externalized and communicated by the Prophet to his community, the revelation becomes a text (oral or written) that is deeply connected with the context of the Prophet's community. The text is narrated, recited, communicated, taught, explained and acted upon. It is through this actualization of the text that the understanding of the text first becomes a reality, and it is on the basis of this actualization that any future understandings and actualizations occur. The text is no longer simply a text. It is now 'enlarged' [Text + Immediate Context of Actualization]. The Prophet's presence in the community, his engagement with the community and the revelation add to the text on an on-going basis, increasing the volume of the actual text as well as its rich array of understandings and supporting praxis.

Level 4: closed text-interpretive communities-context-inspiration

With the death of the Prophet the text becomes final and it becomes closed. The actual closure while beginning with the death of the Prophet (as there are no more revelations) is officially closed with the writing down of the text and production of the *muṣḥaf* (the Codex). This closure does not mean that certain aspects of revelation (non-prophetic, non-linguistic and non-textual) also ceased to exist. Two aspects of the revelation continue. First, praxis that is guided by revelation that begins with the Prophet and his community and is continuously transmitted to subsequent communities. Each community in turn adds to this reservoir of understanding leading to a constantly expanding reservoir of knowledge as we move away from the Prophet and his community. Second, divine guidance is continuously provided by God to those who are God-conscious and are constantly attempting to keep their communities and themselves on the path of God. This amounts to a form of 'inspiration' that continues; it is non-prophetic and non-linguistic.

In this understanding of revelation, the socio-historical context of revelation is a fundamental element of revelation. It is not divorced from the human instrument, the Prophet; neither is it divorced from the community of the Prophet. This fundamental connection of revelation remains even after the death of the Prophet and continues to maintain that link through praxis and interpretive communities. The argument at the heart of this book is based on this understanding of revelation.

Chapter 4

Interpretation based on tradition and textualism

One of the most important types of *tafsīr* is what is known in Arabic as *tafsīr bi al-riwāyah* or *tafsīr bi al-ma'thūr* – interpretation based on tradition or text. I will refer to this as 'tradition-based *tafsīr*'. Tradition-based *tafsīr* means that the interpretation of the Qur'ān should be guided by the Qur'ān, the Prophet and earliest Muslims. In other words, interpretation is hoped to reflect, as far as possible, the original sources of Islam. Moreover, when the source is a reported saying of the Prophet, or a Companion or Successor, the narration (*riwāyah*) should have a 'sound' basis – that is, a sound and complete chain of narrators (*isnād*) whose narrations are truthful and reliable.[1] Only then can the narrated report be accepted as historically authentic and therefore authoritative. A number of scholars (classical and modern) have argued that tradition-based *tafsīr* is the safest and best method of interpretation. Mannāʿ al-Qaṭṭān, a scholar of the modern period, states:

> What we have to follow and hold onto is the *tafsīr* based on text/tradition. This is because it is the path of true knowledge. It is also the safest way of guarding [oneself] against [attributing] error and deviation to the Book of God.[2]

Tradition-based *tafsīr* assumes that it is only those closest in time to the Prophet (*salaf*) and therefore to the revelation who can interpret the text authoritatively. Later generations of Muslims, it is believed, should simply accept this and base their own interpretations of the Qur'ān on those left by the *salaf*.

Authority in tradition-based *tafsīr*

Four different types of interpretation may be grouped under the heading of tradition-based *tafsīr*. These comprise (1) interpretation of the Qur'ān by the Qur'ān, (2) interpretation of the Qur'ān by the Prophet, (3) interpretation of the Qur'ān by the Companions of the Prophet, and (4) interpretation of the Qur'ān by the Successors. In the Sunnī hierarchy of authoritative sources, the first two are considered the most authoritative, with their authority derived directly from the pronouncements of the Qur'ān and the sunnah. The Companions' interpretations, despite their familiarity with the Prophet and the guidance they received directly from him, are lower on the Sunnī scale of authority.

Interpretation of the Qur'ān by the Qur'ān

The Qur'ān is considered to be a unified whole with unity of purpose. This means that difficult sections or verses of the Qur'ān are clarified in another part of the text. The Qur'ān contains verses that are absolute (*muṭlaq*), others that are qualified (*muqayyad*), abrogating (*nāsikh*) or abrogated (*mansūkh*), and others that are aggregated (*mujmal*) or explained (*mubayyan*).[3] An ambiguous verse may have its explanation in another verse or verses.[4] An issue raised by one verse may be elaborated on or explained by another verse. The explanation of one verse by another is called interpretation of the Qur'ān by the Qur'ān, and is considered by many exegetes to be the best and most authoritative form of interpretation.[5] Ibn Taymiyyah (d. 728/1328) says:

> The best method in [*tafsīr*] is that the Qur'ān be interpreted by the Qur'ān. Where the Qur'ān sums up [a point], the same point is elaborated in another place. What is briefly mentioned in one place is explained in detail in another place.[6]

Several verses in the Qur'ān support the view that it is capable of interpreting itself. An example is the interpretation of Q.2:37 by Q.7:23. Q.2:37 states:

> Thereupon Adam received words [of guidance] from his Sustainer, and He accepted his repentance: for verily, He alone is the Acceptor of Repentance, the Dispenser of Grace.

This verse indicates that Adam received some 'words' (*kalimāt*) from God. However, it does not elaborate on what these words were. This elaboration is provided by Q.7:23:

> The two [Adam and Eve] said: 'Our Lord! We have wronged our own souls. If You do not forgive us, and do not bestow upon us Your mercy, we shall certainly be lost'.

Interpretation of the Qur'ān by the Prophet

One of the functions of the Prophet Muḥammad was to explain the Qur'ān. The following verse is taken to provide support for his role:

> And upon you have We bestowed from on high this reminder [Qur'ān] so that *you explain* to the people what has been revealed to them.[7]

Instances are recorded where the Prophet expounded the meaning of certain verses to the Companions when they had problems in understanding them. One such verse is Q.6:82. Some Companions, it is believed, could not grasp what the Qur'ān meant by 'wrongdoing' (*ẓulm*) in the verse:

> Those who have attained to faith and who have not obscured their faith by wrongdoing (*ẓulm*) – it is they who shall be secure since it is they who have found the right path.

Some Companions said to the Prophet: 'O Messenger of God! Who from among us has not committed [any] wrong?'[8] The Companions here understood *ẓulm* in its literal sense of wrongdoing. They were concerned that they might not be counted among those who had found the right path. The Prophet cleared this misunderstanding by saying that the 'wrongdoing' is ascribing divinity to any being other than God (*shirk*).[9]

Although the Prophet was asked questions about the meaning of verses, there is no indication that he held special sessions to explain and elaborate upon the meaning of the Qur'ān. This practice was ad hoc and depended entirely on circumstances. The practice seems to have been that the Prophet simply recited to those present at the time what he received as revelation and assumed that they understood the text. This would have been a reasonable assumption on the part of the Prophet, as the Qur'ān was being revealed within a social context and in a language mostly familiar to his followers. Of course, not all verses would have been equally well understood by everyone, especially those verses with metaphorical expressions. For instance, it is reported that one of the Companions, 'Adiy b. Ḥātim (d. 68/687–688), did not understand the meaning of 'the white thread' and 'the black thread' in the following verse related to fasting:

> And eat and drink until the white thread [of dawn] appears to you distinct from the black thread [darkness of night].[10]

'Adiy b. Ḥātim reportedly interpreted 'the white thread' and 'the black thread' literally and reportedly took with him lengths of black rope and white rope when he went to bed so that he would know when to begin fasting. Bukhārī, in his *Ṣaḥīḥ*, records:

> ʿAdiy b. Ḥātim said: 'When the verse "until the white thread [of dawn] appears to you distinct from the black thread [darkness of night]" [2:187] was revealed, I took two pieces of rope (one black and the other white) and put them under my pillow. I kept looking at the [darkness of the] night [in order to distinguish the white from the black rope and know that it was dawn] but I could not distinguish it. So early in the morning I came to the Prophet (May God bless him) and mentioned that to the Prophet and he said: "It is the darkness of night and light of the day."'[11]

There are two types of interpretation by the Prophet: practical and expository. Practical interpretation is the form in which the Prophet put into practice a Qurʾānic instruction, whereas expository interpretation is that in which the Prophet explained what a particular verse meant. While the 'practical' can be called 'indirect', the 'expository' can be called 'direct'. Most of the Prophet's interpretation to his followers was practical rather than expository. The people around the Prophet understood the plain Arabic language of the Qurʾān and there was no need to go through each word, phrase, sentence or verse. An example of a direct (expository) interpretation is where the Prophet defined the word *miskīn* ('poor') in the Qurʾān:

> The poor person is not the one for whom a date or two or a morsel or two [of food] is sufficient. But the poor person is he who does not [beg or] ask the people [for anything] or show his poverty at all. Recite if you wish, God's statement: 'They do not beg of people at all' (Q.2:273).[12]

An example of an indirect (practical) interpretation would be the performance of daily prayer (*ṣalāt*). The Qurʾān commands Muslims to perform this but gives no details on how to go about it. The Prophet taught his followers how to perform *ṣalāt* by performing it himself. Similarly, the Qurʾān commands Muslims to pay *zakāt*, and the Prophet put the teaching into practice by implementing a system of *zakāt* with instructions.

What is noticeable in the interpretation by the Prophet (as reported in the ḥadīth) is that there is usually no systematic analysis (linguistic or other) of the texts with which he dealt. The Prophet was more interested in conveying the practical implications of the Qurʾān as it applied to a particular circumstance.

There is generally no dispute among Muslim scholars that, second to explication of the Qurʾān by the Qurʾān, the Prophet's perspective on the Qurʾān constitutes its most authoritative and valid interpretation. Referring to these two types of interpretation, Zurqānī (d. 1122/1710) states:

> There is no doubt that [we should] accept these two types [of interpretation]. As for the first type [interpretation of the Qur'ān by the Qur'ān], it is because the Almighty God knows better than others what He Himself intended. And the Book of God contains the most truthful speech. As for the second type [interpretation of the Qur'ān by the Prophet] it is because the best guidance is that of the Prophet (Peace be upon him). And it is his duty to elaborate and explain [the Qur'ān].[13]

The Prophet was the transmitter of God's word and was deeply involved in it, emotionally, spiritually and intellectually. The relationship between the Prophet and the Qur'ān was intimate and reciprocal. The Prophet had experienced the Qur'ān personally, while the Qur'ān itself depicts the Prophet's difficulties and frustrations, his vacillations between optimism and pessimism, and his relations with Muslims and non-Muslims. God's word had been given in a human language, Arabic, through the medium of the Prophet, who was himself overcome by its majesty and power. Herein lies the uniqueness of the Prophet's interpretation, for it is the experience and deep involvement with the 'word' that gave him the authority to interpret the Qur'ān.

Interpretation of the Qur'ān by the Companions

As noted above, some Companions of the Prophet had difficulty in understanding certain Qur'ānic verses. One of the reasons for this difficulty perhaps was that the Qur'ān was read and recited in the Qurayshī dialect, which was spoken in Mecca and the surrounding regions. Since the Prophet and the early Muslims (particularly of the Meccan period) were either Qurayshī or related to the Quraysh, they were familiar with the dialect. As the Prophet's preaching continued to spread beyond the borders of Mecca to Medina, Taif and neighbouring regions, new adherents communicating in other dialects would have had difficulty in understanding some of the Qur'ānic phrases or terms. This would have occurred particularly in the later part of the Prophet's mission, when Arabs from non-Ḥijazī tribes professed Islam.

A second difficulty for the Companions would have been in understanding some of the historical references of the Qur'ān, particularly to stories of prophets (*qiṣaṣ al-anbiyā'*) and nations of the past. Some Companions approached the 'People of the Book' (*ahl al-kitāb*), notably Jews in Medina, and asked them about such events and stories. A number of Jewish converts to Islam, for example Ka'b al-Aḥbār (d. 33/652–653) and 'Abd Allah b. Sallām (d. 43/663–664), were quite active in transmitting the knowledge of the People of the Book, some of which was related to stories of biblical prophets, to the Companions. In the post-prophetic period, several Companions, for example Ibn ʿAbbās (d. 67/686), engaged in discuussion on such matters on a vast scale with the numerous Jewish converts to Islam.[14]

The Companions' interpretation was often rather personal; that is, they expressed what they thought was the most appropriate meaning for the texts they dealt with, usually without attempting to demonstrate the validity of their positions. This is illustrated in the following report by Ibn ʿAbbās, the Prophet's cousin, in relation to Q.110:

> ʿUmar used to make me sit with the elderly men of Badr [those who fought in the Battle of Badr]. Some of them felt that my presence [due to my young age] among them [was] improper and said to ʿUmar, 'Why do you bring this boy to sit with us while we have sons like him?' ʿUmar replied, 'Because of what you know [regarding his knowledge of the Qurʾān].'

Ibn ʿAbbās went on to say:

> One day ʿUmar called me and made me sit with them [elderly Companions]. I think that he wanted to demonstrate to them [why he let me sit amongst them]. ʿUmar asked them: 'What do you say about the interpretation of the statement of God "When comes help of God, and the conquest"?' (Q.110:1). Some of them said: 'We are ordered to praise God and ask for His forgiveness, when God's help and the conquest [of Mecca] come to us.' Some others kept quiet and did not say anything. On that ʿUmar asked me: 'Do you say the same, O Ibn ʿAbbās?' I replied: 'No.' He said: 'What do you say then?' I replied: 'That is the sign of the death of God's apostle, which God informed him of.' God said: '[O Muḥammad] when the help of God comes [to you against your enemies] and the conquest [which is the sign of your death] – you should celebrate the praises of your Lord and ask for His forgiveness, and He is the One who accepts the repentance and forgives' (Q.110:1–3). On that ʿUmar said: 'I do not know anything about it other than what you have said.'[15]

An illustration of the personal nature of these interpretations can be seen in the explanation of the term *muttaqī* (one who is conscious of God) in Q.2:2. In the interpretation of this term in Ṭabarī's *Tafsīr*, each Companion expressed what he thought was the most appropriate meaning. For instance, according to Ibn Masʿūd, *muttaqī* means 'believers'. One interpretation of *muttaqī* by Ibn ʿAbbās was 'those who fear God's punishment and seek his mercy by believing in what He had sent'. Another interpretation of *muttaqī* by Ibn ʿAbbās was that believers should avoid ascribing divinity to others beside God.[16] Other Companions, such as

Abū Hurayrah (d. 58/678) and Abū al-Dardā' (d. 32/652), provided different definitions. The variation in the views expressed and the lack of any form of linguistic or other analysis regarding the meaning of *muttaqī*, for instance, suggests that in such interpretations each Companion was putting forward his personal view or opinion.

The Companions did not use a systematic approach in their understanding and exposition of the Qur'ān. Nor did they feel bound to support their interpretations with evidence from the ḥadīth or by extensive linguistic analysis. Often it was their *ijtihād*[17] that was the basis of interpretation. It was *ijtihād* that relied on what might be called the 'spirit of the Qur'ān and the Prophet' as they understood it.

Interpretation of the Qur'ān by the Successors

With the expansion of Muslim hegemony in the wake of the conquests of the first/seventh century, conversion to Islam from other religions began to take place on a large scale. The death of the Prophet meant that new Muslims had to rely on leading Companions for their understanding of the religion and the Qur'ān. Companions who settled in places such as Iraq, Syria, Egypt and Yemen, or remained in Mecca and Medina, became the authoritative exponents of the meaning of the Qur'ānic text. No doubt the Qur'ān was the fundamental source for the new religion; but for many converts who had not experienced the time of the Prophet and who came from other linguistic and religious backgrounds, it was difficult to access the meaning of the Qur'ān directly. Leading Companions, therefore, played a major role in ensuring that the text was understandable to a new generation of Muslims, many of whom did not know the now-'official' Qurayshī dialect of Arabic. It was the students of the Companions who became the third most important group of exponents of the Qur'ān: the 'Successors'.

As pupils of leading Companions, many Successors became well known as experts in the 'Islamic' disciplines and as teachers, particulary in three locations: Mecca, Medina and Iraq. The leading authority in Mecca was the Companion Ibn 'Abbās, who had several influential pupils. Among these were 'Aṭā' (d. 114/732), Mujāhid (d. 104/722) and 'Ikrimah (d. 105/723). In Medina, Ubay b. Ka'b (d. 29/649) was the leading exponent of *tafsīr* and had many influential students, including Abū al-'Āliyah al-Riyāḥī (d. 90/708), Muḥammad b. Ka'b al-Qaraẓī (d. 117/735) and Zayd b. Aslam (d. 130/747). Ibn Mas'ūd was the leading authority in Iraq. Among his students were al-Hasan al-Basrī (d. 110/728), Ibrāhīm al-Nakha'ī (d. 95/713) and Masrūq b. al-Ajda' (d. 63/682).[18]

Similar to the Companions, the Successors had a somewhat personal approach to the interpretation of the Qur'ān. This was exemplified in the interpretation of the term *muttaqī*, cited again in Ṭabarī's *Tafsīr*. To Qatadah, for example, a *muttaqī* is one who believes in the Unseen, prays and outlays money in the cause of God.[19] Hasan al-Basrī, by contrast, gives the meaning as follows: '*taqwā* (devoutness; God-consciousness) remains with the *muttaqūn* as long as they avoid many permissible things for the fear that they may be prohibited'.[20] Sufyān al-Thawrī says: 'They are called *muttaqūn* because they avoid what is [normally] unavoidable.' Rajā's opinion is, 'Whoever pleases to become a *muttaqī* should be humble.'[21] For ʿUmar b. ʿAbd al-ʿAzīz, '*taqwā* of God is not achieved by fasting in the day and worshipping all night but *taqwā* of God is avoiding what God has prohibited, and performing what God made obligatory'.[22]

In tradition-based *tafsīr*, interpretation by the Successors is considered authoritative. However, there is no agreement among Muslims on the level of authority enjoyed by the Successors in interpreting the Qurʾān. As pupils of the Companions, they are generally considered to be relying on the knowledge of their mentors. Despite this close link with the Companions, even leading authorities on *tafsīr*, such as Ṭabarī, disputed the authority of the Successors. As early as the second/eighth century Abū Ḥanīfa (d. 150/767), the imam of the Ḥanafī school, made clear his position on the issue of authority. He pointed out that, even when it comes to the Companions, he was free to choose from among their views. If this is the case with the Companions, he would have ascribed a much lower degree of authority to the views of the Successors. Abū Ḥanīfa says:

> I will follow the book of God if I find anything in it. If I do not find anything in it I will follow the sunnah of the Prophet and authentic sayings which are well known among the trustworthy people (*thiqāt*). If I do not find anything in the book of God or the sunnah of the Prophet, I will take the opinion of whomever of the Companions I wished and I will leave the opinions of whomever I wished [of the Companions].[23]

As for the Successors, Abū Ḥanīfa said that, if figures such as Ibrāhīm, al-Shaʿbī, al-Ḥasan, Ibn Sīrīn and Saʿīd b. al-Musayyab could exercise *ijtihād*, then he, Abū Ḥanīfa, could do likewise. Abū Ḥanīfa was less interested in giving authority to the Successors than in exercising his own judgement over which views to accept and which to reject. It is clear that he felt justified in exercising *ijtihād*.[24] On the other hand, Ibn Taymiyyah argued that the *tafsīr* of the Successors (within the broad category of *salaf*) should be considered authoritative: 'If they [the Successors] agreed on [the meaning of] something, there is no doubt that this constitutes a [definite] proof.'[25]

From tradition-based *tafsīr* to textualism

A sub-set of tradition-based *tafsīr* is 'textualist *tafsīr*'. In this book, I will use the term 'textualist *tafsīr*' to refer to interpretation that relies on text and tradition *and* at the same time approaches the question of interpretation strictly from a linguistic perspective. In other words, the thinking of the Textualists is dominated by the linguistic tools and criteria developed in classical *fiqh* and *tafsīr*.[26] I am suggesting that tradition-based *tafsīr* does not always have to be Textualist (governed by linguistic criteria alone). Thus, my use of the term Textualist or textualism implies interpretation that ignores or rejects the socio-historical context of the Qur'ān in interpretation.

Broadly speaking, classical and modern Textualists consider the interpretation of the ethico-legal content of the Qur'ān by the early generation of Muslims as the most authoritative. The limits to this interpretation, in their view, were spelt out by early imams, with apparent consensus. From the Textualists' point of view, the ethico-legal texts and the rules derived from them are to be followed in the modern period regardless of changed circumstances. Any attempt to move away from this is tantamount to subversion of Islam.

Modern Textualists, following their classical counterparts, believe that whatever the earliest Muslims propounded regarding the interpretation of the Qur'ān constitutes the most legitimate and authoritative reading. Although it is natural for any religious tradition to elevate its earliest converts to the top of the religious hierarchy, there are many reasons why Muslims, in particular Sunnīs, gave the first generation of Muslims (the Companions) an unusually high degree of religious authority. This is largely related to the momentous and often bitter events that occurred in the community in the first century of Islam. Immediately after the death of the Prophet, disputes arose on a number of important questions. That of political leadership (*imāmah*), in particular, pitted the Muhājirūn (migrant Muslims mainly from Mecca) against the Anṣār (Muslims of Medina). This division was temporarily resolved in favour of the Muhājirūn, with Abū Bakr (d. 13/634), a Meccan Companion, assuming the leadership of the community as the political successor to the Prophet. Other divisions arose later, many of which were rooted in the same issue of political leadership.

The murder of the third caliph, ʿUthmān (r. 23–35/644–655), and the bitter antagonisms that followed should not be overlooked in this context. The Prophet's wife ʿĀ'ishah (d. 58/678), strongly supported by some senior Companions in seeking retribution for the murder of ʿUthmān, stood opposed to ʿAlī b. Abī Ṭālib (d. 40/660), the fourth caliph. This major division within the community pitted Companions against each other, and in the ensuing Battle of Camel in 36/656, led by ʿĀ'ishah and ʿAlī on opposing sides, some very senior Companions were killed. The Battle of Siffin (36/657) between the forces of ʿAlī and Muʿāwiyah (Governor of Syria) and the ensuing arbitration between the two led to the emergence of an essentially rebellious force (known as Khārijīs) against the nascent Islamic state. The Khārijīs pitted themselves against other Muslims who did not share their beliefs, thus inflaming underlying antagonism in the broader community. In particular, their accusation that the third and fourth caliphs ʿUthmān and ʿAlī were 'unbelievers' was seen as highly provocative.[27] The Khārijīs' exaggeration of their differences with other Muslims into accusations of sinfulness only served to incite resentment towards the Khārijīs within the wider Muslim community. This reaction in part also triggered a counter offensive in the form of an emphasis on the sincerity, truthfulness and faith of the Companions and their commitment and service to Islam, and helped elevate their part in the historic paradigm of a 'model' community.[28]

Thus Sunnī Islam adopted the position that the Companions should not be judged by what they did in the conflicts that raged among them in the post-prophetic period.[29] This position was enhanced later by another development of a more intellectual nature: the emergence of several religious disciplines in Islam, in particular that of the ḥadīth. As the reported sayings and deeds of the Prophet, the ḥadīth were central to the understanding of what Islam was for Muslims in general, and for the newly converted in particular, many of whom had not met the Prophet. It was natural that later generations should venerate those who had witnessed the Prophet, his deeds and his workings within the society. In this way the Companions became the bridge between the period of revelation and the emerging second generation of Muslims.

Had the young Muslim community opted to divide the Companions into good and bad, believers and unbelievers, honest and dishonest, and knowledgeable and ignorant, the bridge between the prophetic period and the new generation would have been placed in jeopardy. A significant problem would have arisen: that of the necessity to reject the contributions of unsuitable Companions to the emerging body of religious knowledge. The problem would have escalated once the systematic collection of ḥadīth began, probably towards the end of the first/seventh century. In order to avoid such problems, a degree of sanctity was accorded the entire generation of Companions. This meant, of course, that Sunnī Islam later adopted the view that the Companions *as a group* were trustworthy, honest, sincere and knowledgeable in matters of religion, and were true representatives of the teachings of the Prophet. Further, the Companions *as a group* were the authority on which Muslims should rely in the area of intermediation between the prophetic period and later generations.

Thus, theoretically, any ḥadīth coming from any Companion of the Prophet was to be accepted, as long as the other transmitters in the chain were trustworthy and the narration was sound on the basis of the criteria developed in ḥadīth criticism. By the third/ninth century the idea of the trustworthiness and authority of the Companions as a group had been accepted without question in the Sunnī tradition. Once this had been institutionalized within the tradition, it became relatively easy to build an intellectual edifice around it. Thus, in the *tafsīr* literature, the views and opinions of the Companions also became the authoritative bases for understanding and interpreting the Qur'ānic text. This authority of the Companions was extended further to the Successors (*tābiʿūn*) and the Successors of the Successors (*tābiʿ al-tābiʿīn*) as well, leading to the development of a hierarchy of authority.

In addition to the political and military context of these developments, an understanding of their social context is also important. The emergence of an extremely wealthy class of Muslims who benefited from the conquests, and of their children who grew up in luxurious conditions in the first/seventh century, is important in this regard. The impact of this, even in places like Medina, was an increase in practices considered un-Islamic, such as drinking and music. The Umayyads kept a watchful eye on any sign of significant opposition to their rule, most notably during the reign of Yazīd b. Muʿāwiyah (d. 64/683). Some devout Muslims began to reject not only the political oppressiveness of the Umayyads but also the materialism and moral laxity evident in their communities in places like Hijaz, Syria and Iraq. Increasingly, these Muslims began to devote their time to acquiring knowledge of the religion and to teaching, which led to the development of centres of religious learning around well-known scholars in major cities of the caliphate.

In this period of rapid expansion of knowledge and thought in the Islamic world at the beginning of the second/eighth century, the overall state of interpretation of the Qur'ān could be described as 'fluid'. This fluidity was due to four main reasons: (1) regional differences with varying cultural mixes and degrees of interaction between Muslims, Jews, Christians and Zoroastrians; (2) the individual approaches of the Companions and Successors to the interpretation and application of key texts of the Qur'ān and ḥadīth, and the degree of rigour adopted; (3) the variety of texts, in particular of ḥadīth texts available on specific matters; and (4) the differences in the understanding of those texts.

With conquest and expansion of the Muslim caliphate, senior Companions were established as leaders in centres throughout the Muslim world, for example Basra, Kufa and Damascus. Such Companions, such as Ibn Masʿūd in Iraq, trained students from the generation of Successors, who, in turn, gathered their own students. Regional traditions of authority began to crystallize towards the end of the first/seventh century and the beginning of the second/eighth century. These were not distinct schools of interpretation or even of law; at first they reflected only differences of opinion on religious matters and rulings.

Within this broader context two distinct groups emerged in time: those who supported a reason-based approach and those who supported a tradition-based approach to problems of law and interpretation. Supporters of the reason-based approach argued that the laws of religion were based on reason and could be understood by studying the Qur'ān as well as the ḥadīth. Commandments and prohibitions could be understood by studying the Qur'ān and the circumstances in which it was revealed. This attitude to the Qur'ān and ḥadīth was more evident in Iraq, where some scholars reportedly rejected ḥadīth they considered inappropriate for their time. They did not see such texts as being in accord with their understanding of what was appropriate to the life of the community. For them, the objectives of religious law were an essential part of religion. Reason had to be used in determining what was appropriate and relevant, even though this meant that some texts might be reinterpreted or discarded. These supporters of reason became known in the jurisprudential literature as 'people of analogy' (*ahl al-qiyās*).

In contrast, supporters of the tradition-based approach were mainly associated with Medina. They tended towards containment and restriction of the use of reason. The most obvious example is the scholars of Medina from whom the Mālikī school developed, with its emphasis on text and tradition. This group felt that a high degree of freedom in understanding and applying the text would lead to a religious crisis. They valued stability and permanence in their quest to protect the young religion from morally corrupt and politically pragmatic Muslims. In time, this emphasis on restriction, containment, tradition and being bound by the text, gradually led to the emergence of a Muslim majority that strongly adhered to the text and curtailed flexibility in the interpretation of the Qur'ān.

Systematization of law

During the second/eighth century, emerging from the two broad trends described above (reason-based and tradition-based interpretation), the gradual systematization of the law, its sources and interpretation led to the emergence of schools of law, each of which was associated with a particular scholar and region. For instance, in Iraq, the Ḥanafī school began to be identified with figures such as Abū Ḥanīfa, al-Shaybānī (d. 189/805) and Abū Yūsuf (d. 182/798). In Medina, the Mālikī school was associated with Mālik (d. 179/796). Each region developed its own characteristics, its typical approach to the question of text and reason, and its peculiarities in interpreting the Qur'ān. Since by then the Qur'ān itself was a fixed written document, differences were limited to exploring methods of interpretation. Many problems existed with the ḥadīth literature, however, because of the fabrication of vast numbers of ḥadīth. Sifting authentic from unauthentic ḥadīth was a major task to which scholars in the second/eighth century devoted much time based on criteria they developed. As a result, towards the end of the second/eighth century several collections of ḥadīth were in existence.

An important need at the time was to create harmony between those who argued for a reason-based approach and those who favoured a tradition-based approach. The aims were to systematize the law and maintain unity within the *ummah*. While there was no disagreement between the two trends on the Qur'ān as the most important source of law, there were differences on the degree of flexibility that should exist in the use of reason (*ra'y*) in interpretation and the law. An important tool that was considered useful in this regard was *qiyās* (analogy). *Qiyās* was a by-product of *ra'y* and served to broaden the scope of the law and help interpret and apply the text to community life. Leading scholars of the time, such as Shāfiʿī (d. 204/820), debated the concept of *qiyās*. This attention was due not only to scholarly interest in methodological tools for interpretation and law, but also to the desire to find common ground between the two approaches – tradition-based and reason-based. Despite this, *qiyās*, as a tool of interpretation, attracted considerable criticism during the second/eighth and third/ninth centuries. Finally, due largely to the efforts of Shāfiʿī, a compromise was reached that narrowed the meaning of *qiyās*.

One of Shāfiʿī's key objectives was to emphasize the pre-eminence of tradition and text in law. It was essential, for him, that Muslims should first identify the sources of law in the Qur'ān and the ḥadīth. Given that there were no disputes about the Qur'ān as being the primary source of law, the focus was on the extent to which the ḥadīth should be relied on in determining law. One of the points of debate between Shāfiʿī and his opponents was whether the ḥadīth were equivalent to sunnah. For Shāfiʿī, there was no question that this was so: where ḥadīth were authentic they had to be followed and *qiyās* discarded. This significantly weakened the reason-based approach as it severely limited the free use of *qiyās*.

The process was more complex than simply excluding reason and emphasizing ḥadīth. A reading of Shāfiʿī's treatise, *al-Risālah*, shows that the debate on the issue of the acceptability or otherwise of ḥadīth, as well as on the use of *qiyās*, was vigorous and that Shāfiʿī's views were challenged. Both sides had their own understanding of what was acceptable in the matter of reason versus text. Accusations were made that scholars who followed the reason-based approach discarded the text (ḥadīth). For their part, the adherents of reason accused the followers of the tradition-based approach of being mere literalists who had no idea of how the law should be interpreted and applied. In the end it was the adherents of the tradition-based approach that emerged triumphant in law and even in the realm of *tafsīr*.

The inquisition and the gradual acceptance of textualism

Not long after the disputes between Shāfiʿī and his opponents on text and reason, another significant event unfolded, this time in the realm of theology. The Muʿtazilah, with their heavily reason-based approach to theological matters, began to propound the idea that the Qurʾān was 'created'. The powerful Abbasid caliph Maʾmūn (d. 218/833), who was heavily influenced by their thought, adopted the Muʿtazilī position on the creation of the Qurʾān (known in Arabic as *khalq al-qurʾān*). Not only did Maʾmūn adopt this controversial position but he also began to persecute those who did not follow this position, in the first state-sponsored 'inquisition' (*miḥnah*). Key state functionaries had to adopt the doctrine and many of those who did not were dismissed or persecuted.

Proponents of tradition-based *tafsīr*, in particular Textualists, were among those who vehemently opposed the Muʿtazilī doctrine as innovation and as an unjustified attack on the Qurʾān, the word of God. A leading opponent of the Muʿtazilīs was Aḥmad b. Ḥanbal (d. 241/855), a student of Shāfiʿī and a vocal Textualist.[30] The increased popularity of Aḥmad b. Ḥanbal as a result of his persecution at the hands of the Abbasid state apparatus, under which he remained steadfast, gave him support and sympathy among both the intellectual elite and the general populace. The inquisition came to an end in the caliphate of Mutawakkil (d. 247/861) who turned against the Muʿtazilah. This unexpected turn of events led to a genuine hardening of anti-reason attitudes among the religious and intellectual elite. From then on textualism was on the rise until it came to dominate much of the thinking in law and *tafsīr*. Had it not been for the Muʿtazilah's intolerance and their use of the political muscle of the powerful Abbasid caliphate to impose their theological position on Muslims in general, the Muslim community might have developed differently in relation to reason and text. The Textualists' reaction and the literalism that it generated might not have occurred with the intensity it did in the wake of the inquisition.

The Textualists relied on certain principles in their approach to *tafsīr*. These provided a basis for understanding, interpreting and applying Qurʾānic dicta to the daily life of individuals and the community. Their three principles were, first, that the text provided a fixed and objective foundation to understand the Qurʾān; and, second, that there were many texts in the Qurʾān and ḥadīth that indicated that the religion of Islam was complete.[31] It followed that rules pertaining to individual and social conduct were thus contained in the Qur'ān and the ḥadīth. Their third principle was that there was no need to seek further elaboration, clarification or justification based purely on reason. From then on, the role of reason in understanding and applying the sacred texts was significantly curtailed, particularly in Sunnī Islam.

Chapter 5

Interpretation based on reason

Interpretation based on reason (*tafsīr bi al-ra'y*) has occupied an uncomfortable place in the discipline of *tafsīr*. The aim of this chapter is to show that *tafsīr bi al-ra'y* in fact has an important role to play in Qur'ānic interpretation. In this chapter, I present an overview of the arguments about the legitimacy of *tafsīr bi al-ra'y*.

Tafsīr and *ta'wīl*

The term *tafsīr* is the most commonly used word for interpretation in Arabic, including interpretation of the Qur'ān. However, there is disagreement among linguists as to its origin. Some early scholars used *tafsīr* to mean explanation of words or speech. According to one opinion, the term *tafsīr* is the second form of the Arabic word *fasr*, and means 'to expound, reveal and make apparent the intelligible meaning'.[1] According to Ibn Manẓūr (d. 711/1311–12), *fasr* means revealing what is covered. *Tafsīr*, therefore, would be the revealing of what is intended or covered by a difficult word.[2] It is apparently in this sense that the Qur'ān uses the word in Q.25:

> And no example or similitude do they bring [to oppose or to find fault in you or in this Qur'ān], but We reveal to you the truth [against that similitude or example], and the better explanation (*tafsīran*) thereof.[3]

Here *tafsīran*, as explained by Ibn 'Abbās, means *tafṣīlan* – 'elaboration'.[4]

Another opinion suggests that the origin of *tafsīr* is not *fasr* but *safara* (to unveil or uncover).[5] The phrase *safarat [al-mar'at] 'an wajhihā* means '[the woman] removed her veil from her face'.[6] When the woman is thus unveiled she is referred to as *sāfirah*, which means that certain parts of her body are not covered. Thus the meaning of *tafsīr* may be related to 'uncovering' or 'revealing' what is hidden.[7] Whatever the origin, the meaning of *tafsīr* appears to be closely related to 'revealing'.

Zarkashī (d. 795/1392), a scholar of the principles of *tafsīr*, believes the technical term *tafsīr* is an area of knowledge by which one understands, explains and derives rulings and wisdom from the book of God revealed to the Prophet Muḥammad.[8] Abū Ḥayyān (d. 745/1344) defines *tafsīr* as a discipline that examines the recitation of the words of the Qurʾān, what these words signify, their connotations when they stand alone or in context, and the meanings attributed to them in that particular context.[9] This definition includes most of the relevant disciplines on which *tafsīr* relies: recitation (*ʿilm al-qirāʾāt*); morphology and rhetoric; literal and metaphorical use of the language; abrogation; occasions of revelation; and Qurʾānic narratives.

The second most commonly used term for interpretation of the Qurʾān is *taʾwīl*. *Taʾwīl* comes from the word *awl*, which means a return to the origin of something.[10] Edward Lane explains *taʾwīl* as discovering, detecting, revealing, developing, disclosing, explaining, expounding or interpreting; that to which a thing is, or may be, reduced, or that which it comes, or may come, to be.[11] In the Qurʾān, the word *taʾwīl* is used on a number of occasions. One of the most relevant is the following:

> It is He who has sent down to you [Muḥammad] the Book [this Qurʾān]. In it are verses that are entirely clear, they are the foundations of the Book and others not entirely clear. So as for those in whose hearts there is a deviation [from the truth] they follow that which is not entirely clear thereof, seeking *al-fitnah* [polytheism, trials], and seeking for its interpretation (*taʾwīl*), but none knows its interpretation (*taʾwīl*) save God. And those who are firmly grounded in knowledge say: 'We believe in it; the whole of it; [clear and unclear verses] are from our Lord.' And none receive admonition except people of understanding.[12]

Elsewhere in the Qurʾān, *taʾwīl* is used to indicate exactly what is signified in a dream or in reference to the interpretation of dreams: 'Thus will your Lord choose you and teach you the interpretation of dreams.'[13]

Taʾwīl and *tafsīr* are also used more or less synonymously as the explanation of meaning. It is in this sense that *taʾwīl* was used by many early authorities. An example is the Prophet's reported invocation of God to bestow upon Ibn ʿAbbās the understanding of religion and to teach him *taʾwīl* (interpretation) of the Qurʾān.[14] The great exegete Ṭabarī uses the term *taʾwīl* in this sense. For instance, when he says 'the statement with regard to the interpretation (*taʾwīl*) of the word of the Most High is so and so', he is referring to *tafsīr*. Equally, when the exegete Mujāhid (d. 104/722) says 'The scholars know its interpretation (*taʾwīlahū*)', he means the *tafsīr* of the Qurʾān.[15] Based on such usages, many ulama have argued that *ta'wīl* and *tafsīr* are the same. Abū ʿUbayd (d. 224/838) regards the two terms as synonymous.[16] Others, however, have argued that they are different. For instance, Ibn Ḥabīb al-Naysābūrī (d. 556/1160) states: 'In our times [a number of] exegetes of the Qurʾān emerged who when asked about the difference between *tafsīr* and *ta'wīl* could not indicate [the difference].'[17] The attempts to differentiate between *tafsīr* and *ta'wīl* are often confusing.[18]

In later periods, the term *ta'wīl* acquired a more technical meaning in connection with the debate on whether interpretation should rely on tradition (*ma'thūr*) or on reason or opinion (*ra'y*). In this context, *tafsīr* came to be associated with *riwāyah* (narration, tradition, text), while *ta'wīl* was related to *dirāyah* (understanding, reason, opinion).[19] *Tafsīr* was thus linked to knowledge handed down over time (tradition), whereas *ta'wīl* involved giving preference to one meaning over other possible meanings, supported or not by textual or linguistic evidence. This evidence, where it exists, relies heavily on *ijtihād*, and is arrived at with the aid of extensive linguistic, semantic and contextual knowledge. Thus *ta'wīl* implies the use of inference (*istinbāṭ*),[20] while *tafsīr* depends mainly on reports from the Prophet and the Companions. From a Sunnī point of view, a more controversial meaning of *ta'wīl* is associated with the interpretations of Ismaʿilīs and certain Sufīs, such as Ibn ʿArabī.

Tafsīr based on reason

The emergence within the Muslim polity of religio-political groups in the form of the Muʿtazilah, the Khārijīs or the Shīʿah, or of theological groups, such as the Qadarīs or Jabrīs, intensified interpretation based on *ra'y* (reason). A good example of reason-based interpretation occurs in verses related to 'God's judgeship', which means that God is the ultimate judge. This arose in connection with the agreement by the fourth caliph, ʿAlī b. Abī Ṭālib, that there should be arbitration (known as *taḥkīm*) between him and his opponent Governor Muʿāwiyah immediately after the Battle of Siffin in 36/657. Because of ʿAlī's agreement, a group of his supporters (later to be known as 'Khārijīs') rebelled against him, protesting that 'judgement belongs to God alone' (*lā ḥukma illā li-llāhi*). The rebels' interpretation of verses in the Qurʾān relating to the 'judgeship' of God was based on reason. With the rise of the Qadarīs,[21] the issue of predestination and free will came to be debated, again on the basis of Qurʾānic verses. The Muʿtazilah and Shīʿah,[22] as well as a number of other groups, played their role too. The result was a multiplicity of meanings and a large number of contradictory and irreconcilable views on important religious matters. During this early period, this form of interpretation continued without actual guiding principles.

It was largely in the wake of these disputes in early Islam in the first/seventh and second/eighth centuries that the debate on *tafsīr* based on reason and *tafsīr* based on tradition emerged. Related to this was the discussion on *ʿilm* and *raʾy*. *ʿIlm* meant traditional knowledge (ḥadīth, sunnah, text, precedent), whereas *raʾy* referred to reason or opinion (whether supported by authoritative texts or unsupported). The debate on *ʿilm* and *raʾy* was, however, more closely related to *fiqh* than to the interpretation of the Qurʾān. The labelling of the imam of the Ḥanafī school of law, Abū Ḥanīfa, as a legist of *raʾy*, is related to this debate. Abū Ḥanīfa is considered to have preferred *raʾy* over the text (in this case ḥadīth) in a number of his juristic views. Since this debate was about the place of text and textual authority vis-à-vis reason or opinion in religious matters, it soon involved *tafsīr* methodology, which in any case emerged as a discipline much later than *fiqh*. As Schacht argues, the discouragement of *raʾy* in interpretation of the Qurʾān probably owed much to the discussions among early legists.[23]

In *fiqh*, *raʾy* and *qiyās* (analogy) were severely criticized in the wake of Shāfiʿī's successful attempt to bring the Qurʾān and ḥadīth closer to each other. He sought to give the ḥadīth an authority equal to that of the Qurʾān, and to restrict both *qiyās* and *raʾy* in matters of law in favour of tradition and text. The chaotic situation with regard to the use and misuse of the Qurʾānic text in support of various legal, theological and religio-political views succeeded, in part, in discouraging scholars' use of *raʾy* in interpretation. They came instead to rely on what was considered a more objective and sound basis, that is, text, precedent and ḥadīth, the traditional sources of authoritative religious knowledge (*ʿilm*). *Raʾy* was less easily controlled as it was related to personal preference, opinion or inclination, whereas *ʿilm* could be identified, systematized and understood more objectively.

These early debates within the religio-political, legal and theological groupings, with their fluid approach to the Qurʾān, were encouraged by another group – Arabic linguists who contributed to the debate by writing specialist works on interpretation. Some of these scholars provided a linguistic basis for a reason-based interpretation of the Qurʾān.[24]

Not surprisingly, it was the Muʿtazilī theologians and linguists who provided the strongest linguistic support for reason-based interpretation of the Qurʾān. Many of them wrote specialist works on methodology as well as exegetical works of the Qurʾān. Muʿtazilī theologians, such as Qāḍī ʿAbd al-Jabbār (d. 415/1024), theorized about many aspects of the Muʿtazilī approach to the text. Others, such as Zamakhsharī (d. 539/1144), produced *tafsīr* that applied this approach at a basic level. Their interest in the linguistic analysis of the Qurʾānic text, as well as their methodological sophistication, should be seen as important intellectual contributions to the debate on the interpretation of the Qurʾān.

Opponents of *tafsīr* based on reason

The *ʿilm–raʾy* debate led to the discouragement of *raʾy* not only in *fiqh* but also in the interpretation of the Qurʾān and other *sharīʿah* disciplines.[25] One of the main arguments used to discourage *raʾy* with regard to the Qurʾān appears in the following ḥadīth by Ibn ʿAbbās: 'The messenger of God said: "He who interprets the Qurʾān according to his opinions (*raʾy*) should have his place prepared in the fire of hell."' Another ḥadīth expresses the idea that such *tafsīr* is prohibited by implication: 'He who says something concerning the Qurʾān according to his opinion [even if it] is correct has erred.'[26] The following verse is also used to bolster the argument that the interpretation (*taʾwīl*) of ambiguous or obscure verses cannot be known except to God:

> It is He who has sent down to you [Muḥammad] the Book [this Qurʾān]. In it are verses that are entirely clear; they are the foundations of the Book and others not entirely clear. So as for those in whose hearts there is a deviation [from the truth] they follow that which is not entirely clear thereof, seeking *al-fitnah* [polytheism, trials], and seeking for its hidden meanings, but none knows its hidden meanings save Allah. And those who are firmly grounded in knowledge say: 'We believe in it; the whole of it [clear and unclear verses] are from our Lord.' And none receive admonition except men of understanding.[27]

Since the verse, according to one reading of it, states that the interpretation of ambiguous verses is known only to God, many scholars condemned any attempt at interpreting those verses.

Among the most vocal opponents of *tafsīr* based on reason (and on whose views many Textualists of the modern period rely to justify their rejection of it) are the Ḥanbalī scholars, Ibn Taymiyyah and Ibn Kathīr (d. 774/1373), who attempted to exclude *tafsīr* based on reason from the realm of valid *tafsīr* altogether. Ibn Taymiyyah wrote:

> In brief, he who turns away from the views of the Companions and Successors and their *tafsīr*, and accepts what is contrary to those views is in error. Nay he is a heretic even if he was a *mujtahid* whose errors are forgiven.[28]

Ibn Taymiyyah appears to be more interested in preserving the opinions and views of the pious ancestors (*salaf*) on the interpretation of the Qurʾān, where such views exist. For him, these pious ancestors were the ones to interpret the Qurʾān authoritatively, as they were possessed of true 'knowledge' of its meanings. Similarly, Ibn Kathīr was interested in interpreting the Qurʾān in the light of a generally accepted corpus of ḥadīth.

He believed it was the ḥadīth – not *tafsīr*, history, theological works or even law – that provided the correct and true meaning of the Qur'ānic text.[29]

Ibn Taymiyyah appears to suggest that interpretation based on *ra'y* must be rejected because it does not rely on *'ilm*. In his *Fatāwā*, he quotes a number of Companions and Successors to support his position. For example, the first caliph, Abū Bakr, when asked about the meaning of the phrase in Q.80:31, *wa fākihatan wa abban* ('and fruits and herbage'),[30] responded that he ought not to say anything about the Book of God, which he did not know.[31] Ibn Taymiyyah also quotes the Companion Ibn 'Abbās' refusal to explain when asked about the meaning of *alfa sanatin* ('one thousand years') in the Qur'ān. Ibn 'Abbās reportedly said:

> Those refer to two days which God has mentioned in His Book. God knows what is meant by them better than I.[32]

Ibn Taymiyyah points out that many jurists of Medina were also reluctant to discuss interpretation of the Qur'ān.[33] He mentions Hishām b. 'Urwah, an early scholar of Medina, who said: 'I did not hear my father interpreting (*ta'awwala*) any verse of the Qur'ān at all.'[34]

Opposing the Mu'tazilīs (considered 'rationalists'), who argued for a metaphorical reading of the texts related to God's attributes, Ibn Taymiyyah argued that such verses of the Qur'ān were to be understood and explained only within the confines of a valid textual understanding as provided by the pious ancestors (*salaf*).[35] On the other hand, Mu'tazilīs argued that the verses should be interpreted in order to avoid claiming similarities with God; this meant a metaphorical reading, supported by an approach guided by reason. For example, Qur'ānic phrases such as 'the Most Gracious [God] ascended the throne'[36] would need to be interpreted as 'the Most Gracious [God] established on the throne of his almightiness'. Ibn Taymiyyah objected to such an interpretation and argued that the rationalists had established a number of criteria of their own and imposed those criteria on the Qur'ānic text as well as on God's attributes – an unacceptable innovation.[37] In this view, the rationalists should have limited their interpretation of such verses to those of the pious ancestors (*salaf*).

A closer reading of Ibn Taymiyyah, however, suggests that his rejection of *tafsīr* based on reason is qualified. He argues that the reports he quotes from the pious ancestors are 'sound evidence' that the pious ancestors were not comfortable with engaging in debates on interpretation where they did not have sufficient knowledge (*mā lā 'ilma lahum bihī*).[38] He concludes, however, that someone possessing knowledge of both the language and the religion has the background to comment, but insists that it is the duty of all people to remain silent on subjects about which they have no knowledge.[39] Perhaps Ibn Taymiyyah is saying that there are aspects of *tafsīr* based on reason that he might find palatable.

Ibn Taymiyyah differed from scholars such as Anbarī (d. 328/939) and Qurṭubī (d. 656/1258), who adopted a broad and lenient interpretation of the ḥadīth that appear to proscribe interpretation based on reason. The importance of the views of Qurṭubī and Anbarī is that they created the possibility of an inclusive view of *tafsīr*, a tradition that accommodated even Ibn Taymiyyah and Ibn Kathīr within it.[40]

Proponents of *tafsīr* based on reason

Several prominent exegetes of the Qur'ān have argued that *tafsīr* based on reason is valid, and they question the meaning of the ḥadīth that appears to condemn it. In interpreting the ḥadīth cited above ('He who interprets the Qur'ān according to his opinions (*ra'y*) should have his place prepared in the fire of hell') in favour of *tafsīr* based on reason, Anbarī said:

> This ḥadīth has two explanations. Firstly, he who speaks on problematic passages of the Qur'ān, uttering opinions that are not known from the early generations, namely, the Companions and the Successors, he is exposed to God's anger. Secondly – and this is the firmest and most correct of the two explanations – he who speaks on the Qur'ān, uttering opinions which he knows to be untrue, let him take up his seat in Hell.[41]

As for the other ḥadīth cited above ('He who says something concerning the Qur'ān according to his opinion [even if it] is correct has erred'), Ibn 'Aṭiyyah (d. 542/1147) explained this by saying:

> The meaning of this is that a man asks himself concerning the significance of a passage in God's Book and concedes an answer on the basis of opinion without due consideration of the expressed statements of the 'ulama' and the requirements of the scientific disciplines such as grammar and the principles of interpretation. This ḥadīth does not relate to linguists who explain its language, or grammarians who explain its grammar, or *fuqahā'* who explain its significances as long as each one bases his statements on *ijtihād* founded on the rules of knowledge and deduction. One who speaks thus is not speaking merely on the basis of opinion.[42]

For those who favoured *tafsīr* based on reason, interpretation was not merely preserving the views of the pious ancestors (*salaf*). It also meant recognizing and considering the views of the ulama, the textual sources such as ḥadīth, the law and principles of jurisprudence, and theology. Qurṭubī, for instance, firmly believed that without *ijtihād* there could not be an adequate interpretation of the Qur'ān.[43] Such *ijtihād*, based on tradition and sources and with expert knowledge of the *sharī'ah*[44] disciplines, would not come within the purview of the ḥadīth. Qurṭubī proposes an inclusive view of *tafsīr* that takes in *tafsīr* based on tradition and *tafsīr* based on reason. Though Qurṭubī was a firm supporter of *tafsīr* based on reason, he, like many other scholars, was less interested in philosophical or theological speculation.

The need for *tafsīr* based on reason

The philosopher Ibn Rushd (d. 595/1198) argued that *tafsīr* based on reason (which he called *ta'wīl*[45]) is essential for communicating the message of the Qur'ān. He maintained that the *sharī'ah* addresses people of different intellectual and psychological capabilities. People differ in their comprehension of what the *sharī'ah* conveys, as well as their ability to accept and confirm what they have been told. Some people are more reliant on rational evidence, others more comfortable with simple explanations or statements. For Ibn Rushd, this human diversity necessitates dealing with the Qur'ānic text at different levels. If only one level, the literal, for example, is accepted, then other people may be excluded. On the question of the *ta'wīl* of texts, Ibn Rushd believed there are two types of *sharī'ah* texts: texts that do not contradict what reason demands; and texts in which there is a contradiction between text and reason. While the first type does not pose problems, the second does and therefore should be subjected to *ta'wīl*.[46]

Linguistic considerations

The need for *tafsīr* based on reason is also evident linguistically. It cannot be assumed that all Arabic speakers will find the Qur'ānic text accessible simply because it is written in their own language. Several dialects existed, even in the first/seventh century. The same applies to today's Arabic, in which dialects have multiplied and the differences among them become even more pronounced. In the time of the Prophet, some Companions struggled to understand parts of the Qur'ānic text. The fact that the Qur'ān was revealed in the Qurayshī dialect meant that other Arabs faced difficulties in understanding the verses that used words and phrases specific to the Quraysh. The complexities associated with meaning (as will be explored later) often make it difficult to arrive at a meaning that is universally acceptable. The *tafsīr* tradition demonstrates that, by the second, third and fourth generations of Muslims, help was needed in interpreting the scripture, as increasing numbers of Arabs of distant dialects, and non-Arabic-speaking Muslims, joined the growing body politic of Islam.

Legal considerations

Several Muslim scholars argue that a careful reading reveals that relatively few verses in the Qur'ān could be considered strictly legal in nature. This opinion is shared by a number of Western scholars of Islam, for example Noel Coulson.[47] Estimates of the number of legal verses in the Qur'ān range from 80 to 500, depending on the definition of 'legal'. Even if the most generous figure of 500 is taken, only about 200 relate to personal matters (*al-aḥwāl al-shakhṣiyyah*) and inheritance. Most of the 500 verses refer to *'ibādāt* (forms of worship and ritual), which are considered integral to Islamic law. In other areas of law, such as contract law and criminal law, the Qur'ān makes very few references. The Qur'ān by its nature is not meant to be a legal text, which is demonstrated by its lack of interest in the minutiae of legal matters. Verses with a legal import tend to be incidental or in response to particular situations that the Muslim community or an individual had to address during the 22 years of the Prophet's mission (610–632).

The scarcity of strictly legal verses in the Qur'ān was obvious to many early Muslims, even the first generations. In order to meet the emerging needs of the community on matters of law and governance, Companions such as the second caliph, 'Umar (d. 24/644), relied on interpretation and extension of the Qur'ānic guidance, a process continued by other Companions and Successors. While reliance on both the Qur'ān and sunnah continued throughout the first/seventh and second/eighth centuries, with the added use of *ra'y* or *qiyās*, figures such as the jurist, Shāfi'ī, sought to assist interpretation by drawing on the ever-expanding ḥadīth literature of his time. Shāfi'ī also attempted to close the gap between the Qur'ān and sunnah by arguing that the sunnah, the documentation of which is the ḥadīth, represents explanation of the Qur'ān. After quoting the Qur'ānic verse, 'And we have sent among you an Apostle, one of yourselves, to recite to you our signs, and to purify you, to teach you the Book and the Wisdom' (2:146), and similar verses, Shāfi'ī noted that the term 'wisdom' meant the sunnah of the Prophet. Thus, for Shāfi'ī, the sunnah had to be followed:

> So God mentioned His Book – which is the Qur'ān – and Wisdom, and I have heard that those who are learned in the Qur'ān – whom I approve – hold that Wisdom is the sunnah of the Apostle of God. This is like what [God Himself] said; but God knows best! For the Qur'ān

> is mentioned [first], followed by Wisdom; [then] God mentioned His favor to mankind by teaching them the Qur'ān and Wisdom. So it is not permissible for Wisdom to be called here [anything] save the sunnah of the Apostle of God. For [Wisdom] is closely linked to the Book of God, and God has imposed the duty of obedience to His Apostle, and imposed on men the obligation to obey his orders.[48]

Personal reflection

The need for *tafsīr* based on reason also exists at the level of personal reflection on the Qur'ān. One of the problems associated with the prohibition of *tafsīr* based on reason is whether this is in line with the Qur'ānic commandment to contemplate and reflect upon the text. There are verses in the Qur'ān that clearly state that it is the duty of Muslims to contemplate and reflect upon the message rather than rely on recitation alone:

> Will they not ponder over this Qur'ān or are there locks upon their hearts?[49]

And

> We have revealed unto you a blessed Book so that people may ponder over its messages and that those who are endowed with insight may take them to heart.[50]

These verses suggest that people bestowed with intelligence can interpret the Qur'ān.[51]

Is *tafsīr* based on reason always valid?

At this point it is worth looking at the forms of *tafsīr* based on reason that some Muslims consider to be problematic. The first is interpretation of the text merely by relying on personal opinion and without attending to linguistic, historical or contextual evidence. This can occur in a number of ways. One is when the interpreter imposes on a text a meaning that is less obvious, thus rejecting the most obvious and relevant meaning. In interpretation, the most obvious meaning of a text has an important place and usually should not be discarded in favour of any other without valid reasons or evidence.

A second form is when a meaning is imposed on the text for a personal reason or aim. If the interpreter is seeking justification for a particular view, he or she may give the text a meaning that corresponds to that personal objective. For instance, if the subject is women's rights and the interpreter wants to justify a particular position on monogamy, for instance, he or she may read into a particular Qur'ānic verse the desired meaning, again ignoring all other forms of evidence available.

A third form is where a text has two or more possible meanings and the interpreter chooses one without regard to the context and other Qur'ānic texts available. An example is the verse saying that Muslims should not put themselves in the way of danger (*lā tulqū bi aydīkum ila al-tahlukah*[52]). If the text were taken to mean that a Muslim should not act in any situation where there was the *potential* for danger, this would go against many Qur'ānic verses that emphasize values such as striving to help others even if one's life is in danger. This type of verse should be interpreted not only by looking at the text itself but also by relating it to other Qur'ānic commandments and principles.

A fourth form occurs when an individual has a preconceived idea and intends to support that idea by selecting Qur'ānic texts. In such a case, the person is imposing a particular meaning on the text rather than searching for the most legitimate meaning. Examples of such interpretation abound in the literature, with various theological interpretations fitting into this category. Certain interpretations by Mu'tazilī theologians, such as Zamakhsharī, or some of the esoteric meanings propounded by certain Shī'ī scholars (known as Bāṭinīs), are examples. These latter scholars interpreted the term *baḥrayn* (two bodies of water) in 'He has let free the two bodies of flowing water (*baḥrayn*) meeting together' (Q.55:19) as 'Alī and Fāṭimah. They also interpreted *al-lu'lu'* (pearls) and *al-marjān* (corals) in 'Out of them [the two bodies of water] come pearls and coral' (Q.55:22) as Ḥasan and Ḥusayn, the grandsons of the Prophet and two Shī'ī imams.[53]

These examples of *tafsīr* based on reason could be included in the unacceptable category as they do not attempt to look at the overall meaning of the Qur'ānic text or to explore associated meanings and principles, whether linguistic, historical, social, cultural, moral, ethical or legal. These interpretations are a product of the interpreter's imagination or are largely unsubstantiated opinions. They do not rank with careful interpretation of the Qur'ān that is conducted in the light of the 'spirit of the Qur'ān' and its ethico-legal message.

Interpretation to a substantial degree is personal, regardless of what is known of the actual tools and mechanisms. 'Personal' does not mean that interpretation is based on whim, but that there is a subjective dimension to any interpretation simply because the experiences of those engaged in interpretation are unique. This should not lead us to suggest that, because of this subjectivity, *tafsīr* based on reason should be excluded from the purview of valid *tafsīr*.

We cannot deny that much of the *tafsīr* literature we have today is largely based on reason. If *tafsīr* is to be based *entirely* on tradition, it would be no more than a dry exercise in reading a Qur'ānic verse followed by explanatory ḥadīth or reports from the Companions traced back to the Prophet. Accepting this view of *tafsīr* would also mean rejecting much of the *tafsīr* literature. It is perhaps for this reason that Ibn Taymiyyah, despite his stand on *tafsīr* based on tradition, had to acknowledge that *tafsīr* based on knowledge of the subject matter and not contradicting textual evidence should be considered acceptable.

Many *tafsīr* works that are manifestly based on reason, such as Razī's *Mafātīḥ al-ghayb*, Bayḍāwī's *Anwār al-tanzīl*, Abū Ḥayyān's *al-Baḥr al-muḥīt* and Alūsī's *Rūḥ al-ma'ānī*, nevertheless are regarded as acceptable. We should also include in the acceptable *tafsīr* based on reason, works written by Muslim jurists (*fuqahā'*). These jurists concentrated on verses that were legal in nature and interpreted them from the perspective of a particular legal school. Examples of juristic *tafsīr* include Jaṣṣāṣ' *Tafsīr aḥkām al-Qur'ān*, Ibn al-Arabī's *Tafsīr aḥkām al-Qurān*, Qurṭubī's *al-Jāmi' li aḥkām al-Qur'ān* and Ibn al-Jawzī's *Zād al-masīr fī 'ilm al-tafsīr*.

We must not forget the much-maligned *tafsīr ishārī*, that is, *tafsīr* that adopts the view that there are hidden meanings to be attributed to the Qur'ān. Sūfīs engaged in this form of *tafsīr* from early on. This approach was also adopted by some Shī'ah as well. The Sunnīs gave conditional acceptance to some forms of *tafsīr ishārī*, provided that they did not (a) lead to the derivation of laws and rulings or theological positions, (b) contradict other Qur'ānic or ḥadīth texts, (c) contradict the apparent meaning of the text. Moreover, the interpreter should not claim that the meaning arrived at was the only meaning possible.[54]

The tendency of the *tafsīr* tradition on the whole was to accommodate as much as possible: from interpretations based on tradition to those based on reason. Despite this inclusivity, when it comes to the ethico-legal content of the Qur'ān there is barely any variation in *tafsīr* across the schools of law: on the whole, all interpret them within a textualist framework. This remarkable consistency can be explained partly by the fact that the basics of *fiqh* and the rulings associated with ethico-legal matters were agreed upon early in Islamic history and were given a finality that went unchallenged for centuries.

Chapter 6

Flexibility in reading the text

This chapter highlights the flexibility that existed in *reading* the Qur'ānic text in more than one way in the earliest period of Islam. It suggests that, if this flexibility was provided for reading the sacred text itself, perhaps this should be taken as an indication of some support for flexibility in *interpreting* the Qur'ān, particularly its ethico-legal content. While many Muslims may consider that such flexibility as provided by the Prophet in the recitation of the Qur'ān has no bearing on the question of interpretation, it is useful to reflect on this flexibility to accommodate the needs of the Prophet's contemporaries with reference to their dialectical variations. In this, perhaps there is a lesson for us when we are approaching the issue of interpretation.

Seven *aḥruf*

According to a well-known ḥadīth, the Qur'ān was revealed in seven *aḥruf* (plural of *ḥarf* and translated variously as 'ways' or 'dialects').[1] Linguistically, *ḥarf* has a number of meanings other than 'letter of the alphabet'; for example, extremity, edge or side.[2] This ḥadīth continues to generate debate among Muslim scholars to this day. Suyūṭī (d. 911/1505) states there are 40 different interpretations of this ḥadīth and provides many of them.[3] One of the most common interpretations of the 'seven *aḥruf*' is that they refer to the seven main dialects of Arabic that existed in Arabia at the time of the Prophet. In the literature on the principles of *tafsīr* there is a view that the word '*aḥruf*' refers to the seven 'readings' (*qirā'āt*) of the Qur'ān that are considered authoritative and valid.[4] The problem with this explanation, as pointed out by Suyūṭī, is that only a few words in the Qur'ān, such as *uff* ('ugh!') in Q.17:23 and *'abadah* ('those who worship') in Q.5:60, can be recited in seven different ways.[5] A second difficulty is that the possible ways of reading a word can sometimes exceed seven.[6] It is recorded that the word *uff* in the Qur'ān has been read, or pronounced, in 37 ways, which takes it far beyond the number of readings possible under the ḥadīth referred to above.[7]

According to Abū al-Faḍl al-Rāzī (d. 460/1068), the seven *aḥruf* indicate differences related to seven aspects of the Arabic language. Among these are nouns such as number and gender; the conjugation of verbs into perfect, imperfect and imperative; inflection; omission and addition; replacement; and dialects.[8] Razī gives various examples of these differences, all of which are easily found in the Qur'ān. His explanation of the seven *aḥruf* has many close adherents among scholars, for example Ibn Qutaybah (d. 276/889) and Ibn al-Jazarī (d. 739/1338).[9] Such an approach, however, is heavily reliant on linguistic analysis and a grammatical treatment of the text, which are unlikely to have been the Prophet's intention when he reportedly said that the Qur'ān was revealed according to seven *aḥruf*. It is equally unlikely that the Companions would have thought of the text in this way. Razī's explanation would have been plausible to a scholar of the third/ninth or fourth/tenth centuries, when the grammatical structure of Arabic was being documented and approached analytically.

There are further opinions on the meaning of the seven *aḥruf*, with particular focus on the number seven (*sab'ah*). According to an opinion attributed to Qāḍī 'Iyāḍ (d. 544/1149), seven in the ḥadīth does not literally mean the number seven, but is a term used in Arabic for the concept of 'many'.[10] The Qur'ān uses the word seven in a number of places. For example:

> The parable of those who spend their wealth in the way of God is that of a grain of corn: it grows seven ears, and each ear has a hundred grains. God gives manifold increase to whom He pleases.[11]

Here, as the verse itself indicates ('God gives manifold increase'), the meaning of 'seven' is several hundred or a large number, not literally seven hundred.

Seven *aḥruf*: seven dialects or seven ways?

One of the most probable explanations of the seven *aḥruf* is that they refer to the seven dialects according to which the Qur'ān was revealed. These dialects appear to be those of the tribes of Quraysh, Hudhayl, Thaqīf, Hawāzin, Kinānah, Tamīm and al-Yaman.[12] This could be taken to mean that certain words of the Qur'ān could be read using synonymous terms from these dialects. Such an interpretation is supported by Ibn Mas'ūd's reading of the verse '*inna allāha lā yaẓlimu mithqāla dharrah*' (Q.4:40) as '*inna allāha lā yaẓlimu mithqāla namlah*'.[13] He thus uses the synonym *namlah* for *dharrah*. According to Mannā' al-Qaṭṭān, such dialectical differences are cited as the most acceptable interpretation of *aḥruf*.[14] The reports by Ibn Mas'ūd, Ubayy b. Ka'b and 'Umar

b. al-Khaṭṭāb (see below) also indicate that it was the different ways of reciting sections of the Qur'ān, presumably based on the reciter's own dialect, that led the Companions to seek the Prophet's opinion with regard to the correct recitation of those sections. The emphasis was on the words that were heard, as indicated by the following reports:

Ḥadīth 1

'Umar b. al-Khaṭṭāb reports: I heard Hishām b. Hakīm reciting Sūrat al-Furqān [Q.25] during the lifetime of Allah's Apostle [Muḥammad] and I listened to his recitation and noticed that he recited in several different ways which Allah's Apostle had not taught me. I was about to jump over him during his prayer, but I controlled my temper, and when he had completed his prayer, I put his upper garment around his neck and seized him by it and said, 'Who taught you this *sūrah* which I heard you reciting?' He replied, 'Allah's Apostle taught it to me.' I said, 'You have told a lie, for Allah's Apostle has taught it to me in a different way from yours.' So I dragged him to Allah's Apostle and said (to Allah's Apostle), 'I heard this person reciting Sūrat al-Furqān in a way which you haven't taught me!' On that Allah's Apostle said, 'Release him, (O 'Umar!) Recite, O Hishām!' Then he recited in the same way as I heard him reciting. Then Allah's Apostle said, 'It was revealed in this way,' and added, 'Recite, O 'Umar!' I recited it as he had taught me. Allah's Apostle then said, 'It was revealed in this way. This Qur'ān has been revealed to be recited in seven different ways, so recite of it whichever [way] is easier for you [or read as much of it as may be easy for you].'[15]

Ḥadīth 2

Ubayy b. Ka'b reported: I was in the mosque when a man entered and prayed and recited (the Qur'ān) in a style to which I objected. Then another man entered (the mosque) and recited in a style different from that of his companion. When we had finished the prayer, we all went to Allah's Messenger (may peace be upon him) and I said to him, 'This man recited in a style to which I objected, and the other entered and recited in a style different from that of his companion.' The Messenger of Allah (may peace be upon him) asked them to recite and so they recited and the Apostle of Allah (may peace be upon him) expressed approval of their affairs (their modes of recitation), and there occurred in my mind a sort of denial which did not occur even during my pre-Islamic days. When the Messenger of Allah (may peace be upon him) saw how I was affected (by a wrong idea), he struck my chest, whereupon I broke into a sweat and felt as though I were looking at Allah with fear. He (the Prophet) said to me: Ubayy!

> A message was sent to me to recite the Qur'ān in one dialect (*ḥarf*), and I replied: 'Make (things) easy for my people.' It was conveyed to me for the second time that it should be recited in two dialects (*ḥarf*). I again replied: 'Make affairs easy for my people.' It was again conveyed to me for the third time to recite in seven dialects (*aḥruf*).[16]

Ḥadīth 3

> Bukhārī narrates that 'Abd Allah b. Mas'ūd heard someone reading a verse, which he had heard the Prophet reading in a different way. So he brought the person to the Prophet and he [the Prophet] said, 'Both of you were correct.'[17]

These ḥadīth, which are reported in collections like those of Bukhārī (d. 256/870) and Muslim (d. 262/875), suggest that there were differences in reading the Qur'ān and that these differences were significant to the extent that the 'offenders' were brought to the Prophet. Despite the differences in their recitation, the Prophet seemed to indicate that each recitation was correct and as revealed. The Prophet accepted this diversity without any apparent difficulties. He confirmed this by saying that the Qur'ān was revealed in different ways; that is, the sections could be read in more than one way. To indicate this flexibility, he stated that a verse concerned with mercy should not end with punishment, and a verse that dealt with punishment should not end with mercy:

> Ṭabarī reports from Abū Hurayrah: The Prophet [may peace be upon him] said that this Qur'ān was revealed according to seven *aḥruf*. So read without any feeling of guilt (*ḥaraj*). But do not finish [a verse in which] the mention of mercy exists with [words indicating] punishment. And do not finish [a verse in which] the mention of punishment exists with [words indicating] mercy.[18]

The Prophet supported his view by saying that the Qur'ān was revealed according to seven different ways:

> Narrated by 'Abd Allah b. 'Abbās: Allah's Apostle said, 'Gabriel recited the Qur'ān to me in one way. Then I requested him (to read it in another way), and continued asking him to recite it in other ways, and he recited it in several ways till he ultimately recited it in seven different ways'.[19]

The ḥadīth quoted above indicate that there were differences in the recitation of the Qur'ān, but the exact nature of those differences remains somewhat unclear. Some ḥadīth refer to a particular *sūrah*, i.e. *Sūrat al-Furqān*; in the other *ḥadīth* there is no mention of a *sūrah*. Despite this uncertainty about the exact nature of the differences, all ḥadīth available on the issue suggest the existence of differences and variations in *reading* the Qur'ān at the time of the Prophet.

According to some reports, the Prophet's purpose in allowing different readings was to make the Qur'ān more accessible to the community (*ummah*), as many of the converts were illiterate and would not have been able to cope with a lengthy text unless some form of flexibility was introduced. Ibn Qutaybah said:

> It was among the ways in which God the Most High who made the Qur'ān easier for the community by commanding His Prophet that each tribe read it in its dialect in line with their conventions. Thus a person from [the tribe of] Hudhayl would read *ʿattā ʿīn* meaning *ḥattā ḥīn*. He pronounces it [differently] by changing *ḥā'* to *ʿayn*. The tribe of Asad reads *yiʿlam* [for *yaʿlam*].[20]

For Ibn Qutaybah, this was to allow recitation of the Qur'ān in the dialect of each tribe. Many of those who converted to Islam, particularly after the migration of the Prophet to Medina in 1/622, were from tribes other than the Quraysh, with each tribe having its own way of pronouncing particular words, and even having different registers (vocabularies). Thus, unless some flexibility was allowed to slightly modify the reading of the Qur'ān according to their own conventions, it would have been very difficult for people from these tribes to recite it, or perhaps even to understand some of its parts.[21]

This flexibility was important in making the revelation more accessible to a wider audience. Had it been restricted to a style of recitation that was strictly in line with the Qurayshī dialect, other Arabs, who were proud of their tribes, dialects and customs, would have felt that it was a Qurayshī Prophet receiving a Qurayshī revelation and imposing it on non-Qurayshī Arabs. This is despite the fact that the Qurayshī dialect had achieved a special status in pre-Islamic Arabia because of the importance of Mecca. The town was a commercial and cultural centre and was also the destination for pre-Islamic pilgrimage.[22]

The debates on the seven *aḥruf* provide a reasonable justification for approaching the Qur'ānic text in a more flexible way. If there was scope to read the text of the Qur'ān in different ways during the time of the Prophet, can the meaning of the text be approached in like manner? There is no doubt that in Qur'ānic scholarship the flexibility that existed during the Prophet's time was eventually limited. With the collection of the Qur'ān as a book during the third caliph ʿUthmān's reign (r. 23–35/644–656), the text came to be considered fixed forever, and no flexibility was later contemplated in reading the text, except in so far as the recognized readings (*qirā'āt*) were concerned. Based on the understanding of Q.15:9 ('Verily, it is We who have sent down the *dhikr* [Qur'ān] and surely We will guard it [from corruption]') it has been argued that the text of the Qur'ān is forever protected from textual corruption, such as alteration, since God would not tolerate such corruption of the Qur'ānic text.[23] The different *qirā'āt* are not considered alteration, as they are believed to be based on tradition and prophetic authority. Any reading based on dialects and not authorized by the Prophet was not to be allowed.

Once the Qur'ānic text had been written down and fixed during the time of 'Uthmān, and accepted by the Muslim community, and orders had been given to burn any other material that did not conform to the codex of 'Uthmān, the idea was widely accepted that any departure from the codex was considered corruption of the Qur'ānic text. It was only a matter of time before the dogma developed that any kind of linguistic departure from the original was not acceptable and could not be recited, in spite of evidence that such flexibility was apparently given by the Prophet to early Muslims.

From seven *aḥruf* to one *ḥarf*?

During the reign of 'Uthmān, differences arose among Muslims in regions of the emerging Islamic caliphate as to the recitation of the Qur'ān.[24] Some adopted particular readings and argued that it was their readings alone that were authoritative. For instance, Anas b. Mālik reported:

> [The Companion Ḥudhayfah who] had fought in Syria with the people of Iraq to conquer Azrabayjan and Arminia came to 'Uthmān. He was alarmed by the differences among [the people of Iraq] with regard to the reading [of the Qur'ān].[25]

When several senior Companions became aware of such disagreements on the recitation of the Qur'ān among Muslims, they requested that the caliph take action to ensure that Muslims remained faithful to God's revelation and did not corrupt the accuracy of their scripture. 'Uthmān formed a committee of Companions, many of whom had been associated with the recording of the revelation during the Prophet's time and had also sat on the committee that reportedly 'put together' the Qur'ān during the reign of the first caliph, Abū Bakr. 'Uthmān ordered the committee (comprised of Zayd b. Thābit, 'Abd Allah b. al-Zubayr, Sa'd b. Abī Waqqāṣ and 'Abd al-Raḥmān b. Al-Ḥārith), chaired by Zayd b. Thābit, to compile the Qur'ānic text based on the earlier collection of Abū Bakr's time, a copy of which had been reportedly left with the second caliph, 'Umar, and later with his daughter, and wife of the Prophet, Ḥafṣah.[26]

Once the collection was finalized and copies were made, it was sent to major regions of the caliphate such as Iraq and Syria. ʿUthmān is reported to have issued a decree to burn all Qurʾānic materials that did not accord with the officially approved version of the text.[27]

Muslim scholars dealing with the history of the collection of the Qurʾān tend to minimize the tension between some senior Companions and ʿUthmān on this matter,[28] but the differences, for example between ʿAbd Allah b. Masʿūd and ʿUthmān[29] and between Ubayy b. Kaʿb and ʿUthmān, were apparently quite serious. Each insisted that his version of the Qurʾān was authoritative and that ʿUthmān did not have the right to override their recitations. ʿUthmān, instead of handling the matter gently, treated both Ibn Masʿūd and Ubayy b. Kaʿb harshly, which probably led them to join forces in opposing the caliph.

ʿUthmān's attempt to unify Muslims on one version of the Qurʾān was essentially to avoid schism among Muslims who were adopting different readings of the most important text of Islam. If the differences were caused by disagreements over the seven *aḥruf*, then a reasonable step was to retain only the most basic version – the one that corresponded with the dialect of the Quraysh – in the name of unity.

A further imperative for many scholars of the Qurʾān has been to minimize human involvement in the ʿUthmānic codex by arguing and attempting to prove that any handling of the Qurʾān during the caliphate of ʿUthmān was in accordance with the divine plan for the text in terms of compilation and writing down. The divine protection of the Qurʾān from human intervention may be deduced from Q.15:9: 'Verily it is We Who have sent down the *dhikr* [the Qurʾān], and surely We will guard it [from corruption].'[30]

That the codex of ʿUthmān retains seven ways of reading has been rejected by prominent scholars of the Qurʾān. Ṭabarī, for example, believes that the version includes only one of the seven ways of reading.[31] Those who share his view believe that the seven ways of reading the text existed in the days of the Prophet, Abū Bakr and ʿUmar, and also during the early part of ʿUthmān's caliphate, but that afterwards recitation was restricted to only one, in order to avoid division within the Muslim community and to prevent the dangers associated with such division.

The question of the seven *aḥruf* continues to be problematic in the *tafsīr* literature to this day. Acceptance of the concept of the seven *aḥruf* raises the question of whether the Qurʾānic text we have is exactly the one revealed to the Prophet, and necessitates an explanation of the basis on which ʿUthmān restricted the various readings that had been validated by the Prophet. On the other hand, rejection of the seven *aḥruf* carries with it denial of numerous authentic reports in the collections of Bukhārī, Muslim and other canonical works, and, at the same time, necessitates an explanation of the existence of variant readings in the *tafsīr* literature.

Many Muslims of the modern period would probably prefer to avoid this debate. But for Contextualists today, what is of interest is the degree of flexibility provided even in the reading of the Word of God and, by analogy, in the interpretation of God's Word. The main lesson for Contextualists in the twenty-first century is that, even in the revelation itself, a degree of flexibility was entertained by the Prophet to meet the needs of the Muslims of his time. For them, the same flexibility should be available in understanding and interpreting the Word of God in line with the needs of Muslims today.

Chapter 7

Abrogation and reinterpretation

This chapter focuses on the concept of abrogation (*naskh*) and its relevance to flexibility in interpretation and application of the Qur'ān in different times and circumstances. *Naskh* is one the most relevant notions surrounding the rules provided in the Qur'ān that relate God's word to the life of the believer. Its relevance lies in the fact that, within a very short period of 22 years, at least some of the initial rulings in the Qur'ān changed a number of times to meet the evolving needs of the community. Circumstances changed, and so did moral imperatives; a fact recognized to a certain extent in Islamic legal theory and tradition. However, *naskh* has been given little attention by Muslim jurists and scholars as an important method in dealing with changes to law in a substantial way. It has been studied largely as an object of historical curiosity. Despite this, I believe, that in any discussion of *naskh*, the issue of changes in laws and rulings should be given priority. This is imperative in view of the current problems many Muslims are facing in their efforts to implement what is referred to as 'Islamic law'. Many traditionalist ulama[1] consider that social development and the law need not complement each other. This is an attitude that leads to a mismatch between the law and the social needs for which the law is meant to serve. The traditionalist rationale generally put forward is: 'We have to change to what the *sharī'ah* commands us, not the other way round.' Despite this view, I believe that *naskh* provides a strong basis for the reinterpretation of some texts of the Qur'ān, particularly in the area of its ethico-legal content, in order to best link the Qur'ān to the needs of Muslims today.

Naskh: meaning and form

The literal meaning of *naskh* is to annul, supersede, obliterate, efface or cancel.[2] Technically, it means abrogation of one ruling by a subsequent ruling.[3] The basis for this is found in a number of Qur'ānic verses, the most important of which is:

> Whatever verse [of the Qur'ān] do We abrogate or cause to be forgotten, We bring a better one or similar to it. Know you not that God is able to do all things?[4]

Muslim scholars in general[5] consider that this verse indicates that certain Qur'ānic rulings or verses could be, and in fact were, abrogated. They were superseded by similar or better rulings or verses, although sometimes the abrogating texts differed widely from the initial injunction. Some scholars, such as Hibatullāh (d. 519/1125), identified a large number of cases of abrogation. He states, for instance, that the *zakāt* verse (Q.9:103) abrogated all other urgings to give (*ṣadaqah*).[6] Q.9:5, referred to as 'the sword verse', is said to have abrogated 113 other verses.[7] By the fourth/tenth century, several scholars had identified 235 instances of abrogation, and that number eventually doubled.[8] Further on, the trend was reversed and the number of verses claimed as abrogated was gradually reduced. Suyūṭī decreased the number to 20 and Shāh Waliullāh reduced it further to only five instances.[9] Many of these differences were related to different conceptions of *naskh*.

Naskh occurs in several ways. One is the abrogation of a Qur'ānic ruling by another Qur'ānic ruling. There is no dispute among Muslim jurists, at least those who accept the concept of *naskh*, about the existence of this form of abrogation.[10] The second form is the abrogation of a Qur'ānic ruling by a sunnah (ḥadīth). There are two ways in which this may occur. One is by an *āḥād* ḥadīth (solitary ḥadīth). The majority of scholars believe that abrogation of a Qur'ānic ruling/verse by an *āḥād* ḥadīth should not be permitted because such ḥadīth, in terms of authenticity, do not belong to the category of *mutawātir* (a ḥadīth which is transmitted from a large number of narrators), and thus do not constitute definite proof, unlike the Qur'ān.[11] The second is abrogation by a *mutawātir* ḥadīth.[12] Many early leading authorities, such as Abū Ḥanīfa, Mālik b. Anas and Aḥmad b. Ḥanbal, believed that abrogation of the Qur'ān by the sunnah could occur if it was by a *mutawātir* ḥadīth.[13] This is based on the understanding that the sunnah is a form of revelation (*waḥy*), as the following verse is said to suggest:

> Or does he [the Prophet] speak of [his own] desire. It is only an inspiration (*waḥy*) that is inspired.[14]

Shāfiʿī is one scholar who rejected this form of *naskh*. He argued that, as Q.2:106 stated that the replacement ruling should be similar to or better than the ruling being repealed, and the sunnah could not be equal to or better than the Qur'ān, the sunnah could not replace a Qur'ānic ruling.[15]

A third form of *naskh* is the abrogation of a sunnah by the Qur'ān. This form is regarded generally by scholars of *fiqh* as possible[16] because, in terms of the hierarchy of the sources, the Qur'ān is supreme and the sunnah is second to the Qur'ān. There are several examples of this. For instance, the Prophet prayed facing Jerusalem when he migrated to Medina; this was established by the sunnah but was annulled and replaced by the verse that ordained that Muslims face the Ka'bah (House of God) to pray.[17]

The fourth is the abrogation of a ruling based on a sunnah[18] by sunnah.[19] Jurists regard as permissible the abrogation of rulings that are equal to each other in terms of the status of the ḥadīth and also revocation by a superior ruling (*āḥād* by *mutawātir*, for example).[20] Abrogation is not allowed if the abrogating source is lower in the hierarchy; for example, a ruling based on a *mutawātir* ḥadīth cannot be abrogated by an *āḥād* ḥadīth.[21] The focus of this chapter is on the abrogation of Qur'ānic verses and therefore will not explore these ḥadīth-related categories.

Categories of abrogated verses

Abrogated Qur'ānic verses fall into three categories. The first is where abrogation affects the two aspects of a Qur'ānic text: the ruling, as well as the recitation (*naskh al-ḥukm wa al-tilāwah*). In this type of abrogation, the verse is withdrawn from the Qur'ānic text and its ruling is no longer valid. An example of a 'verse' of which both the wording and the ruling were abrogated is that related to breastfeeding ('suckling' or *raḍā'*)[22] as is indicated in the following report recorded in the *Ṣaḥīḥ* of Muslim:

> 'Ā'ishah, may God be pleased with her, reported that it had been revealed in the Holy Qur'ān that ten clear breast-feedings made the marriage unlawful. This was abrogated [and substituted] by five breast-feedings and God's Messenger, may peace be upon him, died [while this was recited as part of the Qur'ān]. Before [the death of the Messenger], it was found in the Holy Qur'ān.[23]

This text, the so-called verse of *al-raḍā'*, does not exist in the Qur'ān. 'Ā'ishah's comment, if authentic, that the verse was in use even at the time of the Prophet's death suggests that the verse was taken out when the Qur'ān was collected during the reigns of Abū Bakr or 'Uthmān. Given the implication of such a view, many Muslim scholars were reluctant to accept the view that the text was removed from the Qur'ān after the death of the Prophet.

The second category of abrogation affects the ruling of a verse but not its wording (*naskh al-ḥukm dūna al-tilāwah*). This means that the verse remains part of the Qur'ānic text and is recited. However, the ruling it conveys is no longer in operation. An example of this type of abrogation is Q.33:50:

> O Prophet! We have made lawful to you, your wives to whom you paid their dowers; and those whom your right hand possesses out of the prisoners of war whom God has assigned to you; and daughters of your maternal uncles and aunts, who migrated [from Mecca] with you; and any believing woman who dedicates her soul to the Prophet if the Prophet wishes to wed her; this only for you not the believers [at large]. We know what we have appointed for them as to their wives and the captives whom their right hands possess in order that there should be no difficulty for you and God is Oft-Forgiving and Most Merciful.

According to this verse, it was open to the Prophet to take wives from among the listed categories. However, this ruling was reportedly abrogated by Q.33:52, which prescribed that the Prophet should not take any more wives:

> It is not lawful for you [to marry more] women after this nor to change them for [other] wives, even though their beauty attract you except any your right hand should possess. And God does watch over all things.

Although this verse abrogated the ruling of Q.33:50, the latter remains part of the Qur'ānic text.

The third category of abrogation affects the wording of a verse but not its ruling. This means that, although the verse is no longer part of the Qur'ānic text, its ruling remains applicable. An example of a verse the wording or recitation of which was abrogated while the ruling remains is the so-called 'verse of stoning' (*āyat al-rajm*):[24]

> 'Abd Allah b. 'Abbās reported that 'Umar b. Khaṭṭāb sat on the pulpit of God's Messenger [may peace be upon him] and said: Verily God sent Muḥammad [may peace be upon him] with truth and He sent down the Book upon him, and the verse of stoning was included in what was sent down to him. We recited it, retained it in our memory and understood it. God's Messenger [may peace be upon him] prescribed the punishment of stoning to death [to the adulterer and adulteress] and, after him, we also prescribed the punishment of stoning. I am afraid that, with the lapse of time, the people [may forget it] and may say: 'We do not find the punishment of stoning in the Book of God' and thus go astray by abandoning this duty prescribed by

> God. Stoning is a duty laid down in God's Book for married men and women who commit adultery when proof is established, or if there is pregnancy, or a confession.

ʿUmar suggested that the text of this verse existed in the Qurʾān at the time of the Prophet. It does not exist in the ʿUthmānic codex. However, in line with the opinion of all schools of law, the ruling of stoning to death for adultery remains in force.[25]

Among the issues related to *naskh* is whether the abrogating ruling is more or less equal to its predecessor in terms of severity. The two different rulings related to the punishment for *zinā* (unlawful sexual intercourse) provide an example in which the abrogating verse was more severe than the abrogated one. The earlier ruling on the punishment for unlawful sexual intercourse in the case of women appears to have been house arrest. The Qurʾān reads:

> And those of your women who commit unlawful sexual intercourse, take the evidence of four witnesses from amongst you against them; and if they testify, confine them [i.e. the women] to their houses until death comes to them or God ordains for them some [other] way.[26]

This punishment is said to have been abrogated by the ruling related to flogging or stoning. The new ruling is prescribed in the verse, 'The woman and the man who are guilty of unlawful sexual intercourse, flog each of them with a hundred stripes.'[27] The so-called 'stoning verse', '[As for the] elderly person, whether male or female, if they commit unlawful sexual intercourse, stone them [to death]', is said to have prescribed 'stoning', but its recitation is said to have been abrogated. Flogging and stoning are more severe forms of punishment than house arrest.

Some scholars, such as Hibatullāh b. Sallāmah (d. 468/1075) and Abū ʿUbayd, mention that an earlier ruling may be abrogated without being replaced.[28] The following verse is an example:

> O you who believe! When you [want to] consult the Messenger [Muḥammad] in private, spend something in charity before your private consultation. That will be better and purer for you. But if you find not [the means for it], then verily, God is Oft-Forgiving, Most Merciful.[29]

This is said to have been abrogated by the verse:

> Are you afraid of spending in charity before your private consultation [with the Messenger]? If then you do it not, and God has forgiven you, then [at least] perform the daily prayer and give *zakāt* and obey God. And God is All-Aware of what you do.[30]

The issue of *naskh* has to be taken in the context of an evolving Islamic community with changing needs in terms of guidance and rulings. Accordingly, a number of earlier rulings were repealed and substituted by new rulings. The necessary flexibility was provided by *naskh*.

Extreme views of *naskh*

Some scholars, such as Hibatullāh b. Sallāmah and Abū ʿUbayd, exaggerated the existence of *naskh* to an unlikely degree by pointing out that many, possibly hundreds, of verses fell into that category.[31] For instance, Hibatullāh claimed that the first half of certain verses was revoked while the other half remained valid. Explaining Q.7:183, he stated that the beginning of this verse, 'Respite will I grant them (*wa umlī lahum*)', was abrogated by Q.9:5, while the rest of Q.7:183 remained valid.[32] Abū ʿAbd Allah al-Qāsim b. Sallāmah claimed that the first part of Q.5:105 was abrogated by the second half of the same verse.[33] Another extreme example is Ibn al-Arabī's view that the first and last parts of Q.7:199 were abrogated while the middle part remained valid.[34] A further exaggeration in this context was that customs and habits that existed in pre-Islamic times were nullified or abrogated by the Qur'ān.[35] Examples include the prohibition of marriage to one's father's wives, and the rulings on blood money and retaliation. Similarly, abrogation claims were made in the case of permission for Muslims to consume foods previously prohibited to Jews and Christians.[36] However, according to the contemporary scholar Ṣubḥī al-Ṣālih, many ulama had actually taken such matters out of the category of *naskh*.[37]

Naskh and the immutability of ethico-legal content

An important part of the debate on *naskh* is the idea of development or progression in the rulings of the Qur'ān. Textualists and semi-Textualists of today consider that, once a ruling is spelt out in the Qur'ān or in the sunnah, it is immutable and should be followed regardless of time, place or circumstances. In the early development of Islamic theology, especially within the context of the debate on the nature of the Qur'ān as to whether it was created or uncreated, a position emerged according to which the Qur'ān is both eternal and an attribute of God (associated with *kalām* – the attribute of speech). Referring to this belief, the so-called *Waṣiyyat Abī Ḥanīfah* (reportedly composed around 210/825) states:

> We confess that the Qur'ān is the speech of God, uncreated, His inspiration and revelation, not He, yet not other than He, but His real quality, written in the copies, recited by the tongues, preserved

> in the breasts, yet not residing there. The ink, the paper, the writing are created, for they are the work of men. The speech of God on the other hand is uncreated, for the writing and the letters and the words and the verses are manifestations of the Qur'ān for the sake of human needs. The speech of God on the other hand is existing in Him, and its meaning is understood by means of these things. Whoever says that the speech of God is created, he is an infidel regarding God, the Exalted, whom men serve, who is eternally the same, His speech being recited or written and retained in the heart, yet never dissociated from Him.[38]

Further, to emphasize this eternity, Q.85:21–22, 'Nay this is a glorious Qur'ān [inscribed] in a Tablet preserved', were interpreted as the Qur'ān's having being recorded in the 'Preserved Tablet' (*al-lawḥ al-maḥfūẓ*) at the beginning of creation as a permanent record. The argument was that, since God knows past, present and future, God's rulings are immune to change. The implication for those who hold this view, is that the text and rulings of the Qur'ān offer no scope for change.

This theological position is fraught with problems in the light of the debate on *naskh*. A satisfactory explanation has to be given for the obvious presence of *naskh* in the Qur'ān, and for the notion that God changed the very rulings He gave to the community. The explanation that God intentionally gave rulings for different circumstances because He knows that human communities change should not be overlooked. This notion of change can and should play an important part in the discussion of *naskh*. The Qur'ānic revelation occurred over 22 years (610–632 CE), during which the Prophet put his mission in place. Within that period, even though the community remained largely within the confines of Hijaz (around Mecca and Medina), a number of ethico-legal instructions given in the earlier period of the mission were changed once, twice or even three times.

An example of these changes is the ruling related to the consumption of wine. At first the Qur'ān pointed out that drinking wine was a great sin (*ithm kabīr*);[39] it then stated that believers should not come to prayers (*ṣalāt*) while under the influence of wine;[40] and finally the Qur'ān declared that believers should keep away from wine completely.[41] A further instance is provided in the Qur'ān's instructions to the Medinan Muslims on how to deal with aggression from non-Muslim Meccans. When the Muslim community was weak, the Qur'ān urged them to be patient and tolerate the hostility of the Meccans.[42] However, when the Muslims became relatively powerful and able to resist the Meccans, the Qur'ān said that the Muslims might fight in self-defence.[43]

From a Contextualist point of view, with changes like these to ethico-legal rulings in response to different situations, God appears to be providing the community with an important tool with which to change rulings in line with changing needs and circumstances. If that is the case, there is a problem in holding the view that *all* Qur'ānic rulings must be immutable or unchangeable – in the sense that another ruling cannot be devised or implemented to match with broader Qur'ānic objectives. But the principles of jurisprudence (*uṣūl al-fiqh*) did not entertain the idea that Qur'ānic rulings could be changed by later rulings that are not directly from God or the Prophet, despite there being empirical data to the contrary from the time of the Prophet and the Companions.

Many abrogating verses were revealed in Medina, within the last decade of the Prophet's mission. There are several reasons for this. The Muslim community in Mecca was a very small minority. They were unable to defend themselves against the constant persecution by their Meccan opponents and had little control over key decisions being made regarding the governance of the Meccans. This lack of political power is clearly shown by the fact that Meccans who became Muslims during this period were severely persecuted, especially if they were from the lower classes of slaves and other marginalized groups. The biographer of the Prophet, Ibn Isḥāq (d. 150/767), states:

> It was the wicked Abū Jahl who used to incite the men of Quraysh against the Muslims. When he heard of the conversion of a man of high birth with powerful friends, he [Abū Jahl] criticized him vigorously and put him to shame. 'You have left your father's religion', he said, 'although he is a better man than you; we shall make your prudence appear folly and your judgement unsound, and we shall bring your honour low'. If he was a merchant, he said, 'By God, we shall see that your goods are not sold and that your capital is lost'. If he was an uninfluential person, he beat him and incited people against him.[44]

The situation of the Muslims changed significantly with their migration to Medina. In addition to a large number of Meccan Muslims, mass conversions by Medinans meant that the majority of the Medinan population became Muslim, and the Prophet became the de facto religious and political leader of the Muslim community there.[45] The Jewish population of Medina who did not convert gradually left or was forced to leave and their place was taken by an increasingly assertive Muslim community, in terms of numbers and strength.[46] Medina, thus, became a home for the community of believers (*mu'minūn*), with political, economic and military strength. This sense of autonomy meant the community needed rulings to govern itself, to maintain law and order, and to conduct relationships within and beyond its bounds.

With the change from a weak to a relatively powerful and autonomous 'state', the direction of Qur'ānic guidance also changed in some respects. In the early period of Islam in Mecca (610–622), the focus was largely on the spiritual and moral development of the individual. There were also rulings for the support of the poor and deprived.

Beyond instructions like these there was very little in the Qurʾān in the Meccan period about governing the community and maintaining harmonious relationships among the various groups, clans and tribes, as such guidance was not relevant. The shift in emphasis occurred in Medina. The language as well as the tone of the Qurʾān changed in line with the changes in the community. This change, to a certain extent, is embodied in the concept of *naskh*. However, Muslim scholars like Zarkashī, Ibn Ḥazm and Suyūṭī who discussed *naskh*, did not take it to its logical conclusion that, when society changes there is sufficient warrant in the Qurʾān and the sunnah to change certain rulings or at least aspects of their application through reinterpretation. Rulings are useful only so far as they provide a strong and reasonable basis for the proper functioning of society. If they do not fulfil that objective they should be open to change according to changed circumstances.

From a Contexutalist perspective, the logical implication of *naskh* was not seriously considered by Muslim scholars, either in the formative or the post-formative periods of Islamic law. There were several reasons for this. One was the idea that, since the Qurʾān was the 'Word' and attribute of God, it should have the attribute of permanence. Also related to this are the jurisprudential developments that took place early in Islamic history, especially through the contributions of figures like Shāfiʿī, who emphasized that any rulings given in the Qurʾān or in the authentic sunnah should be followed. *Naskh* was thus relegated to a mere historical study of the changes that occurred to rulings during the 22 years of revelation, without explanation or discussion of what stimulated the changes. The legacy of the rise of jurisprudential methodology in the second/eighth and third/ninth centuries, and its failure to recognize the close relationship between *naskh* in the Qurʾān and changing social needs, led in part to the idea that rulings in the Qurʾān cannot be changed by anyone other than God or the Prophet. Other scholars, however, took a more lenient view of change. For instance, the Ḥanbalī scholar, Ibn Qayyim, said that laws should change if the customs, on which the laws were based, changed. Elaborating on this, he wrote a lengthy chapter in his famous *Iʿlām* entitled, 'On changing the *fatwā* and varying it in accordance with change in time, place, situation, intention and customs'.[47] However, it must be recognized that this did not mean that Ibn Qayyim was arguing for changing the rulings provided in the Qurʾān.

Today, Textualists calling for the implementation of rulings in the Qurʾān and sunnah appear to have little interest in exploring the fact that many rulings in those two sources changed even in the formative years of Islam, and how *naskh* was later understood in Islamic jurisprudential methodology.[48]

Ethico-legal content of the Qur'ān: form, moral objectives and abrogation

A key problem for Muslims today in the area of implementing the ethico-legal rulings of the Qur'ān lies in the difficulty of distinguishing between the outward form of Qur'ānic rulings and the moral purpose behind them. The concept of *naskh*, however, can provide a relatively easy way of achieving this. Examination, however, of *naskh*-related verses often reveals that the Qur'ān does not abrogate *the objective* of a ruling, but rather reinforces that objective by amending the ruling itself. In the case of *zinā* (unlawful sexual intercourse) or what the Qur'ān calls *fāḥishah*, a woman committing the offence was, in the early period of Islam, detained within her home until she died.[49] The objective was to prevent the woman from engaging in further unlawful sexual activity. Prevention also remained at the core of the second ruling, flogging,[50] which abrogated the earlier ruling. The deterrent was revoked, not the objective, which remained in force to prevent offences that were against Islamic morality. The same could be said about the rulings on consumption of wine. The objective was to prevent the damage that alcohol abuse could do. None of the other verses revealed in relation to this suggests that the objective of prevention was abrogated. What was abrogated was the means by which prevention was to operate in the community.

One conclusion that may be drawn from this is that a Qur'ānic ruling should be looked at first in order to ascertain its underlying objective. If that objective is understood, then the next stage would be to see how the Qur'ān wanted to achieve that objective. At this point, temporal, cultural and circumstantial differences or contexts may be taken into account. In the early Islamic community, amputation was used to punish and prevent theft.[51] Without changing the underlying objective, one could argue, a Muslim community could today find a means of prevention that is more in line with its own circumstances. The Qur'ānic objective, as stated in the amputation verse (Q.5:38), 'As for the person who steals, whether male or female, cut off their hands in requital for what they have wrought and as a deterrent ordained by God', appears to be prevention of theft, not amputation of the thief's hand. Amputation is simply a means to an end.

Had scholars taken a more flexible approach in the formative period of Islamic law and accommodated the implications of the theory of *naskh* into the jurisprudential methodology, scholars of today would have been saved many difficulties. It is likely that when the law was developed in the first/seventh and second/eighth centuries, Muslim life had not significantly changed: the social, economic, political and legal structures remained largely intact. Differences were not considered serious enough to justify a radical departure from rulings, although Companions like 'Umar

b. Khaṭṭāb (d. 23/644), the second caliph, found some of the rulings given in the Qur'ān and the sunnah to be inadequate within a few years of the Prophet's death.[52] The changes introduced in the area of rulings/law by Abū Bakr and ʿUmar, and later by the Umayyad and Abbasid caliphs and other scholars, were not seriously considered when the jurisprudential theory was developed by scholars such as Shāfiʿī. Instead, the changes were incorporated in the developing body of law and legitimized as part of the 'sunnah', thus rejecting any suggestion that the changes were somehow equivalent to nullification of rulings provided in the Qur'ān and sunnah.

Shāfiʿī's *Risālah* is very clear that, in the presence of any authentic text (Qur'ān and ḥadīth), contrary opinions, whatever their source, should be rejected:

> On all matters concerning which God provided clear textual evidence in His Book or [a sunnah] uttered by the Prophet's tongue, disagreement among those whom these [texts] are known is unlawful.[53]

All had to be subjugated to this theory. Attempts by earlier Companions to introduce changes to rulings in the Qur'ān and the sunnah were sometimes given a cover of legitimacy by the argument that their modifications were in accord with instructions they may have received explicitly or implicitly from the Prophet. The reality, however, is that when he thought circumstances warranted it, ʿUmar clearly contradicted the Qur'ānic instructions in a number of cases, instances being *zakāt* and divorce. In the case of *zakāt*, one of the categories of recipient from the Qur'ānic point of view was *al-mu'allafat qulūbuhum* (those whose hearts are to be reconciled),[54] because their alliance with Muslims was seen as important during the time of the Prophet. The Prophet would give them a share from the *zakāt* funds to obtain and maintain that alliance. This practice continued during the time of the first caliph, Abū Bakr. However, ʿUmar, during his caliphate, refused to give to this group from *zakāt* funds. He reasoned with them that the Qur'ān had allocated them a share at a time when Muslims were weak and their allegiance to Islam was needed; the situation had since changed and the Muslims now had grown strong and were not in need of their allegiance.[55] As for divorce, due to the high rate that was affecting the community, ʿUmar declared the triple divorce (*ṭalāq*) in a single formula to be three divorces, and thus irrevocable.

During the time of the Prophet, however, declaration of 'three divorces' at one time were considered just one and therefore revocable. A contemporary scholar, Mahmassani, stated:

> This [type of] divorce [triple divorce in a single formula] was considered a single divorce and revocable during the time of the Prophet,

> peace be upon him, and the time of Abū Bakr [may God be pleased with him] and for two or three years during the caliphate of ʿUmar b. al-Khaṭṭāb. This was acceptable because people were mindful of divorce. But when people became unmindful regarding divorce, the announcement of triple divorces in a single formula increased among them. [ʿUmar] saw that it was in the public interest [in order to stop that practice] to punish them and make their divorce irrevocable.[56]

ʿUmar's decisions were later given an authoritative gloss by early jurists in order to make them acceptable to jurisprudential theory. Constructs such as the 'justness' of the Companions, their sincerity and devotion to Islam and their Islamic knowledge were used if a particular Companion contradicted what was in the Qur'ān or gave a ruling that went against an instruction in the Qur'ān or the sunnah. An illustration of this is provided by Būṭī in his *Ḍawābiṭ al-maṣlaḥah*; he tries to explain away a number of instances in which ʿUmar gave rulings contrary to the Qur'ān and the practice established by the Prophet.[57] Būṭī, following the approach of jurisprudential theory, states:

> The truth of the matter is that ʿUmar, may Allah be pleased with him, did not go against the text in his *ijtihād* or in a decision he made. What some writers claimed, that some of his *ijtihād* or decisions went against the text of the Qur'ān, is by itself evidence of the fact that ʿUmar followed the text and of his strong desire not to go against the text.[58]

Jurisprudence: from practice to theory

The key principles of jurisprudential theory, as developed by Shāfiʿī and others, remained standard until the modern period. Although a very small number of scholars, for example Shāṭibī (d. 790/1388) and Ṭūfī (d. 716/1316),[59] attempted to take jurisprudential theory beyond the confines of the Shāfiʿian foundations in some respects, they had slight impact on jurisprudential theory. Ṭūfī's view that 'public interest' (*maṣlaḥah*) was a basis for developing law and even for changing laws that were based on the Qur'ān and sunnah was not taken into consideration. Scholars like Ṭūfī were attempting to introduce new approaches at a time when the development of jurisprudential theory was complete and deviations would have been very difficult. Their only recourse was either through *maqāṣid al-sharīʿah* (objectives of the *sharīʿah*) or by using *maṣlaḥah* as a liberating force. By that time, however, the entrenched attitudes of the ulama and the schools of law had formed a formidable barrier to change.

In the modern period, however, the ideas of scholars like Ṭūfī are being revived. Some of the modernists of the early twentieth century used their ideas to argue for change in the interpretation of at least some of the ethico-legal texts of the Qur'ān. More recently, some Contextualists have been increasingly using these ideas in putting a case for reinterpretation of those ethico-legal rulings.

Concluding remarks

Naskh could be considered as one of the most useful tools for relating the Qur'ān's rulings to changing needs and circumstances. I have already shown that, within a very short period of 22 years, the Qur'ān changed a number of its rulings as the circumstances of the Muslim community changed; this fact is given recognition only grudgingly in Islamic legal history and tradition. It is my belief that, in any discussion of *naskh*, the changes to rulings that occurred during the very early period of Islam as a result of changed circumstances should be recognized as a legitimate tool of jurisprudential theory.

The attitude on the part of many ulama, even today, that developments in society do not need to have any effect on law, leads to an unfortunate mismatch between the law and the purposes for which law exists. Their rationale is that people have to change to fit with what the *sharī'ah* commands, not the other way round. Muhammad Asad states:

> We need not 'reform' Islam, as some Muslims think – because it is already perfect in itself. What we must reform is our attitude towards religion, our laziness, our self-conceit, our short-sightedness, in short, *our* defects, and not some supposed defects of Islam. A change there must be, but it should be a change *within* ourselves – and it should go in the direction of Islam, and not away from it.[60]

Despite this view, *naskh* still offers us today a strong basis for the reinterpretation of parts of the ethico-legal content of the Qur'ān in order to relate the Qur'ān even more closely to the needs of Muslims. This is not to argue in any way, however, for an unguided, unprincipled or undisciplined approach. Principles and approaches will have to be developed for this purpose. For today's Muslims, *naskh* can be a means of keeping the objectives of the Qur'ān alive and relevant.

Chapter 8

The meaning of the text as an approximation

If a substantial part of the Qur'ān can only be interpreted in an 'approximate' fashion, then it is possible to argue that an approximate understanding of the Qur'ān as a whole is valid. In this chapter, I will explore three text types in the Qur'ān. In relation to these text types it is difficult to suggest that one can simply arrive at a meaning and be certain that the meaning so arrived at would be the 'true' and 'final' meaning. What some of these texts refer to is not easily accessible to the human mind, and indeed in some cases is simply beyond human experience. In some cases, the literal meaning of the text is not intended at all. What these texts show is that a degree of indeterminacy exists in relation to the meaning of all forms of the Qur'ānic texts.

Several early Qur'ānic scholars attempted to classify the Qur'ānic texts. Ṭabarī, for instance, classified texts from the perspective of *authority to interpret*. His first type was verses that could only be interpreted directly or indirectly by the Prophet. This includes verses related to various commandments and prohibitions. Ṭabarī's next text type included verses whose interpretation is known only to God. These are concerned with future events, such as the 'time of the final Hour', the 'blowing of the Trumpet' or the return of 'Isā b. Maryam (Jesus, son of Mary). The third text type represents verses whose interpretation is open to anyone familiar with the Arabic language.[1] By contrast, Ibn 'Abbās (d. 32/652) reportedly divided the text into four categories from the perspective of '*knowability*': what the Arabs knew of the Qur'ān because it was revealed in their language; interpretation that anyone can know; interpretation that only scholars (ulama) can know; and interpretation known only to God.[2] These early attempts at classifying the Qur'ānic text show that early Muslims were aware that not all Qur'ānic texts should be treated in exactly the same way.

The question of text types is also important from a Contextualist point of view. A possible classification today could be the following four types, from the perspective of how approximate the meaning of the text will be: (1) texts that are related to the Unseen (*ghayb*); (2) historically oriented texts; (3) parables; and (4) practice-oriented texts. The first type concerns God, His attributes and work, Paradise, Hell and the world beyond human experience. The second type is texts related to past nations, peoples, stories, prophets and religions (as well as events during the life-time of the Prophet). The third type, parables, are stories or accounts through which certain lessons can be learned. The fourth category deals with beliefs and values, ethical and moral behaviour, law, rulings and instructions, commandments and prohibitions. It is this last type that is directly relevant to ethico-legal issues (the focus of this book) and will be explored in Chapter 11. The present chapter will focus on the first three types, the objective being to highlight that in these texts we can arrive at approximate meanings only.

Texts related to the Unseen (*ghayb*)

Many verses in the Qur'ān refer to two types of beings in the metaphysical realm: God and His being (such as His attributes and His works), and others, such as the 'Throne' (*arsh*), Paradise (*jannah*), Hell (*nār*), angels (*malā'ikah*) and the 'Preserved Tablet' (*al-lawḥ al-maḥfūẓ*). These texts are concerned with beings that are beyond human experience and comprehension.

Most of the references in the Qur'ān are to God. There are also some verses about Paradise.[3] How does the interpreter approach a verse relating to Paradise, for example? The first step would be to try to understand the meaning of the word (or verse) in our everyday language. In projecting our idea of Paradise on to the Unseen world, we use popular, religious and historical narratives and our imagination. The end product has little to do with the reality of what Paradise is, as far as we know. Whatever meaning the interpreter may give to Paradise, it will remain a human construct and a product of the human imagination.

Since references to the Unseen are not related to the experienced or 'seen' world, we must ask whether such references are understandable or explicable. Similarly, the interpreter does not know what God is like; there is no knowable correspondence between the interpreter's understanding of the term 'God' and what God actually is. The Qur'ān refers to this in several verses, one of which is '*laysa kamithlihī shay*' (There is nothing like unto Him).[4] The Prophet indicated that whatever is in the Unseen realm is not experienced by humans in this life, nor can the imagination grasp it. A ḥadīth *qudsī* (a statement attributed directly to God) states that God has prepared for his righteous servants 'what no eye has ever seen, and no ear has ever heard, and no mind of a man has ever imagined'.[5]

In this type of text, meaning we arrive at and the reality to which it refers do not correspond. We have to be content with approximate meanings conveyed through images borrowed from human experience. As Zamakhsharī (d. 539/1144) explains, texts related to metaphysical concepts are conveyed 'through a parabolic illustration, by means of something which we know from our experience, of something that is beyond the reach of our perception'.[6]

Given this gulf, how can this first text type have meaning for humans at all? The verses related to the Unseen were among the most important in the early Meccan period. We cannot claim that these texts were completely unknown or unfamiliar to the people to whom they were addressed. The Prophet was sent 'to explain what was revealed to them'.[7] The Qur'ān keeps emphasizing that the addressees know what they are being told and that the message is in their language, Arabic:

> We have not sent a messenger except to [teach] in the language of his [own] people, in order to make things clear to them.[8]

Understanding was, therefore, an important aspect of the message. The community, including the Prophet, must have made sense of the Qur'ānic text, including verses related to the Unseen. We cannot say that these texts had no meaning simply because they were related to the Unseen and the world beyond physical experience. However, their sense is limited by human experience and understanding. For instance, if the Qur'ān says that God is 'All-Knowing' or 'All-Hearing', these words are interpreted or understood in relation to our experience, in relation to our understanding of knowing and hearing. It cannot be assumed that there is a correspondence, in terms of reality, between the hearing of a person and the hearing of God. It does not follow, however, that the meaning given to the text or the understanding of the text by the interpreter is false; it is probably the only way such a text can be interpreted in a meaningful way.

If the text is understood in this way the interpreter, however, should not claim to have reached the 'true' meaning of the text, or that all other interpretations are false. The concept of true or false is meaningful if there is an observable correspondence between what is signified and what exists in reality. At the same time, because of this difficulty it cannot be argued that we can say nothing about God. That would be an extreme position, because one of the functions of revelation is explanation. The problem for an interpreter in dealing with texts like these is that an ultimate and 'final' meaning cannot be achieved. Nor can the degree of achievement be established. Therefore, the safest way to approach those texts is at the level of human communication, at the same time acknowledging the approximate nature of that understanding.

The interpreter must still try to find satisfactory meanings of these texts, because those meanings have real implications for the lives of the people to whom they are addressed. People are expected to relate the meanings of these texts to their day-to-day life. Interpretation is therefore dependent on the linguistic conventions of the community, limited though they are for this purpose.

The following is an example of an approximate meaning. The Qur'ān repeatedly says *Allah ghafūr* (God is forgiving).[9] The approximate meaning of *Allah ghafūr* can be understood, but only in everyday terms: if a person commits a wrong against another, the aggrieved person can or may forgive. The details of the forgiveness, the actions to be taken in redress and the behaviour of the parties may differ from one community to another. Likewise, what constitutes a wrong will also differ. But the universal idea of forgiveness exists in all human communities as part of the social order.

On the other hand, we do not know how God forgives, although some of the basic elements of human forgiveness may approximate God's forgiveness. Because God works in an unexperienced world from the perspective of humankind, we cannot say with certainty exactly how God forgives. It is interesting to quote the jurist, Mālik, who, when asked about God's 'ascension to the throne' (*al-istiwā' 'ala al-'arsh*), said: 'The [linguistic meaning of] *istiwā'* is well-known but how [*istiwā'* or ascension applies to God] is imperceptible, and to inquire about how *istiwā'* applies to God is a heresy (*bid'ah*).'

Among the interpreter's tasks with texts related to the Unseen world is, first, to make sense of the linguistic code that is used to express the material. Second, the interpreter also needs to look at how the linguistic code is used within the community, taking into account the conventions, understandings and associations made when these terms are used, not in a vacuum but within the context of ethics, morals, worldview and religious experience. More importantly, the interpreter's task is to not only identify the approximate meaning of the text but also to consider the implications for the people to whom the Qur'ān is addressed. The interpreter's role is not to 'dig' into the text to see what is 'behind' it. It is to find out the relationship between the text and the community and to explain what that relationship means. For instance, the verse 'God is All-Forgiving' has, for humans, only an approximate meaning. The interesting question is what lessons the community should learn from it. That lesson may vary, depending on the interpreter's background, on his or her understanding of the issues, and on how deeply he or she wants to go in seeking the implications. Some scholars, such as Ghazālī (d. 505/1111), said that God's attributes were ideals for human beings to follow. This means that if God is All-Forgiving, then people should wholeheartedly emulate this. There should be institutions and mechanisms in the community to encourage people to forgive and to show the individual and social benefits of forgiveness.

These implications emerge as the interpreter interacts with the text against the historical background of the community, its aspirations and its concerns. One can therefore argue that the implications of the text are constantly changing and that, at a particular time, these implications reflect the needs of a specific community at that time. For this reason, a particular set of implications should not be imposed on a community without taking into consideration its needs and interests. Any durable religion or religious scripture needs to have a built-in system to respond to the fluctuating needs of its followers. It was largely due to the flexibility and adaptability of its message and scripture, the Qur'ān, that Islam spread so rapidly within its first one hundred years. Such adaptability can be attributed to those early interpreters of the text: the first and second generations of Muslims who did not rigidly and dogmatically follow a particular approach to interpretation. Instead, they took the texts as part of their religious experience and translated them with a remarkable degree of flexibility for the people who had not seen the Prophet or witnessed the event of revelation.

Historically oriented texts

The Qur'ān has much material that belongs in this category. These verses refer to events in human history and can be cross-checked with other sources and traditions, where such data are available. With all the linguistic and perceptual limitations surrounding the recording of these events, they remain grounded in the experiential world. When the Qur'ān says that Pharaoh disputed Moses' claim to prophethood,[10] it is referring to an historical event. Similarly, it is possible to verify the Qur'ān's account of what Muslims did on the day of the Battle of Uḥud.[11]

In the *tafsīr* literature, historical events are often interpreted by relying on historical reports. Some of these can be found in the Qur'ān itself, in which case the interpreter is relying on other Qur'ānic verses to explain the event. Sometimes the interpreter may rely on reports attributed to the Prophet that may or may not be historically reliable (authentic), in which case the explanations may be of little value. Beyond the Qur'ān and ḥadīth there are other documents, artefacts and archaeological and anthropological evidence that can be used. An important source is the Bible itself, particularly in relation to Qur'ānic texts that refer to biblical prophets, peoples, places and events.

In the *tafsīr* literature, however, many interpreters were uncomfortable about examining the Qur'ānic texts in the light of non-Qur'ānic and non-prophetic 'knowledge' or information. This could have been due to the perception that any exposition based on sources outside the *sharī'ah* disciplines indicated compromise by reducing the sacred text to an historical text – to the level of mere historicity. Several interpreters of the Qur'ān have tended to avoid addressing historical events unless these were supported by certain authorities or other sources within the Islamic tradition.

Historically oriented texts in the Qur'ān share a common set of characteristics. First, they often lack details, such as names, dates and places. The Qur'ān never gives a specific date for an event. A key reason for this appears to be that references to past events were not intended to give historical information but, rather, to serve a moral or religious purpose related to the life of the community. For instance, the Qur'ān is not interested in where Adam lived, or in which year Moses left Egypt, or when Pharaoh died. It is more concerned with how Moses proclaimed God's message to Pharaoh, with how Pharaoh reacted to Moses' invitation to submit to God, and in Pharaoh's subsequent behaviour towards the people of Moses.

At times, the Qur'ān repeats the same event at different places with different wording. For instance, the story of Noah recurs with varying lengths in Q.7:59–64, 9:70, 11:25–48, 14:9, 22:42, 25:37, 26:105–122, 38:12, 40:5, 31, 50:12, 51:46, 53:52 and 54:9–17. These texts in different parts of the Qur'ān are neither contradictory nor repetitive. The verses place emphasis on different aspects of the event depending on its particular context in the Qur'ān, largely as a lesson to the community of the Prophet Muḥammad.

The interpreter, in expounding an historical event, is expected to try to give as many details as possible from reliable sources. The interpreter of the Qur'ān in the twenty-first century will have to look to other sources in order to see historical references in the Qur'ān in their full historical context. Once these sources are identified, the interpreter should try to reconstruct the events. Drawing on non-Islamic sources does not mean that the sacred text is compromised. On the contrary, insights can be gained into aspects of it that would otherwise be impossible. The interpreter must realize, however, that historical distance and witnesses' perceptions affect the understanding of an event. Nowadays, for instance, there will be as many accounts of, as there are witnesses to, say, a car accident. Limitations of language will further alter an account. Imagining, conceptualizing or perceiving a whole event exactly as it happened is an impossible task.

The historical texts in the Qur'ān, as with texts related to the Unseen, seek to convey a message about how people should live in line with God's instructions. For example, the Qur'ān refers to the people of Shuʿayb and some of his teachings.[12] In order to have a better understanding of his teachings, we need basic historical data because the Qur'ān ignores who these people were, where and when they lived, and what social structures they had. The interest of the Qur'ān lies in how the people of Shuʿayb responded to the teachings and guidance of their prophet, whom they had rejected. The Qur'ān presents this as a lesson to Muslims:

> We sent Shuʿayb, one of their own brethren. He said: O my people worship God; you have no other god but Him. Now a clear sign has

> come unto you from your Lord! Give just measure and weight nor withhold from the people the things that are their due; and do no mischief on the earth after it has been set in order: that will be best for you if you have faith. And squat not on every road breathing threats, hindering from the path of God those who believe in Him and seeking in it something crooked. But remember how you were little and He gave you growth. And hold in your mind's eye what was the end of those who did mischief.[13]

Elaborating on this end, the Qur'ān states:

> To the Madyan [people We sent] their brother Shu'ayb. Then he said: 'O My people. Serve God, and fear the Last Day. Do not commit evil on the earth with the intent of doing mischief'. But they rejected him. Then the mighty blast seized them, and they lay prostrate in their homes by the morning.[14]

Thus, one of the key objectives of the historically oriented texts of the Qur'ān appears to be to teach and to present moral questions. The lessons to be learned from these historical events may be identified by exploring their impact on the first generations of Muslims, and by relating this to the modern reader of the Qur'ānic text.

Therefore, as I indicated above, it is not the interpreter's responsibility to find the meanings that lie 'behind' these texts, but, rather, to explore relevance and provide reasonable accounts of lessons to be learned by contemporary people. From this, a set of principles and values can be construed to guide a current Muslim community in its quest for a clearer identity as it attempts to follow what it believes to be 'true Islam'. By expounding historical events without relating them to contemporary circumstances, the interpreter performs little service to the community of believers. Knowledge of basic facts alone, whether they be historical or otherwise, does not enhance the life of the believer. One of the roles of scripture is to guide the individual and the community to a better life in this world and in the Hereafter. The interpreter of historical texts can facilitate this by relating the past to the present, even if the interpretation leads to an approximate meaning.

The use of biblical sources in relation to Qur'ānic texts has been frowned upon by many interpreters of the Qur'ān, especially recently. Mannā 'al-Qaṭṭān recommends avoiding biblical sources, which he calls '*isrā'īliyyāt*'.[15] In the early stages of Islamic history, many Muslim historians and interpreters had no difficulty in using biblical sources, but from the fourth/tenth and fifth/eleventh centuries onwards resistance began to set in. This can be attributed to several factors. One was the maturing of Islam and the establishment of *sharī'ah* disciplines, such as *kalām*, *uṣūl al-fiqh* and *tafsīr*. Muslims became more confident of their theological positions and of their own distinctive scripture. The expansion of their political and economic power led them to become even more confident vis-à-vis other religions and the peoples of the territories they conquered, including Christians and Jews. With this came the gradual denigration of other religious traditions seen as essentially corrupt or manufactured, and thus somehow beneath the attention of Muslim scholars. Only a few Muslim scholars, Ibn Ḥazm (d. 456/1064) being an example, attempted to study the traditions of other religions. The result of this attitude was that Muslims had to leave behind biblical and other non-Muslim sources. By the time of Ibn Kathīr (d. 774/1373), one of the most ardent opponents of using biblical sources in *tafsīr*, the use of such sources had come to be regarded as anti-Islam. One of Ibn Kathīr's aims in writing his *tafsīr* appears to have been to provide an authoritative one in which the so-called *isrā'īliyyāt* was totally avoided.[16] This attitude by Muslims towards non-Muslim sources remains very strong even today. It has been rare until recently for a Muslim student to undertake a scholarly study of the Bible or of faiths such as Christianity, Judaism or Hinduism. Any suggestion of going back to those materials in expounding some of the historical material in the Qur'ān is likely to be received by most Muslims as tantamount to subverting the Islamic tradition, a view that does not seem to be in accord with the practice of the earliest Muslims.

Parables: *mathal* texts

The Qur'ān uses certain phrases, expressions and texts to illuminate certain concepts and ideas. At the linguistic level this is often to make the text clearer to those to whom it is addressed. In so doing, the Qur'ān takes into consideration their appreciation of literature and literary style. One of these genres is parables (*mathal*). The Qur'ān uses *mathal* in a number of ways. One is to use an image with which the first generation of Muslims would have been familiar. Like a living image, a *mathal* can express and explain things concretely that are otherwise not easily explained or described.

Pre-Islamic Arabs were familiar with *mathal*. The genre was an important part of their literary repertoire in the pre-Islamic period, and they excelled in it. Arab linguists and scholars like Ibn al-Athīr and Māwardī collected a large number of parables, especially in relation to Qur'ānic studies.[17] Most of the important scholarly works on Qur'ānic interpretation, for instance Suyūṭī's *Itqān*, include discussion on *mathal*.[18]

In a number of verses, the Qur'ān says that it uses parables. For example, in Q.59, we read, 'Such are the parables (*amthāl*, pl. of *mathal*) which We put forward to humankind that they may reflect';[19] and in Q.39, 'And indeed We have put forth for people, in this Qur'ān every kind of similitude (*mathal*) in order that they may remember.'[20]

Scholars of *tafsīr* have classified *mathal* in a number of ways. One is whether the word *mathal* is used in the *mathal* itself. Based on this, Qaṭṭān identified three types. First is a *mathal* that is explicit (*al-amthāl al-musarraḥah*); that is, where the word *mathal* indicates explicitly the kind of similarity intended. For example, Q.2:17 declares: 'Their similitude (*mathal*) is that of a man who kindled a fire; when it lighted all around him, God took away their light and left them in utter darkness. So they could not see.'[21] The next verse says: 'They are deaf, dumb, and blind. They will not return [to the right path].'[22] In this *mathal* the Qur'ān is referring to the 'hypocrites' in Medina and portrays their attitude to God's message in a parable.

The second type of *mathal* contains a latent or concealed similarity (*al-amthāl al-kāminah*). In this the word *mathal* or its derivatives do not occur. Nevertheless it expresses in an elliptical manner a meaning signified by a common *mathal*. An example of this is the verse, 'And let not your hand be tied like a miser to your neck, nor stretch it forth to its utmost reach like a spendthrift, so that you become blameworthy and [end up] in severe poverty.'[23] Although this verse does not contain the word *mathal* itself, it expresses the same meaning as in the *mathal* 'moderation is the best way' (*khayr al-umūr awsaṭuhā*).[24] The verse portrays a Muslim who is moderate in spending. The message is conveyed not by asking the people to be moderate, but by contrasting the image of someone who is mean with that of someone who is over-generous. Both images are conveyed in a form with which the culture of Mecca and Medina was familiar. More importantly, because it is expressed as an image, its impact on the people would have been greater.

The third type is the open simile (*al-amthāl al-mursalah*). This refers to a Qur'ānic verse in which the word *mathal* does not occur nor is it a rephrasing of a common *mathal*; but the verse has come to be treated as a common *mathal*. An example is the verse, 'Is not the morning near?' (*alaysa al-ṣubḥ bi-qarīb*).[25] This statement concludes Q.11:81, in which the Prophet Lot is told to leave his people and travel at night, as God's punishment will befall them next morning. The statement, 'Is not the morning near?', indicates the proximity of the dreadful event. The statement is therefore used as a *mathal* to presage the Last Days. Among other examples is the verse, 'None but God can unveil it.'[26] This alludes to the certainty of God's ultimate judgement and to the fact that God alone knows when this is to be. The verse expresses human helplessness in the face of the inevitable.

So far we have looked at some of the formal aspects of *mathal*. In terms of interpretation, we need to understand its functions in the Qur'ān. As Suyūṭī indicates, several scholars, for example Māwardī, Zarkashī and Zamakhsharī, elaborated on this.[27] *Mathal* is used in the Qur'ān as praise; for instance, praising the firm stand of the Companions in their belief in

God and the Prophet. Here the *mathal* likens their stand to a plant which grows firm and high:

> Muḥammad is God's Apostle; and those who are [truly] with him are firm and unyielding towards all deniers of truth, [yet] full of mercy towards one another. You can see them bowing down, prostrating themselves [in prayer], seeking favour with God and [His] goodly acceptance: their marks are on their faces, traced by prostration. This is their parable in the Torah as well as their parable in the Gospel: [they] are like a seed that brings forth its shoot, then He strengthens it, so that it grows stout, and [in the end] stands firm upon its stem, delighting the sowers. [Thus will God cause believers to grow in strength,] so that through them He might confound the disbelievers.[28]

Mathal are also used to express disgust. For instance, in an attempt to repel believers from seeking out others' faults, the Qur'ān compares such a person to one who eats the flesh of his dead brother:

> O you who have attained to faith! Avoid most guesswork [about one another] – for, behold, some of [such] guesswork is [in itself] a sin; and do not spy upon one another, and neither allow yourselves to speak ill of one another behind your backs. Would any of you like to eat the flesh of his dead brother? Nay, you would loathe it![29]

Another example of a *mathal* used to express disgust is in Q.5:175–177. Here the Qur'ān presents a *mathal* about a person to whom God gives knowledge of scripture and religion. The person understands the divine message but refuses to admit its truth because he 'clings to the earth'; that is, he is dominated by a materialistic, earthly outlook on life.[30] The Qur'ān states:

> And tell them the story of the man to whom we vouchsafed Our messages and who then discards them: Satan catches up with him, and he strays, like so many others, into grievous error. Now had We so willed, We could indeed have exalted him by means of those [messages]: but he always clung to the earth and followed but his own desires. Thus his parable is that of an [excited] dog: if you approach him threateningly, he will pant with his tongue lolling; and if you leave him alone, he will pant with his tongue lolling. Such is the parable of those who are bent on giving the lie to Our messages. Tell [them], then, this story, so that they might take thought.[31]

There are many other areas in which *mathal* are used, but their main function is to convey the meaning in a more effective and lively way. For instance, to discourage *ribā* (usury) the Qur'ān says:

> Those who gorge themselves on *ribā* (usury) behave but as he might behave whom Satan has confounded with his touch. That is because they say: 'Buying and selling is like *ribā*', whereas Allah has made buying and selling lawful and *ribā* unlawful. So whosoever receives an admonition from his Lord and desists [from *ribā*] may keep his past gains and it will be for God to judge him; but as for who returns to it [*ribā*], they are destined for the Fire, therein to abide.[32]

To encourage spending money for charity, the Qur'ān conveys the following image:

> The likeness of those who spend their wealth in the way of God, is that of a grain [of corn] out of which grow seven ears, in every ear a hundred grains.[33]

Mathal are also used to present abstract ideas in concrete form. In this example, the Qur'ān is illustrating how hollow it is to spend money just to show off:

> O you who have attained to faith! Do not deprive your charitable deeds of all worth by stressing your own benevolence and hurting [the feelings of the needy], as does he who spends his wealth only to be seen and praised by men, and believes not in God and the Last Day: for his parable is that of a smooth rock with [a little earth on it – and then a rainstorm smites it and leaves it hard and bare. Such as these shall have no gain whatever from all their [good] works: for God does not guide people who refuse to acknowledge the truth.[34]

Mathal is an excellent example of a text type where a literal reading is not intended at all. In fact, a metaphorical reading is crucial for an appropriate understanding of this type of text.

Concluding remarks

Given the variety of text types in the Qur'ān, it is difficult to argue that one can simply look at the Qur'ānic text and understand all of its meaning. Texts that are related to the Unseen (*ghayb*), for instance, cannot be taken at face value by imposing a literal meaning and assuming that the meaning corresponds to the reality. In such cases, we can only arrive at an approximate meaning. Similarly, historically oriented texts require dependence on a large body of external data. Often these sources are biblical, archaeological, anthropological or historical. Qur'ānic references to historical events are, at best, general and lacking in specific dates, places or even names. In such cases, it is difficult to arrive at the 'true' meaning of the text and provide a final and complete interpretation easily. In some cases, it may be almost impossible as the required data may not be available. *Mathal* is perhaps one of the best examples of where the literal meaning of the text is not intended at all.

All three text types demonstrate that the simplistic and reductive view of Textualists today – that we can easily understand the meanings in the Qur'ān, or that there is an objective meaning that we can take hold of – is both problematic and unsustainable. Understanding the meaning of the Qur'ānic text by relying on literalism also ignores complexities associated with the different text types in the Qur'ān and the way meaning is constructed in relation to each.

Chapter 9

Recognition of the complexity of meaning

This chapter focuses on the question of 'meaning' as this is one of the most contested areas in the interpretation of the ethico-legal content of the Qur'ān, if not the most important. The definition of meaning has been debated without consensus by the philosophers of language.[1] It is not possible, given its extent, to summarize the debate in this chapter. Suffice it to say that, from Plato to Wittgenstein and beyond, a number of theories of meaning have been put forward: referential theory; semantic theories; ideational theories; and functional theories. While these theories all contribute in some way to our understanding of meaning and are relevant to the interpretation of the Qur'ān's ethico-legal content, I will not adopt any particular theory here. It is true to say that, to many Textualists, both classical and modern, the referential theory of meaning has been the most relevant and dominant.[2] According to this, the meaning of a word lies in the object to which it refers. This theory anchors language and meaning in the real extra-linguistic world in a stable and determinate way.[3] While it is true to say that this theory is relevant to a specific and limited number of words in the language (for example, names, physical objects, acts and processes), it cannot be said to explain a very large number of words, phrases, sentences and language uses as Textualists usually assume. Much of what I say in this chapter is therefore a critique of the Textualist understanding of meaning, and an argument for adopting an understanding of meaning that is more relevant and appropriate to the interpretation of the ethico-legal content. I believe, given the nature of the language use in the ethico-legal texts, a referential theory of meaning is highly inadequate. I am arguing for the recognition of a degree of indeterminacy and complexity in meaning, of the importance of context (linguistic, socio-historical and cultural), and of the legitimacy of multiple understandings.

For the Textualist, the idea of a single objective meaning is an ideal to be cherished. This objectivity of meaning appears to rely on two key assumptions. First, God's Word (the Qur'ān) is in the Arabic language and the usages of this language, once ascertained, can provide an objective (= true) meaning of the text. For Textualists the efforts of figures like

Ibn ʿAbbās to understand the Qurʾānic text in the light of the pre-Islamic usage of specific Arabic terms provide the linguistic support for this objectivity. Following this line of thinking, many exegetes of the Qurʾān attempted to provide the meaning of the text by relying on such usage and citations. The second assumption is that this objectivity can be achieved if, in addition to the linguistic evidence, the meaning can be supported by statements made by the Prophet, the Companions or the Successors in relation to the specific Qurʾānic text. An 'objective' linguistic interpretation is thus assumed to be reached based on linguistic evidence and historical reports. However, from a Contextualist's point of view, there exists an inherent element of subjectivity and fluidity in understanding the Qurʾān and, in particular, its ethico-legal texts, given its application to different times, places and circumstances. Thus, any talk of objective and true meaning, even if based on linguistic and historical evidence, remains unsatisfactory as it does not take into account the context of the text.

Whereas from the Textualist's point of view one has to approach the Qurʾānic text with complete objectivity, that is, without presuppositions or preconceived ideas, from a Contextualist's perspective, such objectivity is not possible, even if desirable. The interpreter cannot approach the text without certain experiences, values, beliefs and presuppositions.[4] For the Contextualist, the interpreter is acting as an historian, because the Qurʾān is, among other things, an historical document that demands knowledge of a particular period. The presuppositions and experiences of the interpreter can be reflected, for instance, in the texts chosen for study and in the framework used to understand and interpret the texts, as well as in the emphases given to particular sections of the text or shades of meaning. Such emphases may or may not be in line with the understandings of the text dominant at the time of the revelation.

Such a view signals the impossibility of a completely objective interpretation of the Qurʾānic text. Every reader has his or her own values through which they interpret what they read. The interpreter chooses a certain viewpoint, which in turn means that he or she is open principally to the questions arising from that viewpoint. However objectively their subjects may be pursued, historians cannot escape their own understanding.[5] Objective meaning in history cannot be spoken of, for history cannot be known except through the subjectivity of the historian.[6] While all understanding is shaped by pre-existing ideas and experiences, this does not rule out the claim that some conclusions are more reliable and more likely to be accurate than others; that is, they have a claim to knowledge.

Recognition of the complexity of meaning

The issue of meaning is therefore complex: a complexity well known to the classical exegetes of the Qurʾān, such as Ṭabarī, Ibn Qutaybah and

Qurṭubī. By contrast, today among Textualists, even at a popular level, there is a high degree of rigidity about what is considered 'meaning' in the Qur'ān. By rigidity I refer to the tendency (among them) of attempting to limit the meaning of ethico-legal text to one, wherever they could, and argue against the legitimacy of other possible meanings of the same text. This attempt to limit and then preserve meanings to what has been handed down from generation to generation becomes the hallmark of authenticity for the Textualists. Not only do these preserved meanings deter other possible and reasonable meanings, but they also assume that there is no authority in the later generations that can add to the bank of possible meanings.[7]

As far as words are concerned, in Arabic, like any other language, there are many types of words, and not all of them can be treated in the same manner in order to arrive at a meaning. Any language may have words that can easily be learnt, for example names of objects.[8] Most words in the language, however, do not fall into this category. Words that function as verbs, pronouns, other referential words and abstract nouns are not as specific as words for objects when it comes to arriving at verifiable objective meanings for them.

Another complicating factor is that meanings are not concrete objects, to be taken down like books from a shelf; meanings are mental entities.[9] A mental entity when conveyed to another person through language will be received only after some adjustments are made to suit the receiver's psychology and mental capabilities. More importantly, the circumstance of the utterance gives the word a determinate reference. Experience of meaning is an impression or an image. 'To see a sign as enjoining different uses is to see different aspects of it, and that is to have different impressions.'[10] Zemach highlights the complexities of meaning:

> Acceptance or rejection of a sentence depends on holistic considerations: whether you accept a given sentence depends on your willingness to accept many other sentences. Thus it seems that a sentence cannot be tied to one situation only representing (or meaning) a single state of affairs because the reasons for accepting it are global and essentially involve a huge number of other sentences.[11]

From a Contextualist point of view, this indicates that in determining the meaning of words, sentences and much bigger texts, the Textualist idea that one can produce meanings that are externally verifiable and observable is highly questionable. A large number of words in the language actually do not fit into such a neat classification. Many words are related to meanings that can be extremely difficult to clearly specify, and therefore it is not easy to encompass all aspects of their meanings. This leaves a high degree of subjectivity associated with the meaning of a text.

Related to this is the idea of 'indirect' meaning, which is highly relevant to the Contextualist approach.[12] Direct meaning (as opposed to indirect meaning) can be most obvious at word level; that is, what is perceptible and directly accessible to the senses, such as 'book', 'pen' and 'the Qur'ān'. Indirect meaning exists primarily at discourse level and is difficult to grasp, but is extremely important in understanding a text. While the direct meaning comes from the words, the indirect meaning comes largely from the context. They are, however, closely related. In the case of 'spoken word' (even though it may have been reduced to writing, as is the case with the Qur'ān) the context consists of the manner of the utterance and its tone, rhythm and strength; the situation in which the utterance was given; the relative status and relationship of the interlocutors; and the effect intended in the discourse. For a Contextualist, the concept of indirect meaning further complicates the idea of a simple and objective meaning of the Qur'ānic text. The principle, therefore, is that whatever interpretation can be given to the text, that interpretation can never wholly encompass the text. 'No text, however simple or familiar, can be formalized without remainder: there will always be a supplement of signification that is overlooked or reduced.'[13]

Closely related to the idea of indirect meaning is 'context'. Context implies two meanings: one broad and the other narrow. In relation to the Qur'ān, the broad meaning is the overall content of the Qur'ān, as well as the broader framework of the Prophet's life and of the first Muslim community. It includes the worldview presented by the Qur'ān, the values it emphasizes and the overall guidance (which by definition varies depending on how one approaches the Qur'ān) it provides. This broader context gives meaning to many parts of the Qur'ān and any interpreter of the text must be thoroughly familiar with it. Norman Calder emphasizes this point:

> Texts in isolation are not only unproblematic, they are meaningless. The text of the Qur'ān takes on meaning only when it is systematically juxtaposed to certain structures which exist independently (more or less) of the Qur'ān itself; notably the grammatical and rhetorical structures of the Arabic language, but also the scholastic disciplines of law, theology and prophetic narrative.[14]

The narrow meaning of the context relates to a sentence or word that signals an idea in a given part of the Qur'ān. The interpreter needs to consider what comes before and what comes after the verse. As far as discrete units (short phrases or even a single verse or a few verses) are concerned, it may be difficult to determine their overall context. The Qur'ān was not revealed at one time nor in book form, so seemingly connected portions may well have been revealed in different circumstances and at different times. Verses that relate to each case or situation form a unit on their own. These are some of the things that an interpreter must look into to understand a verse or Qur'ānic concept. Unless the interpreter includes what went before and what follows a given verse or idea and makes an effort at understanding the text as a unit, the meaning of the text arrived at is likely to be unsatisfactory.

Recognition of change in meaning

From a Contextualist point of view, the meaning of a word is not static; it changes with developments in the linguistic and cultural environment of the community. Some aspects of meaning become redundant, while other aspects emerge or are emphasized, adding new perspectives to the word. It is possible to argue that even the so-called 'core' meaning of the word does not remain static. A relatively straightforward Arabic word such as *kitāb* (book) highlights the difficulties involved. For a person living in the twenty-first century, the core meaning of 'book' will reflect the common experience of people accustomed to the modern method of producing books. The core meaning of the word is determined *inter alia* by experience and by transfer of definitions.

The word *kitāb*, if it is translated into 'book' as we know it today, is 'a collection of sheets of paper fastened together as a thing to be read or to be written in'; this may be the core meaning of 'book' today.[15] But before paper was invented, 'books' were written on tablets, papyrus or animal skin, to name just a few examples. Later, additional shades of meaning for the word 'book' came to be associated with printing. Today, 'books' also exist in electronic form or on compact disks. As communication technology brings further changes, new layers of meaning will be added. Many other words follow a similar pattern in changes of meaning, leading to the view that a fixed core meaning of a word over a long period of time is a problematic concept.

Considering the ethico-legal text as discourse

For Contextualists, the linguist and literary theorist Tzvetan Todorov's distinction between the two levels at which the text can be looked at, that is, its language and discourse, is important. The former is abstract while the latter is concrete. This distinction is important, as the discourse dimension includes the context in which the text functions at language level. In the words of Todorov:

> Language exists in the abstract; it has a lexicon and grammatical rules as its input and *sentences* as its output. Discourse is a concrete manifestation of language, and it is produced, necessarily, in a specific context that involves not only linguistic elements but also the circum-

> stances of their production: the interlocutors, the time and place, the relations prevailing among these extralinguistic elements. We are no longer concerned with sentences as such, but with sentences that have been produced, or, to put it more succinctly, with *utterances*.[16]

A text like the Qur'ān can only be considered as *just* language at an abstract level. However, the production of the text as revelation in a given socio-historical context highlights the fact that it is primarily discourse (language in context). This discursive aspect of the text gives it a high degree of richness that cannot be found if we consider the Qur'ān simply as language. In order for the Qur'ān to be relevant at different times, and in different places and circumstances, its interpretation (including of its ethico-legal texts) should be considered as both language and discourse. For instance, in the case of verse Q.2:2 (*dhālika al-kitābu lā rayba fīhi*), those who are familiar with Arabic can understand the basic meaning[17] of each word and the literal meaning of the sentence. This can be readily translated into English as, 'This is the book; there is no doubt about it', which is approximately its literal meaning. If one were dealing with this text in purely linguistic terms, this would be sufficient, but this does not tell us much about the overall purpose or meaning of the sentence. This text was revealed in a given context at a specific time *as discourse* for a particular purpose; therefore it has to be approached as discourse. It is at this level that various shades of meaning and shifts in emphasis become relevant.

Many Textualists, both classical and modern, have treated the Qur'ān as language, not discourse. This is evident in a number of early works on the Qur'ān and even in later ones, such as Suyūṭī's *Tafsīr al-Jalālayn*. Although it may be unfair to generalize and claim that classical exegetes totally disregarded the notion of discourse in their interpretations, there is ample evidence that *tafsīr* scholars often defined words and explained grammatical points without looking at the context of each verse – historical, socio-cultural, political, legal or economic. The closest one comes to finding a discourse-oriented *tafsīr* (albeit in a partial way) is that concerned with the *asbāb al-nuzūl* (occasions of the revelation) literature and other contextual material, for example in Ṭabarī. But when it comes to the ethico-legal context of the Qur'ān, even in these *tafsīr* works, the overall emphasis is on language dimension, not discourse. Therefore it could be argued that an emphasis on the ethico-legal aspects of the Qur'ān as not just language, but as discourse also, is a relatively new and promising idea.

Recognizing limits to the meaning of the text

Though the argument above highlights the impossibility of total objectivity in interpretation, this does not mean that I am arguing for total subjectivity and relativity. This would allow any interpreter to read into the text whatever he or she liked. It is here perhaps that one can talk about limits to understanding the ethico-legal texts. Such limits are desirable in order to protect the Qur'ān from being used in an unprincipled manner.

Textualists believe that the Prophet Muḥammad determined the limits on the meaning of the text, as he was the closest to the author of the text – God. They believe that the Prophet's interpretations should be taken as the final word and the limit beyond which one should not go. This position presents several problems. There is no systematic and comprehensive commentary on the Qur'ān by the Prophet in which he specifies the meanings that should be associated with the text. The Prophet left only a few ad hoc comments. Nor is it possible, in the absence of specific comments from the Prophet, to know how he wanted people, the Muslims, to interpret the text.

A second point in relation to the limits of meaning is the context in which the text was produced (or revealed). Since the Qur'ānic text itself is actually a combination of many texts revealed at different times, it is important to look at the context of each individual text. For example, the verses that prohibit *ribā* (usury) were revealed in a given context: the socio-historical and economic context of Mecca and Medina in the first/seventh century.[18] This helps us understand the reason why that prohibition occurred and how it was understood.

A third point in relation to the limits of meaning is the role of the reader. Some have argued in the literature (not necessarily in relation to Qur'ānic interpretation) that it is the reader who ultimately determines what the text means; it is the recipient (the reader) who places limits on its meanings. Accepting this argument implies that the reader can construct meanings for the text in any of a number of ways. As far as the Qur'ānic text is concerned, a general licence without rules is considered unacceptable, as it implies permission to construct meanings in accordance with individual desires and whims in a totally subjective manner.

Another aspect one must consider when trying to interpret a text is the nature of the text itself. It may be argued that a particular type of text, for instance a legal text related to a ruling that is meant to be implemented by the community, must be reasonably clear. Otherwise, those who are supposed to understand it and implement it will face enormous difficulties. At the opposite end of such a text type, there exists what in Arabic is referred to as *mathal* (parable) (see pp. 97–100). Each text type has limits on its meaning, based on the conventions of the text type. A legal text, because of its function, is considered to have a very narrow band of meanings, whereas a *mathal* can have a broader spectrum of meaning. The symbolic character of the latter provides this leeway. Meanings are thus dependent to a certain extent on the type of text.

It may also be argued that cultural context plays a significant role in limiting the meaning of a text. To understand the limits of the meaning of the Qur'ān, it is necessary to understand the cultural traditions regarding the sacred text and its production and reception. Because the text is a social phenomenon functioning within a given society, the meaning of the text depends also on the expectations and conditions of that society.

The meaning of the sacred text is knowable

From a Contextualist perspective, the meaning of the Qur'ān is knowable. However this knowledge is contingent on time, place and circumstance. It can also change from time to time in line with developments (intellectual, political, economic and social) in the community. In the early Islamic period, Muslims debated whether some verses of the Qur'ān were 'knowable' or 'unknowable'. The issue was primarily related to the understanding of the terms *muḥkam* (clear) and *mutashābih* (allegorical), referred to in Q.3:7:

> It is He who has sent down to you [Muḥammad] this Book [Qur'ān]. It contains verses that are clear in and by themselves (*muḥkamāt*), and these are the foundations of the Book – as well as those that are allegorical (*mutashābihāt*). So as for those in whose hearts there is a deviation [from the truth] they follow that which is not entirely clear thereof, seeking *al-fitnah* [polytheism and trials], and seeking for its hidden meanings, but none knows its hidden meanings save God. And those who are firmly grounded in knowledge say: 'We believe in it; the whole of it [clear and unclear verses] are from our Lord.' And none receive admonition except men of understanding.[19]

This verse classifies the Qur'ānic verses into 'clear' (*muḥkam*) and 'allegorical' (*mutashābih*) verses, which presupposes that one can differentiate between them. However, for the scholar of today, at least two problems arise: first, what is the precise meaning of 'clear' and which verses are 'allegorical'?

Ṭabarī explains *muḥkamāt* in Q.3:7 as meaning those verses that have been made 'perfect' – clear by explanation and elaboration.[20] Zamakhsharī offers a similar explanation. He explains as 'clear' those verses that have been perfected in their wording so that they are not open to different interpretations or confusion.[21]

As for the *mutashābihāt*, Ṭabarī explains them as those verses that resemble each other with regard to their recitation but differ in their meanings.[22] Zamakhsharī explains them as those verses that are open to a variety of interpretations.[23]

Second, besides the problem of understanding the concepts of 'clear' and 'allegorical', there is the issue of identifying the 'clear' and 'allegorical' verses. There is disagreement on this in the *tafsīr*. According to one opinion, 'clear' verses are the abrogating verses, that is, verses that are operative.[24] The 'allegorical' verses, according to this interpretation, are those that have been abrogated.[25] According to another, the 'clear' verses are those that have clearly prescribed what is permitted and what is not, whereas the 'allegorical' are verses those whose meanings resemble each other even though their wording differs.[26] A third opinion is that 'clear' verses do not admit of more than one interpretation, while 'allegorical' verses do.[27] A fourth is that 'clear' verses are those whose interpretation the scholars know and whose explanation they understand. The 'allegorical' verses are those whose interpretation is known only to God, for example the time of the end of the world and the final judgement.[28] These divergent views indicate that what is clear and what is allegorical, or which verses are clear and which are allegorical, remains unresolved.

Some argue that the Qur'ān says that it is impossible to know the interpretation of the allegorical texts. This is based on the meaning of the phrase in the above-mentioned verse: 'Only God knows its *ta'wīl*.'[29] If *ta'wīl* is read as 'interpretation', then the allegorical verses can only be interpreted by God. ʿĀ'ishah and Ibn ʿAbbās from among the Companions, and others, such as ʿUmar b. ʿAbd al-ʿAzīz and Mālik, reportedly preferred this reading and argued that those who have knowledge do not have access to the interpretation of allegorical verses which, for them, cannot be interpreted by humans.

However, several early authorities[30] considered that those who are knowledgeable (*al-rāsikhūn fī al-ʿilm*) can actually know the interpretation of allegorical verses. This was based on a variant reading, *wa mā yaʿlam ta'wīlahū illa allāhu wa al-rāsikhūn fī al-ʿilm*, which stops at this point.[31] In this reading, the words allāh and *al-rāsikhūn* are joined together by the conjunction *wa* (and), the effect of *wa mā yaʿlam* to both *allāh* and *al-rāsikhūn*. The meaning then would be that both Allah and those who are knowledgeable know the interpretation of these verses. This view is also supported by the objective of the Qur'ānic revelation, which is that the revelation should be accessible to humankind. If there are verses in the Qur'ān with meanings and interpretations known only to God, then one function of the Qur'ān is lost. Since the Qur'ān was revealed so that people could understand the will of God, one should surely take the verse to mean that the interpretation of allegorical verses was known both to God and to those with deep knowledge of the scripture even if this knowledge is imperfect.

The opposing positions on allegorical verses can be reconciled, however. Even the more inclusive definition given above does not claim that those who have deep knowledge of the Scripture also know the *reality* of what the verses refer to in relation to the Unseen world. If *ta'wīl* is taken as referring to the reality or *true* meaning of a Qur'ānic verse, then the more exclusive view can be accommodated. Many early authorities, such as Ibn ʿAbbās, were confident that they had the capacity to interpret many Qur'ānic verses, including those that referred to the Unseen, as is demonstrated in reports attributed to them. For the purpose of this book, it may be said that interpretation of the Scripture, at the level of explanation of its meanings, includes all parts of the text without exception. This offers considerable freedom to humankind in understanding it.

Legitimacy of multiple understandings

For Contextualists today, throughout the *tafsīr* tradition multiple understandings of one text have generally been quite common, despite the attempts made by various groups, classical or modern, to limit their interpretation to one. When it comes to the ethico-legal context of the Qur'ān, in both classical and contemporary Qur'ānic studies there has been a tendency on the part of many Textualists to argue that only one understanding is true and correct. They limit this 'true' understanding to that backed by *ijmāʿ* (consensus). They see any deviation from consensus as unacceptable.

Early exegetes, such as Ṭabarī, were familiar with the concept of multiple understandings and were able to accommodate diversity into a broad framework of exegetical Islamic scholarship. For instance, Ṭabarī's method of interpretation was to quote a verse and then bring together a number of diverse opinions on the meaning of that verse. This was supported by sayings of the Companions or the Successors without labelling any particular view as invalid, unacceptable or unorthodox. Ṭabarī would then go on to give his preference for one particular view or synthesis of views, while still accommodating diversity.

In contrast, here is a modern example that is used in Textualist discourse. It attempts to impose one single understanding on the reader.[32] The verse in question is Q.5:44: '*wa man lam yaḥkum bimā anzala allāhu fa ula'ika hum al-kāfirūn*'. This is taken by many Textualists (of an Islamist persuasion) today to mean, unambiguously, 'Whoever does not implement what God has revealed [that is, Islamic law] is an unbeliever'. This interpretation is found in the writings of several Islamists, such as Saʿīd Ḥawwā.[33] Terms such as *yaḥkum*, *mā anzala allāhu* and *al-kāfirūn* are taken according to their literal meaning: *yaḥkum* means 'to rule'; *mā anzala allāhu* means the Qur'ān or Qur'ānic laws; and *al-kāfirūn* means the unbelievers.

The apparent simplicity in such a statement should not obscure its many problems. The verse cited here could be read very differently. The reading of the word *yaḥkum* (to rule) is determined by the ideological orientation of the reader. At the same time the connotations associated with *yaḥkum*, the circumstances under which it applies or the context in which this particular verse occurs are treated as irrelevant. An ideologically driven reading here ignores both the historical and immediate contexts in which the verse was revealed, in favour of the ideological interpretation. It also assumes that it is a general statement unrelated to any special circumstances and one that Muslims are to take literally and implement accordingly. Reductionist understandings of this nature are highly problematic but unfortunately quite common in modern Textualist discourse.

To overcome this problem, any reading of the Qur'ānic text should take into account the textual, historical and contextual aspects of the text. This will inevitably lead to a more balanced understanding. It is always easy to treat one verse as a slogan, but this would contribute very little to a proper understanding. In fact, limitations of such an approach are immediately apparent. For instance, the word *yaḥkum* literally means 'to rule' or 'to judge' and is derived from *ḥukm*. But what is a *ḥukm*? What are its implications? How is this rule or judging to be carried out, and at what level: private or state? Is a *ḥukm* in the domain of God or of political leaders? Who is the ruler and who are the ruled? And who is the judge? Many more questions could be asked, and the answers are neither simple nor easily given.

Another example is provided by the phrase, 'what God has revealed' (*bimā anzala allāhu*), in the same verse. Can we simply say that it is the Qur'ān 'as it was revealed'? What is meant by the ruling according to what has been revealed? There are many rulings in the scripture: theological, moral, spiritual, and commandments and exhortations. What aspect of the scripture is thus referred to by this verse? Again, who is the intended audience? How are they to act on this? If this verse refers to the legal aspects of the Qur'ān, what exactly are these? Are they specifically related to *ḥudūd* (prescribed punishments), as many Textualists take it to mean today, or is the issue much broader? Are there any specific rulings on this in the Qur'ān, or are they matters of interpretation that we think are clear, unambiguous and legally binding? Again, answers to these questions are not always clear. When a reader has been trained within a particular ideological framework, such difficult questions and issues that do not accord with that framework are likely to be ignored. For instance, if Sayyid Quṭb, in his *Ẓilāl*, says that the meaning is 'so and so', his followers will adopt his reading because they wish to look at the text through his eyes and from his ideological standpoint.

Literal meaning as a starting point for interpretation

A key point in the interpretation of the Qur'ānic text is the original language in which the Qur'ān was revealed – Arabic. Any interpreter of the Qur'ān should be fluent in the language and be able to read, write and understand it, not just at a functional level but also at a linguistic and an advanced literary and stylistic level. The Qur'ān is the Qur'ān only in Arabic; when it is translated it becomes an interpretation. In translation, many features that exist in the original language disappear and it can be almost impossible to translate subtle associations that arise due to the grammatical, semantic or stylistic complexities of Arabic. The implications of this are important in developing theological doctrines or legal rulings. If the features of Arabic are not available to the interpreter, the intended meaning may prove elusive.

All texts, revealed or not, require interpretation, and the strategies followed may be largely common. Such a need for interpretation does not imply that the scripture is not divine. The divine message is in a language that we use, and, in order to understand and interpret it, we have recourse to principles and rules that we use in dealing with other texts. This does not diminish the transcendental or revelatory nature of the text. Historically, many interpreters of the Qur'ān relied heavily on the literal method of interpretation, examining each word in the text and identifying its literal meaning or, at sentence level, giving the sentence a direct word-for-word interpretation. They sought to remain faithful to the 'literal' meaning of each word and true to the syntactic and semantic features of the language.

At the word level, meanings are generally understood by the linguistic community. This common understanding associated with the word is its literal meaning. It must be emphasized, however, that determining this literal meaning and making it absolutely clear is often attended by significant difficulties. These difficulties may be related to the nature of the words themselves. Commonly used concrete nouns, such as 'tree', 'man', 'girl' or 'book', are readily understood. But with most abstract words, such as 'justice' or 'morality', specifying a clear literal meaning becomes more difficult. Even if a literal meaning is given to such a word, significant ambiguity will remain. Considerations other than linguistic ones are needed to arrive at an appropriate meaning for such words.

Too much emphasis on the literal meaning of the Qur'ānic text can lead to accusations of 'literalism'. Literalism can be of two forms: (1) a 'soft' literalism, where the literal meaning is emphasized and becomes the basis for the exploration of the entire meaning of the text, and (2) 'wooden' literalism, which is a rigid understanding of the literal meaning of the words without any regard to the complexities associated with meaning. The problem with 'wooden' literalism is that the scripture is not written in a scientific language in which there is one-to-one correspondence in meaning between the terms and the objects or realities to which they refer. Moreover, since the Scripture is largely devotional, the spiritual encompasses concepts such as morality, spirituality and the transcendent God.

Thus, the language used is often symbolic, figurative and anthropomorphic. If these are presented in the wooden or rigid literalistic fashion, then meanings can emerge that conflict with the spirit of the religion.

There are advantages in following the literal reading as a starting point. One is that it is a constraint on unrestricted imaginative leaps to new meanings. A number of Muslim interpreters of the Qur'ān have relied heavily on rather imaginative interpretations. This has included not only allegorical and mystical, but also theological and religio-political 'leaps' into interpretation. Such unrestricted activity in terms of finding hidden meanings is a problematic way of dealing with the scripture. Literal interpretation can also help in developing theological doctrines and systems on a sounder basis. It provides some objectivity and firm criteria by which the scriptural validity of theological or legal doctrines, of ideas and institutions, can be ascertained by a given language community. On the other hand, many Qur'ānic texts, if literally interpreted, may not provide a satisfactory meaning. This applies to a large number of parables, to metaphorical and figurative language, to a number of texts related to the Unseen, and to a significant part of the ethico-legal content.

Validity and authority in interpretation

In approaching the interpretation of the Qur'ān, the question of authority and the extent to which the results of interpretation can be used by the Muslim community is important. Any successful interpretative effort (for the purpose of religious practice) will have to be undertaken by people who share the essential beliefs, worldview and values of the Muslim community in general. There can be two levels of commitment by an individual engaged in interpretation. At one level are the fundamentals of the religion, upon which there is a high level of consensus. This consensus covers belief in one God, in Muḥammad as His prophet, and in the Qur'ān as revelation from God, as well as other basic beliefs. At the second level are further tenets of Islam, such as universal humanitarian values, accountability to God, the relationship of God to creation, the need for and importance of religion to human development, and the legal implications of the Qur'ān.

As long as the interpreter adopts and believes in the fundamentals of religion, their substantiated views should be regarded as potentially valid and to be taken seriously. Those who do not meet the criteria, for example non-Muslims, may contribute to the interpretative effort in a purely academic sense. Their understanding may be drawn on but cannot be taken as authoritative for the purpose of religious practice. Within the Muslim community itself, however, there are those who share fundamental beliefs and values but differ from other Muslims on various substantive but not fundamental issues. In fact, the degree of diversity found among

Muslims today can be associated with such non-fundamental issues. Although there have been attempts by Muslims (in both the classical and modern periods) to reject certain scholars' views as heretical, the tendency within the *tafsīr* tradition has been to accept them as potentially valid and acceptable. For instance, Zamakhsharī, although he was a champion of Muʿtazilī theology, continues to be accepted by the wider circle of interpreters of the Qurʾān and the Sunnī Muslim community. Similarly, Rāzī, who was fond of bringing positions of his own theological school (Ashʿarī) into Qurʾānic interpretation, is still widely accepted. As long as the fundamentals are adhered to, differences on non-substantive issues should not be taken as a basis for excluding the views of any scholar.

If new interpretative efforts are to succeed and become accepted in a given community, it is important for the interpreter to share as much as possible of the mutable aspects of the religion as well, which include certain aspects of one's worldview, as well as cultural norms and values in line with developments in society. The community of interpreters of which the interpreter is a part, thus shares a body of values, beliefs and assumptions. This community of interpreters functions in two very important ways: as a context for new interpretations to emerge, and as a means to check and validate emerging interpretations. Since many new interpretations may be subjective, it is important to have a process to offset or validate this subjectivity. The critical appraisal of new thinking is usually part of the scholarly process.[34]

A question that arises in this context is the degree to which interpretation is guided by the theological views of the interpreter. If by theological views we mean the fundamentals of Islam, these should certainly guide the interpretation. There should be some meshing of the community's fundamental religious expectations and the interpretation of foundation texts. Failure to achieve synchronicity may result in reductionism, which reduces all scripture to the literary, sociological, anthropological or psychological rather than focusing on the religious and theological aspects that give the text its status as sacred. At the same time it is important to free interpretation from dogmatic theology; that is, approaches that are totally uncritical and that lack any knowledge of the historical context and heritage of Islam, or those that simply rely on dogma to affirm faith.

Chapter 10

Socio-historical context and interpretation

This chapter highlights the need to emphasize the socio-historical context of the Qur'ān in its interpretation. This context is of fundamental importance in order to make the ethico-legal texts of the Qur'ān meaningful and relevant to contemporary Muslims. The socio-historical context provides a basis for understanding the connection between the Qur'ānic ethico-legal instructions and the reasons for introducing such instructions in the seventh-century Hijaz. Despite the importance of this context, it has until recently been marginalized in both law and exegesis.

Muḥammad al-Ghazālī (d. 1996), a contributor to exegetical thinking, believed that Muslims, after the first few centuries of Islam, shifted their attention from reflection on the text of the Qur'ān to the recitation of its words, perfecting the recitation and focusing on the mechanics of reading. For Ghazālī, this shift of focus gradually led to the recitation of the Qur'ān today as having no purpose but *barakah* (grace or blessing). He saw this approach to the Qur'ān in most parts of the Muslim world, and believed that it goes against the Qur'ān's exhortations to reflect on and comprehend the text, as well as to recite it.[1] He argued that the very purpose for which the Qur'ān was revealed has disappeared from the sight of many Muslims, who read what they do not comprehend.[2] Ghazālī believed that we must emphasize reflection and understanding:

> One must read the Qur'ān carefully, contemplatively, which leads to the understanding of each sentence accurately. Each person should make all efforts to understand its meaning and comprehend its goals. If there is any difficulty [with the text] he should ask those who have knowledge. Reading, understanding and reflection of the Qur'ān are required at all times.[3]

Part of this reflection should be an effort to link the past with the present. Such a link requires exploration of two dimensions of the meaning of the Qur'ānic texts concerned: the 'historical' and the 'contemporary'. Historical refers to the meaning at the time of the Prophet and earliest Muslims; contemporary refers to the meaning of the Qur'ān for people today.

Until now, Muslim interpretation of the Qur'ān has largely assumed that the interpreter's function is to explain the historical meaning of the text by philological and grammatical analysis. The question we could now ask is, 'Can the meaning of the Qur'ānic text in the Prophet's time be somewhat different when looked at from another point in time?' or 'Can the meaning of a text change?' Such questions were not considered highly significant to interpreters of the Qur'ān in the pre-modern period; nor did they seem justified, as they implied that the meaning of the Word of God could be changed. The general view among the scholars of *tafsīr* and law was that, since the text was fixed, the meaning was more or less fixed too. This is not to suggest that there was only one approach in the *tafsīr* tradition to the question of meaning, but that the tendency of the tradition was to maintain as much stability as possible, particularly in the interpretation of the ethico-legal texts of the Qur'ān.

Recognition of the socio-historical context in interpretation

The socio-historical context of the Qur'ān in the pre-Islamic and early Islamic periods should not be ignored. Understanding this context of the Qur'ān requires a detailed knowledge of the Prophet's life, both in Mecca and Medina, the spiritual, social, economic, political and legal climate, and the associated norms, laws, customs, manners, institutions and values of the region, in particular Hijaz. These also include housing, clothing and food, and social relations, such as family structure, social hierarchy, taboos and rites of passage. The importance of these aspects is supported by the frequency with which the Qur'ān refers to them.

Historically, the socio-historical context played a less significant role in the interpretation of the Qur'ān after the establishment of the discipline of Islamic law by the third/ninth century. Before then, some emphasis had been placed on the non-linguistic, largely historical, context. This was achieved mainly through the *asbāb al-nuzūl* (occasions of revelation) literature. While the *asbāb* purport to explain the immediate contexts of certain verses, one could argue that their ability to provide an understanding of the actual socio-historical context is limited. Many *asbāb* are contradictory and others are historically suspect. In light of these limitations, the more we know about the communities of Hijaz and Arabia in an anthropological sense, the clearer will be the socio-historical context of the Qur'ān and its verses.

Emphasizing the importance of this context, the Qur'ān makes many references to the cultural and material world of Hijaz and Arabia in general: physical characteristics, events, attitudes, people and how they responded to God's call, and the institutions, norms and values of the people there. The region of Hijaz is a reflection of the cultures that existed in Arabia and surrounding regions. These ranged from Mediterranean cultures, including Jewish and Christian, to southern Arabic, Ethiopian and Egyptian, all of which to varying degrees influenced Hijaz and its people. As a consequence, the socio-cultural life of the world of Hijaz at the time of the Qur'ān was highly diverse. Understanding this will help today's reader make connections between the Qur'ānic text and the environment that gave rise to the revelation.

Looking at the Qur'ān in its wider context: an overview

The starting point for understanding the context of the Qur'ān is Hijaz in the seventh century CE. Mecca, where the Qur'ān began to be revealed, was a town in the middle of a mountainous region that had very little water and no agriculture. At its centre was the sacred Ka'bah (House of God). Medina was different. It was an oasis that relied on agriculture. Life around Mecca was harsh. While both Mecca and Medina were settled communities, the region contained many nomadic tribes constantly on the move in search of water and vegetation for their animals. Raids were common, and the settled communities had to enter into agreements with nomadic tribes in order to protect themselves and their caravan trade. The associated insecurity, coupled with the general hardships and uncertainties of daily life, gave the Meccans a rather fatalistic view of the world.

Christian, Jewish and pagan communities were scattered throughout Arabia. Many Christian communities existed in the north of Arabia and Abyssinia and parts of southern Arabia. Judaism also had a presence in Yemen, Medina and Khybar. Mecca itself was largely pagan and its people worshipped a large number of deities housed in the Ka'bah. A small number of people in Mecca shunned the worship of idols and believed in one supreme God. Even in Medina the non-Jewish people (the two tribes of Aws and Khazraj) were largely pagan. The Jewish influence in Medina had been strengthened through intermarriage, shared neighbourhoods, adoption and conversion. Despite these different religious traditions, there was substantial interaction between the people of Hijaz and those in other parts of Arabia. This generally occurred through trade and visits to Mecca by Arabs wishing to pay their respects at the Ka'bah. The interaction of Meccans and Medinans with other communities meant that ideas associated with one supreme God were well known.

This interaction gave rise to a rich resource of legends, myths, ideas, historical figures, images and rituals, which the Qur'ān used to relate its narratives, norms and values to the context of Hijaz. The stories of the prophets it chose to narrate were relevant to the region, be they from biblical or other sources. The Qur'ān appropriated local practices, such as fasting, for the emerging community. At times, the Qur'ān 'Islamized' formerly pagan practices. *Ḥajj* (pilgrimage), which the Meccans had practised in pre-Islamic times, was 'purified' and reintroduced, stripped of its polytheistic practices but with little change otherwise.

Many of the pre-Islamic values in Hijaz also came to be accepted as part of the new religion. On the whole, what the culture considered to be important and of positive value was accepted – for instance, values such as patience in the face of adversity or 'manliness' (*muruwwah*). What the culture normally considered improper or indecent (*faḥshā'*) was rejected. This included extravagance, lack of generosity, breach of trust, hypocrisy, suspicion, vanity, boasting, ridiculing of others, slander, murder, adultery, cheating in trade, usury, hoarding and gambling. In commanding Muslims to reject such attitudes and behaviours, the Qur'ān presents a picture of what was occurring in the society at the time. Many of the foods consumed were also accepted by the Qur'ān, with exceptions such as wine and pig meat.

Where the institutions of pre-Islamic Arabs were in conflict with its new religious vision, the Qur'ān rejected them or adapted them. In the case of adoption, for instance, the Qur'ān would not allow an adoptee to be treated as a biological son or daughter. This is illustrated in the famous case of the Prophet's marriage to the divorced wife of his adopted son, Zayd. The Qur'ān even recognized norms surrounding war and peace that existed then. Slavery existed and was accepted as normal. The pre-Islamic holy months became Islamic. Sacrifice was also accepted as Islamic, on the condition that the sacrifice should be made only to the one God, not to other deities. The unity of God (*tawḥīd*) was the overriding concept.

An example of an area that the Qur'ān dealt with on numerous occasions is in relation to women. Distinctions on the basis of gender and class remained part of society. There are numerous statements in the Qur'ān that suggest that females were valued less than males in the culture. While rejecting some manifestations of this, the Qur'ān retains what it could not do away with due to social and cultural constraints. For example, it disapproves of people who do not welcome the birth of a female child. It also prohibits female infanticide. Several other references, however, suggest that in some respects, from the Qur'ānic point of view, women did not have quite the same status as men. For example, the evidence of two women was regarded as equal to that of one man in certain cases. Men were allowed authority over and guardianship of women. Despite these instances, the Qur'ān does not treat gender as having clear-cut answers; the message is plain that women in the society of Hijaz endured greater hardships than did men and their status was somewhat low. The Qur'ān, however, did not condone blatant discrimination against women; its emphasis was on fairness and justice. It did much to alleviate the suffering of women as a whole and to protect their interests, as it did to ease the burden on other weak and disadvantaged groups in the society of Hijaz, such as slaves and the poor.

Socio-historical context: the example of the laws of inheritance

The clearest examples of the connection between the Qur'ān and its context are found in the verses that deal with ethico-legal matters. An example of this is the 'verses of inheritance':

> Allah [thus] directs you as regards your children's [inheritance]: to the male, a portion equal to that of two females: if only daughters, two or more, their share is two-thirds of the inheritance; if only one, her share is a half. For parents, a sixth share of the inheritance to each, if the deceased left children; if no children, and the parents are the [only] heirs, the mother has a third; if the deceased left brothers [or sisters] the mother has a sixth. [The distribution in all cases [is] after the payment of legacies and debts. You know not whether your parents or your children are nearest to you in benefit. These are settled portions ordained by God; and God is All-Knowing, All-Wise.
>
> In what your wives leave, your share is a half, if they leave no child; but if they leave a child, you get a fourth; after payment of legacies and debts. In what you leave, their share is a fourth, if you leave no child; but if you leave a child, they get an eighth; after payment of legacies and debts. If the man or woman whose inheritance is in question, has left neither ascendants nor descendants, but has left a brother or a sister, each one of the two gets a sixth; but if more than two, they share in a third; after payment of legacies and debts; so that no loss is caused [to any one]. Thus is it ordained by God; and God is All-Knowing, Most Forbearing.[4]

These verses are generally understood in Islamic law as specifying the shares to be given to the heirs of an estate. On the whole, where there are males and females at *the same level*, such as sons and daughters or brothers and sisters, females receive less than males. Islamic law does not question why this should be so and why there should be a gender difference in allocating the shares. Exegetes of the Qur'ān, following the views of the legists, took the view that it was normal to differentiate on the basis of sex in allocating shares of an estate. They did not attempt to relate this differential treatment to the socio-historical context *of the time*.

In the pre-modern period, the social structure and context in Muslim communities often meant that men had greater economic responsibilities and therefore should receive larger inheritances. In pre-Islamic Hijaz, women were often economically dependent on male relatives, although there were exceptions, such as the Prophet Muḥammad's wife Khadījah, who was much wealthier than the Prophet himself. Politically, women played no significant role in running the affairs of the clan, tribe or town. After the Prophet's death, this position was further weakened by Muslims adopting the norms and values of a number of newly conquered regions, such as the Sassanid empire. By juxtaposing Qur'ānic instructions, the situation of women in Hijaz in the early first/seventh century and the norms and values of conquered regions, Muslims began to develop ideas about women, some of which may not have had the support of the Qur'ān itself. It seems that the way women were viewed gradually worsened and this was later consolidated through incorporation of such views in law and exegesis. Women, in later Islamic periods and in many communities, were often considered incapable of providing even good advice and counsel in matters related to governance and public life. Intellectually, they were regarded by many male scholars as weak, and their opinions not worthy of consideration. These ideas continued to dominate the thinking of many men, including scholars of religion, up until today. Commenting on verse Q.2:282, in which two female witnesses are required in place of one male, the exegete Rāzī stated:

> Women's nature is dominated by forgetfulness owing to a predominance of cold and wetness in their physical constitution. When two women are joined, forgetting is less likely than the occurrence of forgetting in just one woman. Therefore two women are to take the place of only one man so that if one of them forgets the other could remind.[5]

In understanding the Qur'ānic texts related to women, it is important to place the inheritance verses in the broader cultural context of Hijaz, which can be found by exploring the socio-cultural aspects referred to above. On the other hand, the meaning of the verse for a Muslim of the twenty-first century can be determined by looking at the contemporary context. Today, in many Muslim communities, women are economically independent thanks to educational and employment opportunities. They attend school and university like their male counterparts, and equip themselves to play important roles in society. Early ideas about the intellectual inferiority of women have been proved to be baseless; in fact, women are ahead of men on many fronts in educational achievement. In many countries, women can become heads of state or assume other senior positions and this is despite the arguments put forward by some Muslims, who argue that women should not assume such positions. In the light of the transformation of the roles and status of women, should we still argue for maintaining the only reading of the inheritance verse entertained by Muslim scholars over the past 1,400 years, or should we attempt to explore other possible readings? My argument is that we have no reason not to.

Socio-historical context and cultural language

In dealing with ethico-legal matters, the cultural context of Hijaz was a point of departure for both the Qur'ān and the Prophet. The Prophet never claimed that he came to eradicate all the cultural elements from Hijaz. His main task was to teach new ideas primarily related to God, God's relationship to people and His creation, moral values and life after death. By and large, the way of life of the people of Hijaz and their worldview were retained. The innovations introduced by the Prophet were primarily in theological, spiritual and ethical areas. Hijaz also provided the worldview of the first recipients of the Qur'ān – the Companions.

The Qur'ān contains its own culturally specific language appropriate to its worldview. By this I mean the symbols, metaphors, terms and expressions that were used in Hijaz. Even in describing the Islamic concept of Paradise, the Qur'ān uses language that is closely associated with the local culture and popular imagination: flowing rivers, fruit, trees and gardens. Each culture has its unique ways of describing specific issues, ideas and values, and these ways may not always be translatable into other contexts. For instance, in relation to the veiling of women, the people of Hijaz in the first/seventh century used a language that was understandable in that culture. This relied upon a range of understandings about women and their role in the society, how women were perceived, how men and women were expected to relate to each other, the type of women who were supposed to engage in veiling, and ideas about sexuality, morality and decency.

In dealing with ethico-legal matters, the language of the Qur'ān is primarily ethical, not legal. This can be seen in the way the Qur'ān expresses its ideals, commandments, prohibitions and instructions. However, this ethical language was later transformed into a legal language as Islamic law was developed in the first three centuries of Islam. In addition to its ethical language, the language of the Qur'ān is also theological in the sense that it talks about God, humankind, the relationship of humankind to God and the fundamental questions about human existence in relation to God. I would argue therefore that the Qur'ānic language should be categorized primarily as 'ethical-theological'. Reducing this ethical-theological language to purely legal language has, in my view, been one of the most unfortunate events in the history of Qur'ānic exegesis. An emphasis on legal matters was needed when Islamic law was being developed in the first/seventh, second/eighth and third/ninth centuries and jurists were seeking an authoritative basis for developing law and devising a system of jurisprudence. However, this emphasis was taken too far when manifestly ethical texts came to be considered purely legal. To reduce the language of the Qur'ān to the purely legal – as the Textualists have done and usually do today – is, in my view, a disservice to the language and spirit of the Qur'ān.

Socio-historical context and what is mutable and immutable

Fresh interpretation of the ethico-legal texts raises the issue of mutability and immutability in Islam. For many Muslims, merely thinking about changing Qur'ānic rules is tantamount to unbelief (*kufr*) or heresy. However, there are debates in Muslim tradition on the issue of mutability and immutability that may help us. At one level, an example is that of *muʿāmalāt* (transactions) and *ʿibādāt* (worship). The former is seen as negotiable/mutable, the second as non-negotiable/immutable. This is based on the view that rules and regulations related to worship are injunctions from God and the Prophet; no human being other than the Prophet has the authority to change them. Therefore, rules related to *ʿibādāt* should be considered immutable. Opposed to this is the *muʿāmalāt*, which includes things like buying and selling, which is based on local custom or practice and thus is negotiable/mutable. Early scholarly discussions on changing laws according to local customs are evident in Ḥanafī law, for instance.

At another level is consensus (*ijmāʿ*). Shāfiʿī, for example, argued that it was only on the fundamentals of religion that consensus could be achieved.[6] This view allows for a large area, where consensus cannot be achieved, to be seen as mutable. Early discussions on these questions have been dismissed in the contemporary discourse, particularly by Textualists, who insist that everything in the Qur'ān is immutable.

Related to this is the assertion by Textualists that the *sharīʿah* as such is immutable and therefore must remain unchanged, and that Muslims must change according to the *sharīʿah*. First, the meaning of *sharīʿah* is not made clear. It could mean the sources of *sharīʿah* (such as the Qur'ān and sunnah) or the Islamic laws based on those sources. Second, if by *sharīʿah* is meant the laws and rulings mentioned in the Qur'ān or sunnah, then significant change has undeniably occurred. Third, Muslim scholars from the earliest period to the present day have debated change and decided that in some areas change is negotiable while in others it is not. For jurists such as Shāṭibī, Islamic law (including traditionally immutable categories, such as *ḥudūd*) serves certain purposes. For example, for him laws related to the social sphere are formulated in the public interest. Others, such as Ibn Qayyim, have recognized that prevailing customs may influence both the formulation of law and changes to law, based on the purpose of that law.[7]

However, although mechanisms for change were recognized, few voices were heard in the past advocating substantial changes to existing laws of the Qur'ān or sunnah. Among the few who did advocate such change was Ṭūfī (d. 716/1316). He argued that the ḥadīth, 'No harm shall be inflicted or reciprocated' (*lā ḍarar wa lā ḍirār*),[8] supported the absolute priority of 'public interest'. Laws – even those drawn from the Qur'ān or the sunnah – could be changed if the change served the public interest.[9] Ṭūfī's ideas were not taken up by scholars and remained ignored.

Many Textualists argue that Muslims of the twenty-first century have no authority to change anything in the *sharī'ah* or even to reinterpret it. This argument appears unsustainable on several fronts. First, reinterpretation and change are not new in Islam. It occurred in the Qur'ān and sunnah during the formative period and at the time of the Companions. It was practised by many leading jurists and theologians. For example, 'Umar b. al-Khaṭṭāb changed a number of rulings clearly stated in the Qur'ān and sunnah. An example is 'Umar's refusal to distribute the land of Iraq as booty to the Muslim army after its conquest, even though there is an instruction in the Qur'ān that appears to command Muslims to distribute such booty.[10] But when circumstances changed and the 'public interest' demanded it, 'Umar believed he could choose a different way.[11] In other words, if a practice or ruling fulfilled a specific social function, reinterpretation was possible if the context of the ruling changed.

Concluding remarks

Values change according to social, economic, political, legal and intellectual circumstances. When this happens, there should be a change in how we approach the foundation texts that relate to those values. The Qur'ān was given in a specific context, within the framework of a worldview that was appropriate to first/seventh-century Arabia, and in a language and symbolism that its audience understood. The Qur'ān should be seen as embedded in the context in which it was received.

Despite the importance of the socio-historical context for understanding the Qur'ān, many Muslims view this dimension with suspicion. In general, Muslims believe the Qur'ān is applicable at all times and in all places and circumstances, regardless of the differences in cultural context. Thus, for many Muslims, any discussion of the socio-historical context of revelation is a threat to the religion and its traditions.

Unless we recognize the importance of the socio-historical context of the Qur'ān, our reading and understanding of it would be context-free to a large extent. It is this socio-historical context that shows us how the text was received by the first generation of Muslims and in what circumstances. Appreciation of this will help us determine which areas of the ethico-legal content remain highly relevant to us today and which parts may have become somewhat less relevant. Institutions, ideas and practices that may have been significant in the context of the first/seventh-century Hijaz may or may not enjoy the same significance today. Despite the importance of the socio-historical context, it has received little attention in contemporary Islamic discourse until recently.

Chapter 11

Ethico-legal texts and a hierarchy of values

As indicated in earlier chapters, the first generation of Muslims enjoyed a high degree of freedom in interpreting the Qur'ān. Major figures, such as the second caliph, ʿUmar b. al-Khaṭṭāb, departed from the Qur'ānic text in favour of what was considered 'right' at the time. This freedom was facilitated largely by the absence of a governing methodology and attendant principles and procedures for interpreting the Qur'ān. This meant that the early Muslims were relatively free to relate the text to prevailing conditions. These early Muslims, from the Companions and the Successors onwards, were highly dependent on an intuitive exploration of the text that reflected what the Qur'ān meant for them and how they should respond to it. Thus we see the emergence of what could be called a 'proto-Contextualist' interpretation.

An example of this is in the area of *zakāt*. As one of the pillars of Islam, Muslim jurists consider rulings related to *zakāt* as immutable. However, ʿUmar adopted a more pragmatic approach. For instance, Q.9:60 specifies that the recipients of *zakāt* must belong to eight categories, one of which is 'those whose hearts are to be reconciled'. The Qur'ān includes in this a number of tribal leaders whose political support for the Prophet Muḥammad and Islam was considered important in early Islam. These leaders were given a fixed share from the proceeds of *zakāt*, a practice that existed during the time of the Prophet and the reign of Abū Bakr (r. 11–13/632–634), the first caliph. However, ʿUmar refused to give these tribal leaders *zakāt*, saying that Islam was no longer in need of their support. This was a clear departure from a Qur'ānic instruction, but ʿUmar's reasoning was that the objective behind the Qur'ānic instruction counted most; when circumstances changed, there was no need to apply the instruction literally.[1] Many such decisions by ʿUmar, the Companions and other leading figures of the following generation can be traced in early Islamic legal and ḥadīth literature.[2]

A theoretical basis for this proto-Contextualist interpretation can also be found in the *maqāṣid al-sharīʿah* (aims and objectives of *sharīʿah*) literature. The *maqāṣid* is, in fact, a development in the area of law rather than of *tafsīr*. Its emergence was partly in response to the literalism that dominated the interpretation of law in the post-formative period of Islamic law (after the first/seventh and second/eighth centuries). Even though, in the twenty-first century, the *maqāṣid* tradition is taken by a number of Muslims to be a panacea for problems in adapting the ethico-legal content of the Qur'ān to the modern period, a closer look at the *maqāṣid* literature shows that it actually did not go far enough for it to be an alternative methodology to deal with the problem of literalism in law or in interpretation. The views of leading figures of *maqāṣid*, such as Ghazālī or even Shāṭibī, were too restrictive to be considered as a basis for liberal interpretations of the Qur'ān. Only a few scholars, such as Ṭūfī,[3] saw the possibility of freeing interpretation from literalism. He argued that *maṣlaḥah* (public interest) should become the basis for the interpretation of the ethico-legal content of the Qur'ān. Ṭūfī's radical approach did not, however, enjoy sufficient popularity for it to become the basis of any real redefinition of law, nor for it to supply a methodology of *uṣūl* for interpreting the text. It was too isolated an approach and too radical to be palatable to scholars accustomed to the safety of traditional *uṣūl* (principles of jurisprudence). In the twentieth century, Muḥammad al-Ṭāhir b. ʿĀshūr attempted to broaden the *maqāṣid* tradition,[4] which was taken up by several scholars associated with the Islamization of Knowledge Movement[5] initiated by Ismail al-Faruqi.

One of the stumbling blocks to interpretation based on *maqāṣid* is the apparently clear instructions in the Qur'ān, such as a clearly spelt out ruling or law. The *uṣūl* methodology, in general, does not allow for any reinterpretation of such a text. For instance, when the Qur'ān says, 'The thief, male or female, amputate their hands',[6] this is taken as a clear ruling that does not allow for any reinterpretation. According to *uṣūl* methods, such texts have to be followed literally, regardless of changes in time, place and circumstances. This creates an unsolvable problem: if the interpretative endeavour is to accommodate *maqāṣid*, the ruling related to the 'clear instruction' may have to be modified in line with the *maqāṣid* of that ruling. But the necessity of following the text negates such a modification. *Maqāṣid* is thus often reduced to a form of empty rhetoric as far as ethico-legal texts are concerned.

In the modern period, an extension of the proto-Contextualist interpretation of early Islamic history has been advocated, although indirectly and under a different labelling, by Fazlur Rahman, who perhaps typifies this approach. His contribution to the development of an alternative methodology of interpretation of the ethico-legal texts in the Qur'ān seeks to relate the text to its context, both of the revelation and of the Muslims of today. Rahman argues against traditional approaches to interpretation prevalent among classical legists and exegetes, who, he says, often treat the Qur'ān as 'piecemeal' and make no attempt to understand it and the Prophet's message in a holistic way. That is, against the background of an Arab society that had a particular worldview, values, institutions and culture.[7]

Although Rahman seems to argue for developing a hierarchy of values in dealing with the ethico-legal content of the Qur'ān and its interpretation, he does not explicitly state that such a hierarchy is essential to an alternative methodology of interpretation. He does, however, address the question of values (or what he calls 'general principles').[8] He even refers to some values, for example justice, as being superior to specific rulings given in the Qur'ān, an instance being the verse that permits a man to marry up to four women. Rahman, however, does not provide any particular set of ideas to develop this hierarchy of values apart from stating that one should first elicit general principles from specific rulings in the Qur'ān and sunnah by giving full consideration to their socio-historical context. Rahman then goes on to argue that, on the basis of these, Muslims should develop what he calls a 'unified and comprehensive socio-moral theory'.[9] It is on the basis of this theory that one is then expected to interpret the ethico-legal content of the sacred text. In doing so, Rahman is suggesting the nucleus of a method that I am referring to as Contextualist.

For Rahman, the first and most important step in developing this methodology is the eliciting of general principles via two basic movements; therefore his method is known as the 'double movement theory'.[10] In the first movement, the socio-historical context of the Qur'ān is considered in exploring specific Qur'ānic cases in order to arrive at general principles such as justice or fairness. Rahman does not speak of one principle. Instead, he is interested in a set of general principles that would later govern specific cases. In the second movement, these general principles are used as a basis to formulate rules and laws relevant to the modern period. In formulating such rules and laws one must be thoroughly familiar with the specific conditions of the modern period.[11] The importance of Rahman's double movement methodology is that he takes into account the conditions of the time of the revelation and those of the modern period, and thus relates the text to the needs of the community.

Towards a hierarchy of values

By incorporating the precedents of 'proto-Contextualist' interpretation of the early Islamic period, some aspects of the *maqāṣid* tradition, and Rahman's value-based approach to the Qur'ān, it is possible to develop a hierarchy of values that will enable us to guide a Contextualist interpretation of ethico-legal texts. Although there is a range of values in the

Qur'ān, which also includes aesthetics and epistemology, the main interest to us here is the ethical value of 'right action'. There are many reasons why 'right action' is taken as a guiding principle in reading the text and relating it to the life of Muslims. The Qur'ān considers right action as the basis of religion. It states, 'There is no compulsion in religion. For what is right and what is wrong has been made clear [in the Qur'ān].'[12] From the outset of the Qur'ānic revelation to the conclusion of the Prophet's mission, values relating to right action were recurrent themes in the Qur'ān. Thus a moral continuum was in formation over the period of revelation (610–632 CE). An unambiguous message of the Qur'ān is its insistence that its followers must do right and actively refrain from doing wrong or, in Qur'ānic terms, they must 'enjoin good and forbid evil',[13] as in the following verse:

> And [as for] the believing men and the believing women, they are guardians of each other; they enjoin good and forbid evil and keep up prayer and pay the poor-rate, and obey God and His Apostle; [as for] these, God will show mercy to them; surely God is Mighty, Wise.[14]

Given this emphasis on 'right action', generation after generation of Muslims have emphasized this theme and developed an extensive body of law based on right action. More importantly, in the modern period, what dominates the interpretative endeavours of Muslims interested in relating the Qur'ān to contemporary needs, is the identification of right action. Are all ethico-legal instructions in the Qur'ān relevant today? Or have some lost their relevance? In regard to right action, what is the degree of obligation on the believer? Is the right action obligatory, recommended or simply permissible? Given that my focus in this book is on the Qur'ān, the following will deal with the Qur'ānic values, not those of the sunnah. Since the sunnah is considered by many Muslims to be an 'interpretation' of the Qur'ān,[15] any hierarchy developed from the Qur'ān will not be too distant from the priorities of the sunnah.

A hierarchy of values in the Qur'ān for the interpretation of the ethico-legal content

Because of the rather fluid nature of the notion of 'right action', identifying all Qur'ānic values is difficult. Nevertheless, a careful reading focusing on the concept of right action provides an extensive list of values that can be classified and prioritized in order to arrive at some form of hierarchy that reflects the Qur'ānic emphasis. For such an exercise, there is no option but to go through the Qur'ān, using available indexes and dictionaries.[16] Detailed concordances are still relatively few, so it is necessary to rely on the text itself to identify these values, as well as on supporting material from *tafsīr* as well as *fiqh*.

Drawing on the Qur'ān and other sources, I have identified a large number of values related to 'right action'. Having experimented with various classifications, I adopted the following as a reasonably representative list of categories that covers most values of 'right action', which does not violate fundamental beliefs of the Qur'ān. They are in the following order of importance: obligatory, fundamental, protectional, implementational and instructional. In developing this hierarchy of values I took into consideration the following: the essential beliefs of Islam; the six pillars of faith (*īmān*); the five pillars of Islam; and what is clearly prohibited or permitted in the Qur'ān, such as the prohibition of murder or theft, or the permissibility of consumption of certain food items. In developing the categories, I have also taken into consideration what is unanimously accepted within the Muslim tradition. Much of this also relies on ideas developed in Islamic jurisprudence with regard to the five categories of human action.[17] Therefore, I will now identify criteria on the basis of which we can ascertain the degree of importance that should be attached to each category of value.

Obligatory values

The first level is 'obligatory values'. Such basic values are emphasized throughout the Qur'ān. They cover the Meccan and Medinan periods, and do not seem to be culturally dependent. In line with this, Muslims of all backgrounds on the whole consider them an essential part of Islam. There are three sub-categories of such values:

(1) Values related to the system of belief, for instance belief in God, the prophets, Holy Scripture, the Day of Judgement, accountability and life after death. This is related to what is traditionally known in Islam as '*īmān*' (belief).

(2) Values related to devotional practices emphasized in the Qur'ān, such as prayer, fasting, pilgrimage and contemplation of God. Muslim scholars generally consider this category to be *'ibādāt* (forms of worship). Since these values are emphasized frequently, and are not culturally dependent, they can be taken as universally applicable.

(3) The clearly spelt out and unambiguous specifics of what is permissible (*ḥalāl*) and what is prohibited (*ḥarām*). Regardless of the circumstances, it seems that what the Qur'ān *categorically* prohibits must remain prohibited and what it categorically declares lawful (*ḥalāl*) must remain lawful. Very few such texts exist in the Qur'ān. It would be reasonable to argue that such values are, in principle, universally

applicable. The Qur'ān is unequivocal about those who engage in attempting to make lawful what God has prohibited, or vice versa:

> And, for what your tongues describe, do not utter the lie, [saying] 'This is lawful and this is unlawful', in order to forge a lie against God; surely those who forge the lie against God shall not prosper.[18]

> Say: Tell me what God has sent down for you of sustenance, then you make [a part] of it unlawful and [a part] lawful. Say: Has God commanded you, or do you forge a lie against God?[19]

> O you who believe! Do not forbid [yourselves] the good things which God has made lawful for you and do not exceed the limits; surely God does not love those who exceed the limits.[20]

Even the Prophet was reprimanded for apparently prohibiting what God had made lawful:

> O Prophet! Why do you forbid [yourself] that which God has made lawful for you; you seek to please your wives; and God is Forgiving, Merciful.[21]

Terms such as *uḥilla* or *uḥillat* (it has been made lawful), or *aḥalla* (He made it lawful) or *aḥlalna* (We made it lawful), indicate that something is categorically made lawful, and thus should remain so forever, as in the following verses:

> Lawful to you is the game of the sea and its food.[22]

> It is made lawful to you to go into your wives on the night of the fast.[23]

> This day [all] the good things are allowed to you; and the food of those who have been given the Book is lawful for you and your food is lawful for them; and the chaste from among the believing women and the chaste from among those who have been given the Book before you [are lawful for you].[24]

> The cattle quadrupeds are allowed to you except that which is recited to you.[25]

On the other hand, what is categorically prohibited must remain so. There are several instances in which the Qur'ān deliberately uses terms such as '*ḥarrama*' (He [God] prohibited) and its derivatives to indicate prohibition. Examples of such prohibitions include eating carrion, blood or the meat of swine,[26] the practice of *ribā*,[27] or marrying one's mother, daughter, sister, paternal aunt, maternal aunt, brother's daughter or sister's daughter.[28]

In a similar vein, the Qur'ān says:

> And the divorced women should keep themselves in waiting for three courses; and it is not lawful for them that they should conceal what God has created in their wombs, if they believe in God and the last day.[29]

> Divorce may be [pronounced] twice, then keep [them] in good fellowship or let [them] go with kindness; and it is not lawful for you to take any part of what you have given them, unless both fear that they cannot keep within the limits of God.[30]

> O you who believe! It is not lawful for you that you should take women as heritage against [their] will.[31]

In these examples, the Qur'ān uses terms to the effect that something is unambiguously 'prohibited'. Faced with such a declaration, the practising Muslim does not have any choice but to follow. Questions of cultural specificity do not help. In fact, the *ḥalāl* and *ḥarām* appear to be one of the fundamental aspects of the religion and are considered to be among its immutables. However, such clearly spelt-out instances of *ḥalāl* and *ḥarām* are very few in the Qur'ān. This is not to be confused with the long lists of *ḥalāl* and *ḥarām* one finds in standard Islamic legal texts, often based on the *interpretation* of the Qur'ān and sunnah or arrived at on the basis of analogical reasoning (*qiyās*) or consensus (*ijmā'*). We are concerned here with what is specified in the Qur'ān.

In order to keep such immutables to a practicable level, the *ḥalāl* and *ḥarām* should not be extended beyond what the Qur'ān and the historically reliable sunnah have *clearly* and *unambiguously* prohibited. Emphasizing the need to keep such *ḥalāl* and *ḥarām* to a minimum, Muhammad Asad, commenting on Q.16:116 says:

> In accordance with the doctrine that everything which has not been expressly forbidden by the Qur'ān or the explicit teachings of the Prophet is *eo ipso* lawful, this verse takes a clear-cut stand against all arbitrary prohibitions invented by man or artificially 'deduced' from the Qur'ān or the Prophet's sunnah.[32]

Fundamental values

A survey of the Qur'ān indicates that certain values are emphasized as basic 'human' values. An example is protection of a person's life, family or property. Many early ulama were aware of such values and their discussions on them exist, primarily in *uṣūl* literature. Ghazālī, for instance, discusses what he calls *kulliyyāt* (universals or 'five universal values').[33] These five universal values refer to protection of life, property, honour, progeny and religion. For many scholars of *uṣūl* these values constitute the key objectives of *sharīʿah*.[34]

The fundamental values, therefore, are those that are emphasized repeatedly in the Qurʾān and for which there is substantial textual evidence to indicate that they are among the foundations of Qurʾānic teaching. There is no specific text (Qurʾān or sunnah) which declares that each of these is a 'fundamental' value that has universal applicability. However, according to Wael Hallaq:

> The knowledge of these universals is enshrined with certainty in the collective mind of the Muslim community as well as in the minds of Muslim individuals. This certainty is engendered by virtue of the fact that these principles have been attested to by a wide variety of pieces of evidence, which, in their totality, lead to certitude, although when taken individually they do not rise above the level of probability.[35]

The five universal values referred to above were arrived at using a method of 'inductive corroboration'[36] by eminent jurists such as ʿIzz b. ʿAbd al-Salām and were taken up by later jurists and scholars. Although limited to five by earlier scholars such as Ghazālī or even Shāṭibī, one could argue that it is possible, following the method of inductive corroboration, that a number of new values could be developed. For instance, 'protection of the disadvantaged' or 'protection of freedom of religion' could be considered universal values today. There are numerous individual verses in the Qurʾān, which, if inductive corroboration were used, might support the universality of these values.

For instance, major constituents of legal theory, such as consensus (*ijmāʿ*) and public interest (*maṣlaḥah*), are made up of universals (*kulliyyāt*). Such universals constitute the foundations of the *sharīʿah*[37] and each of them is formed on the basis of a multiplicity of particulars (*juzʾiyyāt*), all of which attest to one meaning or theme embodying the universal.[38] Following this method, one could derive values that protect a range of basic human rights not previously covered by the scholars of law. Examples include freedom of speech, equality before the law, freedom from torture or inhumane punishment, freedom from arbitrary arrest, detention or exile, presumption of innocence if accused, protection of the environment, and protection of the rights of the disadvantaged. While these are referred to as 'fundamental values' that are 'universal', it must be emphasized that this is an area that can be expanded and contracted based on the needs of the generation and the issues and concerns that emerge in that generation. A good example, as referred to above, is the new rights that are being created in the context of human rights, which many Muslims and non-Muslims alike consider today to be universal.

Protectional values

'Protectional values' are values that provide legislative support to the 'fundamental values'. For instance, protection of property is a fundamental value but that value has no meaning unless put into practice. This can be done not by merely stating the value but also by requiring a means of 'protecting' that value, by prohibiting theft or *ribā*. While a fundamental value does not depend on just one 'proof' (text) for its validity, the protectional value often depends on one or a few 'textual proofs'. This does not reduce the importance given to it in the Qur'ān, since the strength of the protectional value is largely derived from the fundamental value and the specific command relating to the protectional value itself. Since protectional values are essential to the maintenance of fundamental values, universality is also extended to the protectional value.

Implementational values

Implementational values are specific measures used to implement protectional values. For instance, the prohibition of theft is to be implemented in a society by taking specific measures against those who do not refrain from engaging in such activity. The Qur'ān says:

> As to the thief, male or female, cut off his or her hands: a punishment by way of example, from God, for their crime: and God is Exalted in power.[39]

When the Qur'ān decreed these measures in the first/seventh-century Arabia, it took the cultural context of the time into account. Since capital punishment and other forms of bodily punishment and/or communal disgrace were entrenched, measures that would be highly effective in that context were required. The measure itself does not appear to be a fundamental objective of the Qur'ān, as the Qur'ān almost always indicates that the aim is the prevention of a person from engaging in unacceptable behaviour. If one has already committed an offence, what is important is that one should repent and refrain from further offence. Evidence for this 'preventative' approach comes from two sources. First, the Qur'ān, immediately after specifying the preventative measure (the punishment), suggests that repentance could lead to a waiving of the measure. However, Islamic law did not take full cognizance of this, generally speaking, and emphasized enforcement of the punishment. The following examples help clarify the point. Having stated that the punishment for theft is the amputation of a hand (Q.5:38), which is the implementational value, the Qur'ān goes on to say:

> But whoever repents after his iniquity and reforms [himself], then surely God will turn to him [mercifully]; surely God is Forgiving, Merciful.[40]

According to Rāzī, repentance could waive punishment.[41] This also seems to be the view of Shāfiʿī[42] and of Aḥmad b. Ḥanbal.[43] Ibn Qayyim also offers a similar opinion in his *Iʿlām*.[44] As for the implementation of the punishment for *zinā* (unlawful sexual intercourse), in the case of the Companion Māʿiz, Ibn Qayyim is of the view that it was the latter's insistence on punishment and repeated requests that led the Prophet to impose the punishment.[45] The implication is that Māʿiz could easily have repented and avoided the punishment.

Similarly, having stated that those who engage in *zinā* must receive 100 lashes and that those who accuse chaste free-women of unlawful sexual relations should be given 80 lashes, the Qur'ān adds: 'Except those who repent after this and act aright, for surely God is Forgiving, Merciful.'[46]

In the same manner, having specified retaliation for murder, the Qur'ān adds: 'But if any remission is made to any one by his [aggrieved] brother, then prosecution should be made according to usage, and payment should be made to him in a good manner; this is an alleviation from your Lord and a mercy.'[47] This allows for 'remission' and for 'following what is right'. If imposing the punishment were the key objective, further options would not have been given.

In the case of the crime of 'waging war against God and His Prophet' (or brigandage), having declared that the punishment is 'that they should be murdered or crucified or their hands and their feet should be cut off on opposite sides or they should be imprisoned',[48] the Qur'ān states that repentance again can be a way of avoiding punishment:

> Except those who repent before you have them in your power; so know that God is Forgiving, Merciful.[49]

Similarly, on the issue of committing *fāḥishah* (indecency; unlawful sexual intercourse) the Qur'ān commands Muslims that if they (the two) repent and reform, they should be left alone and presumably no further punishment should be inflicted:

> And as for the two who are guilty of indecency from among you, give them both a punishment; then if they repent and amend, turn aside from them; surely God is Oft-Returning [to mercy], the Merciful.[50]

All of these instances indicate that the measure itself, whether amputation, flogging or execution, does not appear to be the *primary* objective of the Qur'ān in relation to these crimes. What is more important from its point of view is avoidance of the crime in the first place, and then repentance if a crime is committed. However, punishment should be in place to deter those who may be inclined to engage in such activities.

As for the practice of the Companions, in a case involving theft the second caliph, ʿUmar, was about to amputate the left hand of a person who had committed a crime for the third time. ʿAlī b. Abī Ṭālib, as ʿUmar's adviser, advised against this and suggested he impose whipping and imprisonment instead.[51] It is interesting to note ʿAlī's reasoning in this regard:

> I feel ashamed to face God having left him [the thief] without anything [hand] by which he can eat and drink or clean himself when he wants to perform the obligatory prayer. It is not appropriate to cut off his foot leaving him with nothing on which he can walk.[52]

Despite a clear Qur'ānic text, ʿAlī, foremost among those who understood and followed the Qur'ān, suggested that it was better if the prescribed punishment (*ḥadd*) was not imposed in this case. This suggests that punishment by amputation was not an objective in itself, and that there was some scope for *ijtihād* in applying Qur'ānic injunctions on *ḥadd*.

In *fiqh*, jurists were aware that such harsh punishment, if implemented widely, could lead to problems of the sort ʿAlī referred to in the example above. Considerations such as these (in some cases, no doubt, reliant on ḥadīth) led to the enormous increase in conditions set out by jurists for the implementation of *ḥadd* punishments like amputation, flogging and stoning. This made the punishment of theft, for example, virtually obsolete, for all practical purposes. The contemporary scholar of law, Muḥammad Saʿīd al-ʿAshmāwī, expresses this succinctly:

> These Qur'ānic punishments are so surrounded by conditions that in practice they are practically inapplicable; moreover, to these general conditions are added particular conditions for each penalty. Take for example theft: the object of theft must be marked by the seal of the owner and be in a well-guarded place, which excludes pilfering, open plundering and pick-pocketing; it must have a money value; the robber must not be in great need; finally, for the majority of jurists the Qur'ānic punishment for theft cannot be applied if the robber has some 'quasi-ownership' on the goods stolen, as is notably the case with public goods.[53]

Instructional values

Instructional values in the Qur'ān constitute measures taken in relation to a problem quite specific to circumstances at the time of the revelation. Given that the category of instructional values is, from my point of view, the most numerous, difficult, varied and diverse, I will address this category in some detail.

The bulk of Qur'ānic values appear to be instructional. The texts that deal with these values use a variety of linguistic devices: the imperative (*amr*) or the prohibitive (*lā*); a simple statement indicating the right action intended; or a parable, story or reference about a particular incident. The following are a few examples of such instructions:

Instruction to marry more than one woman in certain circumstances

> And give to the orphans their property, and do not substitute worthless [things] for [their] good [ones], and do not devour their property [as an addition] to your own property; this is surely a great crime. *And if you fear that you cannot act equitably towards orphans, then marry such women as seem good to you, two and three and four*; but if you fear that you will not do justice [between them], then [marry] only one or what your right hands possess; this is more proper, that you may not deviate from the right course.[54]

Instruction that men are 'maintainers' of women

> *Men are the maintainers of women* because God has made some of them to excel others and because they spend out of their property; the good women are therefore obedient, guarding the unseen as God has guarded; and [as to] those on whose part you fear desertion, admonish them, and leave them alone in the sleeping-places and beat them; then if they obey you, do not seek a way against them; surely God is High, Great. And if you fear a breach between the two, then appoint [a] judge from his people and a judge from her people; if they both desire agreement, God will effect harmony between them, surely God is Knowing, Aware.[55]

Instruction to be good to specified people

> *And be good to parents* and to the near of kin and the orphans and the needy and the neighbor of [your] kin and the alien neighbour, and the companion in a journey and the wayfarer and those whom your right hands possess; surely God does not love him who is proud, boastful.[56]

Instruction not to take unbelievers as 'friends'

> They desire that you should disbelieve as they have disbelieved, so that you might be [all] alike; therefore *take not from among them friends* until they flee [their homes] in God's way; but if they turn back, then seize them and kill them wherever you find them, and take not from among them a friend or a helper. Except those who reach a people between whom and you there is an alliance, or who come to you, their hearts shrinking from fighting you or fighting their own people; and if God had pleased, He would have given them power over you, so that they should have certainly fought you; therefore if they withdraw from you and do not fight you and offer you peace, then God has not given you a way against them.[57]

Instruction to greet one another

> And when you are greeted with a greeting, *greet with a better [greeting] than it or return it*; surely God takes account of all things.[58]

It is here that one has the most difficulty in relating the text to the life of the believer today. Do such instructional values transcend cultural specificity, and therefore are they to be followed regardless of time, place and circumstances? Should one attempt to 'recreate' the circumstances of the value, in order to put it into practice? For instance, the Qur'ān refers to slaves and instructs Muslims how to treat them.[59] Should one insist on retaining the social structure in which slaves form an essential part of the Muslim community? More importantly, how should a believer at a particular time respond to these instructional values?

In many instructional values the Qur'ān takes for granted a certain socio-historical background against which it provides these values. For instance, in the case of the value declaring 'men are maintainers of women' (Q.4:34), the Qur'ān is taking into account the situation of women and men at that time in Arabia. While there were exceptions, women were, generally speaking, excluded from important decision-making in Hijaz society. They did not take an active part in raids or battles. Many were financially dependent on men and a common belief in that society was that women needed to be 'protected' by men. Hence, the Qur'ānic instructional value, 'men are maintainers of women', is in fact expressing a value that existed at the time. Under similar circumstances, this instructional value remains operative. There is no emphasis on this value elsewhere in the Qur'ān and there are no other values that state categorically that this should remain so forever. However, in the development of Islamic values, this value was taken to be normative and still is today among more traditionalist Muslims.

Given the ambiguities associated with instructional values, we should explore them to see if a particular value is universally applicable or binding, and if so to what degree. Three criteria may be used for such exploration. Through analysis one can gauge the universality, applicability and obligatory nature of such instructional values. The three criteria that are relevant in this context, in my view, are the *frequency* of the occurrence of the value in the Qur'ān, its *salience* during the Prophet's mission, and its *relevance* to the culture, time, place and circumstances of the Prophet and the first community of Muslims.

Frequency

Frequency refers to how often an instructional value is mentioned in the Qur'ān and can be measured by identifying the frequency of related core terms relevant to the value. This is not a simple task because a particular value, for instance as simple as 'helping the poor', may be mentioned in the Qur'ān using a variety of concepts, such as 'to help the needy', 'to provide food for the destitute' and 'to look after the orphans', which are all relevant terms and concepts, phrased differently. One therefore has to survey the Qur'ān to identify these related terms or concepts in order to give a reasonably accurate estimate of the frequency of occurrence. The higher the occurrence, the more importance should be given to the value. Even this will be an estimate because it is almost impossible to identify all possible associated terms relating to the value.

Salience

The concept of salience refers to whether the value in question was emphasized throughout the Prophet's mission. A high salience indicates a high level of significance of the value in the Qur'ān. From the beginning of the Prophet's mission, a key value was 'helping the disadvantaged', as suggested by both Watt and Rahman, for instance.[60] This was an important idea or theme in both the Meccan and Medinan periods. However, if a value is mentioned once and then discarded, or if another value that opposes it is supported and promulgated, then we may assume the value has no particular relevance in the overall framework of the Qur'ān.

In studying the concept of 'salience' over a period, it is important to utilize historical reports or stylistic or linguistic features of the text and their immediate context. This helps determine an approximate dating for the text. The aim is not to arrive at an exact date, for instance Year 2 or Year 10 of *hijrah*. As long as there is some sense of when in the Prophet's mission this particular value was presented, there will be grounds to say that the particular value was used or emphasized in a particular period of the mission. For instance, we may divide the Meccan period into early, middle and late. The Medinan period can be divided up similarly. This avoids the problem of access to the availability of accurate historical information to determine exact dating of the text. Based on work already done by Muslim and non-Muslim scholars, we can classify the relevant verses into such periods, and gain a sense of the duration and prominence that the value enjoyed. The information we have on the stylistic features of the Qur'ān, its linguistic characteristics and its thematic development also helps determine questions related to salience. The higher the salience, the more importance the Qur'ān attaches to the value.

Relevance

Since the Prophet's mission was initially directed at the people of Hijaz, there is an essential relationship between the mission and the culture of Mecca, Medina and the surrounding regions. Clearly the Prophet did not come to abolish all existing cultural precepts, values and practices and to create a tabula rasa. It is therefore reasonable to assume that many of the Prophet's sayings and actions were relevant to the culture of the time. Relevance here does not mean that all Qur'ānic values are culture-specific. 'Relevance' is a much broader concept, highlighting the relationship between the mission and the society it was intended for. In the way I am using the term, there are two types of relevance: relevance to a particular culture that is time-bound, and restricted to a particular place or circumstance; and universal relevance to any culture (within the orbit of Islam) regardless of time, place and circumstance. It is the second type that is of primary interest to this subject. Whereas the relevance of the first type is time- and place-specific, the relevance of the second type is not and thus transcends the cultural limitations of Hijaz.

Knowledge of the cultural context of the revelation plays a major role in determining the relevance of the text to the modern period. Once we are comfortable with the idea of an underlying value and have determined this for a given text, the next step is to determine how that value is related to the culture of the time. How do we determine whether a particular value is culture-specific? This requires observation of the period and the socio-historical context, as well as of the functions of the society, its habits, customs and cultural constructs. We then need to compare these with a society of today. In comparing two different periods in analysing cultural constructs, we can observe both permanent and changing aspects.

It is important to understand that, within the cultural context of a certain historical period, certain things may be accepted without question. Capital punishment, for instance, was very much part of pre-Islamic and early Islamic society and was the penalty for many offences. It was part of the pre-revelation tribal system to inflict such punishment; maximum pain was acceptable as appropriate redress. For example, it was natural for the Qur'ān to demand punishment, such as amputation, in the context of a crime against wealth and property. What happens if this ethos changes? One has then to reflect on the relevance of the value and see if the value itself was the objective, or if the value was used merely to achieve a more fundamental value, such as protection of property. If the analysis indicates that the particular value being explored is actually culture-specific, one may argue that the extension of the value to cultures that are significantly different may not be what is intended by the text. However, the underlying value (which is of a more general nature and is acultural) may be extended to other cultures.

Some general rules in relation to the instructional values which could be derived from the above are:

- The more frequently a value recurs in the Qur'ān, the more likely it is to be universally applicable.
- The greater the coverage of the value, the more likely it is to be a universal one.
- The more general the relevance of the value, the more likely it is to be a universal one.
- If a value meets the three criteria (at the extreme positive end of the continuum), the value (most likely) is equivalent to a universal value and its applicability is universal and thus binding.
- If the value meets the three criteria (at the extreme negative end of the continuum), the value (most likely) is a religiously non-universal value (culture-specific), and its applicability is contingent on circumstances.

Example of an instructional value

From the very beginning the Qur'ān emphasized freedom of belief as part of its message. This position was maintained consistently from the time in Mecca when Muslims were weak, to the time in Medina when they had become a strong political force. However, towards the end of the Prophet's mission, this general principle seems to have been set aside in relation to the polytheists (*mushrikūn*). The polytheists no longer had a choice: if they did not accept Islam and believe in God and the Prophet, they were to be fought until they complied. This appears to have been a specific measure employed against a specific party under specific circumstances. The following verses emphasize freedom of belief:

> Say: O unbelievers! I do not serve that which you serve. Nor do you serve Him Whom I serve. Nor am I going to serve that which you serve. Nor are you going to serve Him Whom I serve. *You shall have your religion and I shall have my religion.*[61]

> *There is no compulsion in religion*; truly the right way has become clearly distinct from error; therefore, whoever disbelieves in Satan and believes in God he indeed has laid hold on the firmest handle, which shall not break off, and God is Hearing, Knowing.[62]

> But if they dispute with you, say: 'I have submitted myself entirely to God and [so] every one who follows me'; and say to those who have been given the Book and the unlearned people: 'Do you submit yourselves?' So if they submit then indeed they follow the right way; and *if they turn back, then upon you is only the delivery of the message and God sees the servants.*[63]

> And if your Lord had pleased, surely all those who are in the earth would have believed, all of them; *will you then force men till they become believers?*[64]

> He said: O my people! tell me if I have with me clear proof from my Lord, and He has granted me mercy from Himself and it has been made obscure to you; *shall we constrain you to [accept] it while you are averse from it?*[65]

> *But if you turn back, then indeed I have delivered to you the message* with which I have been sent to you, and my Lord will bring another people in your place, and you cannot do Him any harm; surely my Lord is the Preserver of all things.[66]

> *But if they turn back, then on you devolve only the clear deliverance* [of the message].[67]

This value, the right to believe in God or in a particular religion, remained central to the Prophet's mission up to Year 9/630. There was no compulsion to accept Islam. In fact, as the above-mentioned verses and other similar verses[68] indicate, the Qur'ān totally rejects any kind of compulsion. The Prophet's duty was to convey the message; it was up to the people to believe or not to believe.

Although many tribes or clans maintained their pre-Islamic religions, the Prophet concluded peace treaties with a number of them. As long as they were not aggressive towards the Muslims, a harmonious relationship existed between the Prophet and these tribes or clans. Jews, Christians and idolaters were all able to retain their religions without intervention as long as they did not engage in hostile activity against Muslims. This situation appears to have changed in Year 9/630 with the revelation of Q.9 (*al-Tawbah*). The idolaters/polytheists (*mushrikūn*), who did not have a peace treaty with the Prophet, were given four months to enter the fold of Islam or face the consequences. Those who had concluded peace treaties with the Prophet and had not engaged in aggression against Muslims were given until the expiry of the existing treaty. Once this had expired, the idolaters were to be resisted and killed unless they accepted Islam. Similarly, those who did not believe in God or in the Day of Judgement, and did not prohibit what God and His Messenger had prohibited, and those of the People of the Book who did not believe in the true religion (*dīn al-ḥaqq*) were to be fought against until they paid the *jizyah* (tax), which had to be paid to Muslims as a sign of disgrace.[69]

This departure from tolerance of religious difference appears to be due to the changed circumstances of the Muslim community at the time. Although they were virtually in control of large parts of Arabia, there remained pockets of idolaters and others who threatened to resist. Since the Prophet's mission was coming to an end, it would appear that the Qur'ānic imperative was to eradicate idolatry and any form of resistance by bringing all into the fold of Islam. This was to be achieved either by forcing idolaters to accept Islam or by compelling non-idolaters (such as the People of the Book) to accept the primacy of the new religion via taxation. The non-compromising language of the sūrah is evidence of a hardening attitude to religious and political opposition. If the concept of a hierarchy of values is applied here, one can say that the Qur'ānic instructional value (coercion of the polytheist to submit to Islam) is one that is specific to the circumstances of the time in which the revelation occurred. It is not a value according to which any idolater or unbeliever is to be killed. The universal values of protection of life and of freedom of belief should thus receive priority over culturally specific values.

Concluding remarks

In this chapter, I have presented a framework for thinking about Qur'ānic values, in particular how they relate to the ethico-legal dimension – a dimension that is an important aspect of the Qur'ān and for which there is an abundance of texts. One of the difficulties we face in the classical traditions of *tafsīr* and *fiqh* is that scholars of *tafsīr* tend to use legal language and methodology when it comes to the interpretation of the ethico-legal texts. Scholars explore the Qur'ānic text in line with the five categories of action as spelled out in *fiqh*: obligatory, recommended, permissible, reprehensible and prohibited. Thus, their conclusions in relation to the ethico-legal texts are identical to the results of jurists. This strong connection between *tafsīr* and *fiqh* makes it difficult for Muslim scholars today to advocate a high degree of flexibility with respect to the interpretation of ethico-legal texts. The reason for this is that, in the minds of many Muslims, the conclusions the jurists arrived at in the formative period remain the standard by which any interpretation should be measured. However, I have argued that this connection should be broken and a more flexible approach to such texts in *tafsīr* adopted. To this end, I have set out in this chapter a hierarchy of values that could facilitate this.

Chapter 12

Epilogue

The current status of the *sharīʿah* disciplines, be they ḥadīth, *uṣūl al-fiqh* or *tafsīr*, does not seem to be particularly encouraging as far as any fundamental changes to their existing paradigms are concerned. Once the *sharīʿah* disciplines were developed and reached their maturity in the fourth/tenth and fifth/eleventh centuries, they generally lost their vitality and creativity over time. Only rarely did scholars 'test the waters' and challenge the existing paradigm. Confrontations between tradition and reassessment of that tradition were usually won by the established order.

The methods developed by leading figures such as Bukhārī (d. 256/870) and Muslim (d. 261/875) were considered to be the pinnacle of ḥadīth criticism. No significant refinement or reinvestigation was felt by the ulama to be necessary. Modern Western critical scholarship on ḥadīth has, until recently, been largely ignored in the Muslim world because of its questioning of the authenticity of ḥadīth, and because of its methodology. To date there have been few signs of the rethinking of methodological aspects of ḥadīth criticism within Islamic scholarship.

Nor does the situation with the principles of jurisprudence (*uṣūl al-fiqh*), for example, give cause for optimism. Once Shāfiʿī's principles of jurisprudence (in his famous *Risālah*) had been accepted by various leading scholars and developed in the fourth/tenth and fifth/eleventh centuries, the discipline was considered to have reached its maturity. From the sixth/twelfth century onwards, scholars were expected to function largely as collectors and compilers of the views of earlier scholars. Thus, we have summaries upon summaries of *uṣūl*.[1] It is true that on rare occasions, scholars attempted to go beyond the limits of the discipline, for example Shāṭibī (d. 766/1388). However, he too found himself bound by the rigidity of the paradigm of his time. Nonetheless, in his *al-Muwāfaqāt*, Shāṭibī attempted to construct a system of what he termed *maqāṣid*. This work, although it remains an important contribution to the discipline, has had minimal influence on subsequent generations. The existing *uṣūl al-fiqh* methodology and its framework remained authoritative up to the modern period.

Like Shāṭibī, Ṭūfī (d. 716/1316) also attempted to rethink some of the issues of *uṣūl al-fiqh* by emphasizing the concept of *maṣlaḥah* (public interest). This radical concept, advocated in his *Risālah*, had very little impact on later generations. Even in the modern period, Ṭūfī's *Risālah* has not been taken up by the ulama in general. His approach is too radical as it goes against the Shāfiʿian foundations on which the discipline of *uṣūl* is largely based. Any acceptance of Ṭūfī's approach will require significant changes to the existing *uṣūl al-fiqh* methodology, which the ulama are unwilling to contemplate.

Tafsīr, being one of the most versatile disciplines in Islam, has escaped to some extent the suffocating dogmatism of other disciplines. The tradition of *tafsīr* has incorporated diverse methods, approaches and principles, from the purely grammatical to the theological and symbolic. Even here, many of the new approaches utilized in *tafsīr* were labelled by the 'guardians' of orthodoxy as invalid, problematic or, worse, as *kufr* (unbelief).

In order to further Islamic thought and develop it in line with the needs and concerns of Muslims in the twenty-first century, bold steps need to be taken, in particular in relation to bridging the ever-widening gap between the Islamic disciplines and the daily needs of Muslims. Part of this is questioning and then finding solutions to the problems of Islamic thought created over the past several hundred years in the post-formative period of Islam. Notions such as mutability and immutability, religious versus non-religious, and sacred versus non-sacred, all may need to be rethought. Many approaches to Islamic disciplines not considered sacred in the formative period have since become sacred. Yet the calls for reinterpretation in any of these have been rejected by the conservative ulama, who consider themselves the 'guardians' of Islam. Those with the courage to take such a bold step are often labelled agents of Orientalism or of the West, aiming to subvert Islamic tradition.

There are at least three approaches to the question of tradition: a traditionalist position, which essentially argues for unquestioning continuation of the tradition as it is; a continuation of the tradition but with an increasing degree of flexibility; and a rejection of key aspects of tradition in favour of a fresh start. Traditionalism has been staunchly maintained by the proponents of *taqlīd* (blind imitation of early scholars) in various schools of law. The middle approach is represented by scholars such as Fazlur Rahman, who argues for continuity. He emphasizes the importance of a solid grounding in the tradition as a prerequisite for Islamic scholarship.[2] The third position maintains that the early practices and rulings have little to offer in a new framework or paradigm for Islamic disciplines.[3] The popularity of traditionalism flourishes in an environment of anti-intellectualism among a significant sector of the conservative ulama. Their frame of reference remains the long period of general lack of creativity in the history of Islamic disciplines that spans the past 700 years.

Despite this, there are scholars today who argue for rethinking of this tradition. Nasr Hamid Abu Zayd, for example, who sought to rethink some aspects of *tafsīr* methodology, faced many difficulties. In fact, partly because of his views (and of course, his clash with the religious establishment on several issues in Egypt), he was branded an apostate and forced into exile in the Netherlands. Earlier, Fazlur Rahman experienced a somewhat similar fate. In the 1960s Rahman came under pressure from his fellow Pakistanis, scholars and laity alike, because of his views on the Qur'ān, *tafsīr* and Islamic tradition. He too, was forced into exile and went to the United States where he remained until his death in 1988. The disturbing message from these examples is that those who argue for change and for rethinking established views can expect to survive mainly outside the Islamic world, often in academic institutions in the West, where they have a relatively high degree of intellectual freedom. A further repercussion of this is that such scholars are usually writing for an international audience in a language not commonly used by the majority of Muslims (English or French, for instance). Thus the impact of their works in the Islamic world remains limited.

The foregoing is the broad context in which this book has been written. It addresses a concern of many Muslims: can one be faithful to the Qur'ānic revelation while attempting to relate it to the needs of Muslims today? Can Muslims legitimately *rethink* aspects of methodology and the approaches to interpretation transmitted to us historically? This book is a response to these calls for rethinking interpretation of the Qur'ān in the modern period – rethinking advocated by various scholars from a range of backgrounds and perspectives. The book provides an argument for the legitimacy of such an exercise.

The fundamental problem for us remains of relating a sacred text from a distant 14 centuries ago to a world that has changed dramatically. From the establishment of the classical schools of Islamic law, Muslim scholars felt little need to interpret the Qur'ān, in particular its ethico-legal content, in step with changes in the wider community. The early achievements in constructing a system of law in Islam, and the extension of this law to all matters of life, have given the impression that the Qur'ān is capable of meeting the needs of Muslims at any given time or place. Some people ask the question, 'If the Qur'ān has provided answers for all aspects of life so far, why should it not continue to do so, and why should not the methodology that has been adopted so far be appropriate for today?' While the Qur'ān provides guidance to a Muslim at all times, the methodology that is used to arrive at this guidance requires revision and change as circumstances and times change. The methodology that has been in place (in particular in the ethico-legal area) is facing enormous challenges today, challenges – that I contend – it cannot cope with.

Changes in societies across the globe in the twentieth century, and now in the twenty-first century, have been more significant than at any other period in the history of the Muslim *ummah*. Advances in astronomy and astrophysics are changing our views about the universe. Questions of human rights, which have developed over the past 50 years, have now become part of the discourse of all people, including Muslims. Similarly, questions regarding gender equality have placed many Muslim societies in an uncomfortable light. Until the twentieth century, gender *inequality* was not considered a problem of any significance in the Muslim world, but with the changing nature of society, its systems and institutions, women are now increasingly sharing all aspects of life with men.

Technological change is also transforming the way we understand the human body. Recent advances in genetic engineering and biotechnology are taking us to a world of which we know very little. Genetic manipulation and engineering is becoming commonplace and with that, ideas we have so far cherished about humanity, creation, God's intervention in human affairs, health and disease are being reconsidered. This is raising complex ethical, moral and legal questions that many Muslim scholars are ill equipped to deal with. As a result, classical ideas, methods and approaches need to be rethought. Change in some aspects of life is forcing Muslims to rethink some of the traditional views about the way they practise their religion. Some find this such a threat that their response is to disengage from intellectual challenges. For their part, Muslim scholars have to face this challenge square on.

It is in this context that I approach the question of the interpretation and relevance of the Qur'ān. The present book is not a complete solution to the problems Muslims are facing in relating the Qur'ān to the modern period. Rather, it is an argument for rethinking some of the traditional ideas in the area of interpretation of one particular aspect of the Qur'ān – its ethico-legal content – a project to which other scholars are also contributing. It suggests certain things that Muslims may need to do in order to relate the Qur'ān to the present time. Although it provides some ideas within which a rethinking can take place, it nevertheless should be considered as one part of a larger picture.

Most *tafsīr* literature are still modelled on traditionalist lines. For the great majority of the scholars writing on *tafsīr* today, the imperative is to be faithful to the tradition, while practising Islam in the modern world. Despite this need, the preservation of aspects of tradition and orthodoxy at the expense of a meaningful relationship between the Qur'ān and the people is found in almost all Muslim communities.

The neglect of the historical and social context in which these ethico-legal texts were revealed was a neat and easy way to provide textual 'proof' or 'evidence' for specific rulings that were arrived at in *fiqh*. In fact, the developing of law on the basis of textual evidence was so dominant in the formative period of Islamic law that it was considered untouchable. The purpose was to give the impression that the laws being developed were directly based on the texts of the Qur'ān and the traditions of the Prophet. The result of this thinking was that, even if there were no clear texts in the Qur'ān or the tradition, texts only distantly related to a ruling were used as supporting evidence for a law. In relation to the ethico-legal texts of the Qur'ān, this approach remained an important part of the Muslim exegetical and legal tradition.

Considerable difficulties arise, however, when we have to deal with the ethico-legal texts of the Qur'ān to solve problems that are new and specific to the modern era and we find the approach of both the classical *tafsīr* and *fiqh* inadequate. Scholars must therefore ask: 'Can a new framework be developed instead?' One answer, admittedly an extreme one, is that we do not need to look at so-called 'modern' problems as the answers arrived at in the pre-modern period can be applied just as well. A second, and equally extreme answer, is that we should discard the inheritance of the past, ignore difficult texts in the Qur'ān and the sunnah, and somehow develop what we think is appropriate for our own time. This answer divorces the Qur'ānic text from contemporary life. The third answer lies somewhere between and argues that we need to maintain a strong relationship between the solutions we are seeking and the Qur'ānic text. It is this third answer that I think is most relevant to the question of Qur'ānic values and ethico-legal matters. If we are to deal with contemporary issues, such as human rights, women's rights, how a society should be governed, the relationship of Muslims to non-Muslims and the questions of jihad and war, there has to be a new way of approaching, interpreting and understanding the Qur'ān. It is taking into account this issue that I propose the following model for the interpretation of the ethico-legal texts of the Qur'ān. The model in a sense is a summary of the ideas presented in the book. Readers may find the details related to specific components of the model throughout the book.

Brief explanation of the elements of the model

In the model outlined on p. 150, meaning is interactive: the reader is a participant in producing the meaning of the text, not a passive recipient who simply 'receives' meaning. The following are the interpretive stages and allows for meaning to be actively developed. They allow those interpreting the Qur'ān to place the text into a context and then interpret it more constructively.

Model of Interpretation

Text
Stage I
Encounter with the world of the text

Stage II
Critical analysis
Linguistic
Literary context
Literary form
Parallel texts
Precedents

Stage III
Meaning for the first recipients
Socio-historical context
Worldview
Nature of the message: legal, theological, ethical
Message: contextual versus universal
Relationship of the message to the overall message of the Qur'ān

Stage IV
Meaning for the present
Analysis of present context
Present context versus socio-historical context
Meaning from first recipients to the present
Message: contextual versus universal
Application today

Stage I

Encounter

- A broad and general familiarization with the text and its 'world'.

Stage II

At this stage, we are interested in what the text says about itself without relating it either to the first recipient community, or to the present, through the exploration of several aspects of the text:

- Linguistic: this relates to the language of the text, the meaning of words and phrases, syntax of the verse or verses and in general all linguistic and grammatical issues connected to the text. It also covers the *qirāʾāt* (different ways in which particular words and phrases can be read).
- Literary context: how the text in question (verse, verses) functions within a particular surah or more broadly the Qurʾān. For instance, what comes before and what comes after the verse or verses; the composition and structure of the text as well as its rhetorical style.
- Literary form: identifying whether the text is historical, a prayer, a proverb, a parable or a law. The literary form of the passage and its meaning are connected.
- Parallel texts: exploring whether there are other texts that are similar to the text under consideration in the Qurʾān and, if so, the extent to which they are similar or different.
- Precedents: identification of texts that are similar in content or import and whether these texts were revealed before or after the text under consideration.

Stage III

Relating the text to the first recipients of the Qurʾān:

- Contextual analysis: the historical and social information that would shed light on the text in question; analysis of the worldview, culture, customs, beliefs, norms, values and institutions of the first recipients of the Qurʾān in Hijaz. This would involve seeking to understand specific people the text addresses, where they were located and the time/circumstances in which the specific issues (political, legal, cultural, economic, for instance) arose.
- Determining the nature of the message the text conveys: legal, theological or ethical.
- Exploring the underlying messages and the specific messages that appear to be the focus of the text; and investigating whether the message is likely to be a universal one (not specific to a situation, people or context) or a particular message relevant to the context of the first recipient community and where in hierarchy of values the value/message is located
- Considering how the underlying message is related to the broader objectives and concerns of the Qurʾān.
- Evaluating how the text was received by the first community and how they interpreted, understood and applied it.

Stage IV

Relating the text to the present context:

- Determining the current concerns, problems, needs that appear to be relevant to the message of the text under consideration.
- Exploring the present social, political, economic and cultural context relevant to the text.
- Exploring the specific values, norms and institutions that have a bearing on the message of the text.
- Comparing the present context with the socio-historical context of the text under consideration to understand the similarities and differences between the two.
- Relating how the meaning of the text as understood, interpreted and applied by the first recipients of the Qur'ān to the present context taking into account the similarities and differences between the two contexts.
- Evaluating the universality or specificity of the message the text conveys and the extent to which it is related or unrelated to the broader objectives and concerns of the Qur'ān.

The points above will lead to the application of the message of the text under consideration to the present context and allow for a higher degree of application to the contemporary environment.

Classical *tafsīr* covered reasonably well Stages I and II and some elements of Stage III. Much of Stage III and Stage IV were not seen as important or relevant for the purpose of interpretation of the ethico-legal content of the Qur'ān in the pre-modern period.

Over the past 1,400 years, many layers have been built up over the Qur'ānic text and over rulings presumably developed in the name of the Qur'ān itself. Today, when Muslims talk about 'Islamic law', they refer primarily to *fiqh*. Rarely do they see the need to go back and examine the actual text of the Qur'ān. More importantly, the Qur'ān is read in line with the decisions and rulings that were arrived at in classical *fiqh*, not the other way around.

If we follow that way of interpreting the ethico-legal texts of the Qur'ān, we will make little headway in relating the concerns and problems of today to the guidance available in the Qur'ānic text. Mediating the guidance through *fiqh*, through juristic rulings, puts an unnecessary constraint on the Muslim of the twenty-first century in finding a closer connection between the Qur'ān and his or her own existence and reality. This is where a new way of looking at the text becomes important. This book provides a framework within which we can think about interpretation, the Qur'ān and our contemporary realities. I have sought to problematize the connection between the literal reading of a text and rulings based on a literal reading. I have argued that the literal reading of the text is an insufficient and ineffectual way to understand the Qur'ān. A literal understanding of the text does not provide the certainty some assume.

'Meaning' can be looked at in many ways. For the classical scholars, ambiguity of meaning was to be avoided where possible in the interests of formulating a clear-cut, easily implemented system of law. One of the ways in which classical Muslim scholarship on law and *tafsīr* developed laws that were clearly related to the text was by narrowing the range of meanings available for the text. In this book I argue that meaning is often indeterminate. This is not to say that the text was incomprehensible to its contemporaries or those who followed closely after its transmission. By 'indeterminate' I mean that we cannot narrow the range of meanings available to only one or two: we must keep the option open of finding new meanings and understandings for subsequent generations.

As I have tried to demonstrate throughout this book, erecting limits to the Qur'ān is unwarranted, even in relation to its ethico-legal texts. For the very first Muslims, the text of the Qur'ān was clearly related to their experiences and social institutions. There was no conflict between their circumstances and what the text required of them. However, when circumstances change, certain aspects of the meanings that we attribute to the text should also change, at least in their emphases. In other words, we are talking about the openness of the text to contemporary reality.

If meaning is fluid and susceptible to change, that is, it is dependent on time, linguistic context and socio-historical circumstances, then that has to be an essential part of our approach to the text. I have also tried to demonstrate that not all texts in the Qur'ān are to be read in the same way, because there is a high degree of fluidity in certain types of verses, for instance texts related to the 'Unseen'. The meanings we attribute to the 'Unseen' are mere approximations because we are dealing with something of which we have no experience and that we cannot even imagine. Despite this, the Qur'ān contains a vocabulary that is familiar to us in relation to the Unseen realm, thereby relating the 'unknowable' to our lived experience, but at the same time showing that there is a gap between the reality that the texts refer to and the human experience.

I have also tried to demonstrate that the approximation of meaning also applies to other types of text. My aim has been to challenge the strongly held idea that a literal meaning of a text can be arrived at easily and with certainty. If we can show that the bulk of the Qur'ānic texts can be seen as indeterminate in meaning, there is no reason why the same approach should not apply to the ethico-legal texts. The meanings of those texts are also inherently unstable, in the sense that certain aspects of meanings we attribute to them have in fact changed over time. These changes have been dependent on the social, political, historical and intellectual contexts that existed in Muslim communities at different times. Some aspects of the meaning of a text have been emphasized, while others have been given less importance. This emphasis and de-emphasis is a continuous process related to specific contexts, despite arguments to the contrary that there has been no change over 1,400 years. Even in the very early period of Islam, changes took place, and I have provided examples of this throughout the book.

In the past, preventing multiple meanings succeeded only when a society's political, economic, intellectual and social development was slow and there was historical continuity. However, even then, we find Muslim scholars challenging the status quo and putting forward new ideas for broadening the scope of *ijtihād* or the tools to develop the law. On the other hand, rapid developments in the modern world offer significant challenges to Muslims. These developments have threatened the stability of the pre-modern nexus between a society's development and the suppression of multiple meanings in the ethico-legal texts. We now see attempts by Muslim scholars to approach the Qur'ānic ethico-legal texts in new ways. Some are attempting to find a new way of connecting the developments in a society with the foundation texts of Islam, in particular the Qur'ān. This book also contributes to this project. It proposes a framework for anchoring a society in the Qur'ānic text. The book aims to provoke further discussion and analysis among Muslim intellectuals and other scholars of the Islamic texts; it does not set out to provide definitive, unproblematic 'answers'.

To this end, I have attempted to explore the idea of a hierarchy of Qur'ānic values, with particular reference to ethico-legal texts. These ideas do not necessarily go against the classical traditions of *fiqh* or *tafsīr* or the essential beliefs (*arkān al-īmān*), such as God, life after death, or what is spelt out as *ḥalāl* or *ḥarām*. These meanings are part of the basic structure of Islam, although in their interpretation there may still be ambiguities. However, in the more problematic parts of the ethico-legal texts, such as the instructional values or implementational values, where there is a high degree of ambiguity and complexity, we should be confident of developing ideas that will guide interpretation in new directions. This is not to discard the traditions of *fiqh* and *tafsīr*, but to recognize that a simplistic approach to the behaviour of a Muslim vis-à-vis the Qur'ān is problematic. The book attempts to emphasize the dynamism that has withered since the post-formative period of Islamic disciplines.

Glossary

ahl āl-kitāb People of the Book (Jews, Christians).
ahl al-sunnah The Sunnīs; 'orthodox' Muslims.
ahl-i-ḥadīth Followers of ḥadīth.
ahl-i-Qur'ān Followers of the Qur'ān.
aḥruf Translated at different times as 'letters', 'ways' or 'dialects'.
'ālim (pl. ulama) Scholar of Islam.
al-lawḥ al-maḥfūẓ The 'Preserved Tablet'.
al-lu'lu' Pearls.
al-marjān Corals.
al-mu'allafat qulūbuhum Those whose hearts are to be reconciled; new converts to Islam.
al-shirk Ascribing divinity to false powers.
arkān al-īmān Essential beliefs; pillars of faith.
'arsh Throne of God.
asbāb al-nuzūl Occasions of the revelation.
barakah Grace; blessing from God.
bid'ah Innovation in religious matters.
dirāyah Understanding; reason; opinion.
fāḥishah Indecent act; unlawful sexual intercourse.
fiqh Jurisprudence, the science of religious law in Islam; Islamic law.
fuqahā' Jurists in Islamic law.
ghayb What is hidden, unseen and inaccessible.
ḥadd Punishment for certain crimes in Islamic law.
ḥadīth An account of what the Prophet said or did or of his tacit approval of something said or done in his presence.
ḥadīth qudsī What God, speaking in the first person, addressed to the Prophet outside the Qur'ānic revelation.
ḥajj Annual pilgrimage to Mecca.
ḥalāl Permitted or permissible in Islamic law.
ḥarām What is prohibited in Islamic law.
ḥijāb Veil; headcover.
hijrah Emigration of the Prophet from Mecca to Medina in 622 CE.

ḥikmah Wisdom; underlying reason.

ḥudūd Plural of *ḥadd*.

ḥukm A rule or injunction that seeks to regulate the conduct of individuals who are capable of bearing legal obligations.

ʿibādah Various forms of worship and rituals in Islam.

ijmāʿ Consensus.

ijtihād Exercise of individual judgement in order to arrive at a solution to a problem in Islamic law.

ʿilm Knowledge; the opposite of *jahl* (ignorance).

ʿilm al-qirāʾāh The discipline of recitation of the Qurʾān.

imam Leader of the prayer; leader of an Islamic community.

imāmah Imāmate; leadership of the Muslim community.

īmān Faith; belief. In Islam, faith has three components: the internal conviction in the heart, the verbal expression and the performance of what is believed in action.

isnād Chain of authorities – an essential part of the transmission of *ḥadīth*.

jāhiliyyah Period of ignorance; pre-Islamic period.

jannah Paradise; garden.

jizyah Tax imposed on *dhimmīs* (protected non-Muslim minorities).

kāfir (pl. *kāfirūn*) A person who refuses to submit himself to God; a disbeliever in Allah.

kāhin Soothsayer.

kalām Speech; scholastic theology.

kalām allāh Speech of God.

kalimah (pl. *kalimāt*) Spoken word; utterance.

khalq al-qurʾān Creation of the Qurʾān; the famous debate over whether the Qurʾān is created or not, which occurred during the Abbasid period.

kitāb Book; scripture.

kitāb allah Scripture of God.

kufr Unbelief.

kulliyyāt Universals or 'five universal values'.

malak Angel.

mansūkh An abrogated verse.

maqāṣid al-sharīʿah 'The aims or purposes of the law.'

maṣlaḥah Public interest.

mathal Parable, proverb or popular saying.

miḥnah 'Testing' or 'trial'; inquisition.

miskīn Poor; destitute.

muʿāmalāt Transactions.

mubayyan Explained.

mufassir Interpreter of the Qurʾān.

muḥkam Clear; unambiguous.

muḥkamāt Clear, unambiguous verses.
mujmal Aggregate.
mujtahid A person engaged in *ijtihād.*
mu'minūn Believers; Muslims.
muṣḥaf The name given to a complete text of the Qur'ān considered as a physical object; codex.
mushrikūn Polytheists.
mutashābih (pl. *mutashābihāt*) Obscure; not clearly intelligible to the human mind; allegorical.
mutawātir ḥadīth A ḥadīth that, at every stage of transmission, has many narrators.
naskh Abrogation.
qirā'āt Recitation.
qiṣāṣ Retaliation.
qiṣaṣ al-anbiyā' Stories of the prophets.
qiyās Reasoning by analogy, the fourth source of Muslim law.
ra'y Opinion.
ribā Usury, interest or unlawful addition or gain.
riwāyah Narration; in modern Arabic usage has become an equivalent of story, novel or play.
sab'at aḥruf The seven ways; seven dialects.
ṣaḥābāh Companions of the Prophet.
saj' The rhythmic style practised by the pre-Islamic Arab soothsayers.
Salafiyyah Neo-orthodox brand of Islamic reformism, originating in the late nineteenth century and centred on Egypt, aiming to regenerate Islam by a return to the tradition of the 'pious forefathers'.
ṣalāt Five daily obligatory prayers; prayer.
ṣawm Fasting.
sharī'ah Rules and regulations governing the lives of Muslims, derived in principle from the Qur'ān and ḥadīth.
sunnah Normative behaviour of the Prophet. It is used sometimes to refer to ḥadīth.
Sunnīs A religio-political group in Islam (as opposed to Shī'ah); mainstream Muslims.
sūrah Designation used for the 114 independent units of the Qur'ān often translated as 'chapter'.
tābi'ī Successors; generation followed by Companions.
tafsīr An interpretation, generally of the Qur'ān. In most cases a work titled *tafsīr* will follow the text of the Qur'ān from beginning to end.
tafsīr bi al-ra'y Interpretation based on reason.
tafsīr bi al-riwāyāh Interpretation based on text/tradition. It implies that the interpretation of the Qur'ān should be guided by the Qur'ān itself, or the Prophet's instructions and his actual interpretations, or by his Companions and Successors.

taḥkīm Arbitration.
ṭalāq Divorce.
taqdīm Bringing forward.
taqlīd Blind imitation.
ta'wīl Interpretation; often used for mystical interpretation of the Qur'ān and dealing basically with the hidden meanings of its terms and concepts.
ulama Scholars of religion.
ummah Community.
uṣūl al-fiqh Works of *uṣūl al-fiqh* are concerned with the sources of the law (*fiqh*) and the methodology for extrapolating rules from revelation.
uṣūl al-tafsīr Principles of exegesis.
waḥy Revelation.
waḥy ghayr matluw Unrecited revelation.
waḥy matluw Recited revelation.
zakāt Obligatory payment by Muslims of a determinate portion of specified categories of their lawful property for the benefit of other enumerated classes.
zinā Adultery; fornication.
ẓulm In the moral sphere, it denotes acting in such a way as to transgress the proper limit and encroach upon the right of some other person.

Notes

1 Introduction

1 This is the area that is the primary focus of Islamic law. Based on such Qur'ānic texts and ḥadīth, Muslim scholars over the past 14 centuries have developed a body of laws usually referred to as 'Islamic law' or 'sharī'ah'.

2 This approach emphasizes the legal dimension of such texts as well as literal meaning.

3 The formative period of Islamic law is approximately the first two centuries of Islam, that is first/seventh and second/eighth centuries.

4 This is a term I will be using throughout this book. Those scholars who adopt a 'Contextualist' approach to the interpretation of the Qur'ān consider that it is important to interpret the Qur'ān by taking into account the socio-historical context of seventh-century Arabia as well as the contemporary context of Muslims today. See Fazlur Rahman, *Islam and Modernity: Transformation of an Intellectual Tradition*, Chicago, IL: University of Chicago Press, 1982, pp. 3–10; Farid Esack, *Qur'ān, Liberation and Pluralism*, Oxford: Oneworld, 1997, pp. 49–81.

5 See, for instance, Sayyid Abu'l A'la Mawdudi, *Towards Understanding the Qur'ān*, trans. Zafar Ishāq Ansari, Leicester: Islamic Foundation, 1995; Sayyid Quṭb, *Fī zilāl al-Qur'ān*, Bayrūt: Dār al-Shurūq, 1412/1992.

6 See, for some of such approaches to the Qur'ān, Suha Taji-Farouki (ed.), *Modern Muslim Intellectuals and the Qur'ān*, Oxford: Oxford University Press, 2004; Charles Kurzman, *Liberal Islam: A Source Book*, New York: Oxford University Press, 1998.

7 See, for instance, Rahman, *Islam and Modernity*, pp. 1–11.

8 In some of Mohammed Arkoun's writings, he has been arguing for a similar approach.

9 Daniel W. Brown, *Rethinking Tradition in Modern Islamic Thought*, Cambridge: Cambridge University Press, 1996, p. 48.

10 Amina Wadud-Muhsin, 'Qur'ān and Woman', in Charles Kurzman (ed.) *Liberal Islam*, New York: Oxford University Press, 1998, p. 129.

11 Mohammed Arkoun, *Rethinking Islam: Common Questions, Uncommon Answers*, trans. Robert D. Lee, Boulder, CO: Westview Press, 1994.

12 Esack, *Qur'ān, Liberation and Pluralism*, 1998; Farid Esack, *The Qur'ān: An Introduction*, Oxford: Oneworld, 2002.

13 Khaled Abou El Fadl, *Speaking in God's Name: Islamic Law, Authority and Women*, Oxford: Oneworld, 2001.

2 The context of the debate on interpretation

1 Nasr Hamid Abu Zayd, *al-Naṣṣ wa al-ṣulṭah wa al-ḥaqīqah*, Dār al-Bayda': al-Markaz al-Thaqāfī al-ʿArabī, 2000; Abou El Fadl, *Speaking in God's Name*; Asma Barlas, *'Believing Women' in Islam: Unreading Patriarchal Interpretations of the Qur'ān*, Austin, TX: University of Texas Press, 2002; Esack, *Qur'ān, Liberation and Pluralism*; Rahman, *Islam and Modernity*.

2 This section largely relies on the author's article submitted for publication in the *Encyclopedia of Religion*: Abdullah Saeed, 'Qur'ān: Tradition of Scholarship and Interpretation' (2005).

3 Practical exegesis is where the Qur'ān uses a particular term or concept (for example, *ḥajj* or pilgrimage) that the Prophet then illustrates by his actions – by performing it, for instance, and not necessarily explaining it in the form of an exegetical ḥadīth.

4 'Companions', or '*ṣaḥābah*', refers to the followers of the Prophet Muḥammad, who witnessed his mission and met him personally, and who died as Muslims. They are also sometimes referred to as the first generation of Muslims.

5 The Successors (*tābiʿūn*) are the generation of Muslims who followed the Companions or those Muslims who knew one or more of the Companions but not the Prophet himself.

6 Andrew Rippin, 'Tafsir', in Mircea Eliade (ed.) *The Encyclopedia of Religion*, New York: Macmillan, 1987, pp. 236–244.

7 Ibid.

8 Claude Gilliot, 'Exegesis of the Qur'ān: Classical and Medieval', in Jane Dammen McAuliffe (ed.) *Encyclopaedia of the Qur'ān*, Leiden and Boston: E.J. Brill, 2002, vol. II, pp. 99–124.

9 Shāh Waliullāh, *The Conclusive Argument from God*, trans. Marcia K. Hermansen, Leiden: E.J. Brill, 1996, p. xxviii.

10 J.M.S. Baljon, *Modern Muslim Koran Interpretation*, Leiden: E.J. Brill, 1961, p. 2.

11 J.M.S. Baljon, *Religion and Thought of Shah Wali Allah*, Leiden: E.J. Brill, 1986, p. 165.

12 Shāh Waliullāh, *al-Fawz al-Kabīr fi usul al-tafsīr*, Bayrūt: Dār al-Bashā'ir, 1407/1987, p. 112.

13 Ibid., p. 108.

14 Baljon, *Modern Muslim Koran Interpretation*, p. 3.

15 The work began in 1879 and was left unfinished at the time of his death in 1898. This *tafsīr* faced fierce resistance not only from ulama but also from Ahmad Khan's staunch admirers and friends.

16 A summary and analysis of Ahmad Khan's views on *tafsīr* is given by Christian Troll in his *Sayyid Ahmad Khan: A Reinterpretation of Muslim Theology*, New Delhi: Vikas Publ. House, 1978, pp. 144–170.

17 Muḥammad Rashid Riḍa and Muḥammad ʿAbduh, *Tafsīr al-Qur'ān al-ḥakīm al-shahīr bi-tafsīr al-Manār*, 12 vols, Bayrūt: Dār al-Maʿrifah, n.d., vol. I, p. 24.

18 Ibid., p. 19.

19 Ibid., p. 25.

20 Ibid., p. 20.

21 Ignaz Goldziher, *Introduction to Islamic Theology and Law*, trans. Andras and Ruth Hamori, Princeton, NJ: Princeton University Press, 1981.

22 Joseph Schacht, *An Introduction to Islamic Law*, Oxford: Clarendon Press, 1964.

23 Brown, *Rethinking Tradition in Modern Islamic Thought*, p. 48.

24 Baljon, *Modern Muslim Koran Interpretation*, p. 21.

25 Riḍa and ʿAbduh, *Manār*, vol. I, p. 340.

26 Quṭb, *Fī ẓilāl al-Qur'ān*, vol. I, p. 76.
27 Q.9–19.
28 Q.27:17–20.
29 Baljon, *Modern Muslim Koran Interpretation*, pp. 22–24; Khalifa Abdul Hakim, *Islamic Ideology, the Fundamental Beliefs and Principles of Islam and their Application to Practical Life*, Lahore: Institute of Islamic Culture, 1993.
30 Troll, *Sayyid Ahmad Khan*.
31 Muhammad Iqbal, *The Reconstruction of Religious Thought in Islam*, Lahore: K. Bazar, 1958, p. 85.
32 Baljon, *Modern Muslim Koran Interpretation*, pp. 43–44.
33 Ismail al-Faruqi, 'Towards a New Methodology for Qur'ānic Exegesis', *Islamic Studies*, vol. 1, no. 1, 1962, p. 36.
34 Ibid., pp. 36–37.
35 Ibid., p. 37.
36 Ahmad Hasan, *Early Development of Islamic Jurisprudence*, Islamabad: Islamic Research Institute, 1970, p. 222.
37 N.J. Coulson, *History of Islamic Law*, Edinburgh: Edinburgh University Press, 1964, p. 12.
38 Mawdudi, *Towards Understanding the Qur'ān*, p. 1.
39 Quoted by Ismail K. Poonawala, 'Muhammad Darwaza's Principles of Modern Exegesis', in G.R. Hawting and Abdul-Kader A. Shareef (eds) *Approaches to the Qur'ān*, London: Routledge, 1993, pp. 236–237.
40 John Burton, *The Collection of the Qur'ān*, Cambridge and New York: Cambridge University Press, 1977, p. 57.
41 Q.53:3–4.
42 This debate on the relationship between the Qur'ān and ḥadīth is more related to the issue of *ijtihād* and *taqlīd* and to what extent the rulings specified in the authoritative texts can or cannot be modified. For many modernists such a close relationship (for instance, both being revelation) would only hinder the Muslim from becoming more attuned to the modern worldview, outlook and thought.
43 Q.8:67.
44 Q.80:1.
45 Muḥammad b. Idrīs al-Shāfi'ī, *al-Risālah*, ed. Aḥmad Muḥammad Shakir, Bayrūt: al-Maktabah al-'Ilmiyah, 1980–1999, p. 78. ('God mentioned [in the above verses in fn. 18] the Book, which is the Qur'ān, and *al-ḥikmah* [literally wisdom]. I have heard from those whom I approve from among the learned that *ḥikmah* is the sunnah of the Apostle of God.')
46 Q.2:129, 151, 231; 3:164; 4:113; 33:34; 62:2.
47 Riḍa and 'Abduh, *Manār*, vol. I, p. 472.
48 Ibid., vol. V, p. 402.
49 Brown, *Rethinking Tradition in Modern Islamic Thought*, p. 44.
50 Ibid.
51 Ibid.
52 The first Ahl-i-Qur'ān movement was started in Lahore by 'Abd Allah Chakralawi (d. 1930), who began to use the term Ahl-i-Qur'ān in 1906. In addition to this, a second group of Ahl-i-Qur'ān, the Amirtsar group, led by Khwaja Ahmad Din Amirtsari (d. 1936), also continued its work in promoting the ideas of Ahl-i-Qur'ān.
53 Brown, *Rethinking Tradition in Modern Islamic Thought*, p. 40.
54 Ibid., p. 44.
55 Ibid., p. 45.

56 Ibid., p. 48.
57 Mannāʿ al-Qaṭṭān, *Mabāḥith fī ʿulūm al-Qurʾān*, Bayrūt: Mu'assasat al-Risālah, 1414/1994. pp. 329–331.
58 For example, Q.4:82; 23:68; 38:29; 47:24.
59 Q.4:82; 47:24.
60 Amina Wadud-Muhsin, *Qurʾān and Woman*, Kuala Lumpur: Fajar Bakti, 1992.
61 Philip Rice and Patricia Waugh (eds), *Modern Literary Theory*, London and New York: E. Arnold, 1989, p. 3.
62 Fatima Mernissi, *Women and Islam*, trans. Mary Jo Lakeland, Oxford: B. Blackwell, 1991; Barlas, *'Believing Women' in Islam*; Wadud-Muhsin, *Qurʾān and Woman*.
63 Mernissi, *Women and Islam*.
64 Fatima Mernissi, 'A Feminist Interpretation of Women's Rights in Islam', in Charles Kurzman (ed.) *Liberal Islam*, New York: Oxford University Press, 1998, 126.
65 Amina Wadud-Muhsin, 'Qurʾān and Woman', p. 129.
66 Rahman, *Major Themes of the Qurʾān*, p. xi.
67 Rahman, *Islam and Modernity*, p. 133.
68 Ibid., p. 1.
69 Ibid., p. 2.
70 Ibid.
71 Ibid.
72 Ibid., p. 4.
73 Ibid.
74 Abou El Fadl, p. 5.
75 Ibid.
76 Ibid., p. 6.
77 Ibid., p. 264.

3 Revelation and interpretation

1 'Revelation' is understood in terms of verbal or quasi-verbal communication by God to recipients who then pass on what they have received. 'Traditional Islamic concept of revelation' means the dictation theory of revelation held by Muslims, according to which the Prophet Muḥammad received the revelation in the Arabic language and passed it on to his followers in Arabic without any change or modification.
2 Kenneth Cragg (ed.), *Troubled by Truth*, Edinburgh: The Pentland Press Ltd, 1992, p. 3.
3 Rahman, *Major Themes of the Qurʾān*.
4 Abu Zayd, *al-Naṣṣ wa al-ṣulṭah wa al-haqīqah*.
5 Esack, *Qurʾān, Liberation and Pluralism*.
6 Fazlur Rahman, *Revival and Reform in Islam*, ed. Ebrahim Moosa, Oxford: Oneworld, 2000.
7 Fazlur Rahman, *Islam*, Chicago, IL: The University of Chicago Press, 1966, p. 31.
8 Rahman, *Islam and Modernity*, p. 5.
9 Rahman, *Islam*, pp. 30–1.
10 According to ʿĀ'ishah, the Prophet's wife, during the period of *jāhiliyyah*, Waraqah became a Christian and wrote in Hebrew. He would also quote, discuss or write about the Gospel. Bukhārī, *Ṣaḥīḥ al-Bukhārī*, trans. Muhammad Muhsin Khan, Riyadh: Dār-us-Salam Publications, 1996, p. 51.

11 Even in Islamic times, the alleged association of poets to *jinn* continued. For instance, the poet Farazdaq's *jinn* was ʿAmr. H.A.R. Gibb and J.H. Kramers (eds), *Shorter Encyclopaedia of Islam*, Leiden: E.J. Brill, 1961, p. 523.
12 Q.37:36.
13 Q.21:5.
14 A number of *kāhins* were fairly well known in the pre-Islamic period. In fact, most of the tribes had a *kāhin*, who would be approached about future events or dreams.
15 Q.69:41–42.
16 Q.11:40–48.
17 Q.2:131–136.
18 Q.19:10–11.
19 Q.5:113–119.
20 Q.15:32; 38:75, 77–78.
21 See for example, Q.7:101; 11:120; 12:3; 18:13; 40:78.
22 Toshihiko Izutsu, *God and Man in the Koran*, Tokyo: Keio Institute of Cultural and Linguistic Studies, 1964, p. 154.
23 Ibid.
24 Abu Hamid al-Ghazālī, *Ihya Ulum-id-Din*, trans. Fazul-ul-Karim, Lahore: Islamic Publications Bureau, n.d., Book one, p. 268.
25 Followers of the Ashʿarī movement, founded by Abū al-Ḥasan al-Ashʿarī (d. 324/935–936).
26 Followers of the Muʿtazilah school of theology. The Muʿtazilah movement was founded in Basra in the first half of the second/eighth century by Wāṣil b. ʿAṭā' (d. 131/748), subsequently becoming one of the most important theological schools of Islam.
27 al-Fakhr al-Rāzī, *al-Tafsīr al-kabīr*, Beirut: Dār Iḥyā' al-Turāth, 3rd edn, n.d., Part 27, p. 187.
28 Q.42:51.
29 Q.41:12.
30 Q.16:68–69.
31 Q.28:7.
32 Q.5:113; 4:163.
33 Q.8:12.
34 Zamakhsharī's interpretation of Q.42:51 in Helmut Gätje, *The Qur'ān and its Exegesis*, Berkeley, CA: University of California Press, 1976, p. 45.
35 Q.28:30.
36 Q.7:143.
37 Q.7:143–144.
38 Q.26:195.
39 Q.26:192–195.
40 Q.75:16.
41 Q.75:17.
42 Q.12:2. See also Q.20:113, 'Thus have We sent this down – an Arabic Qur'ān'; Q.39:28, 'It is a Qur'ān in Arabic without any distortion therein'; Q.42:7, 'Thus have We sent by inspiration to you an Arabic Qur'ān'; Q.43:3, 'We have made it a Qur'ān in Arabic, that you may be able to understand'; Q.46:12, 'And this Book confirms [it] in the Arabic language.'
43 Gätje, *The Qur'ān and its Exegesis*, p. 53.
44 Izutsu, *God and Man in the Koran*, p. 152.
45 Bukhārī, *Ṣaḥīḥ al-Bukhārī*, pp. 49–50.
46 Allamah Sayyid M.H. Tabataba'i, *The Qur'ān in Islam*, London: Zahra Publications, 1987, p. 65.

47 Q.10:37–38.
48 Q.11:13.
49 Tabataba'ī, *The Qur'ān in Islam*, p. 65.
50 Q.4:82.
51 Q.26:192–195.
52 Q.16:101.
53 Esack, *Qur'ān, Liberation and Pluralism*, p. 53.
54 Q.4:87; 20:9; 39:23; 51:4.
55 Q.3:64; 6:115.
56 Q.7:158; 18:27; 18:109.
57 Q.2:243; 3:41.
58 Izutsu, *God and Man in the Koran*, p. 152.
59 Q.20:133; 53:36; 87:18; 87:19.
60 Q.7:145; 7:150; 7:154.
61 Q.62:5.
62 Q.37:117.
63 Q.19:30.
64 Q.57:26.
65 Q.2:113.
66 Q.98:1–3.
67 Q.2:231; 4:105; 4:113.
68 Q.18:27.
69 Q.21:10.
70 Q.2:176; 3:7; 4:105; 6:154–157; 16:64; 29:47.
71 Gätje, *The Qur'ān and its Exegesis*, p. 58.
72 William A. Graham, *Beyond the Written Word*, Cambridge: Cambridge University Press, 1993, p. 89.
73 Rahman, *Islam*, p. 31.
74 As Rahman points out:

> orthodoxy, through the Hadith or the 'tradition' from the Prophet, partly suitably interpreted and partly coined, and through the science of theology based largely on the Hadith, made the Revelation of the Prophet entirely through the ear and external to him and regarded the angel or the spirit 'that comes to the heart' an entirely external agent.
>
> Rahman, *Islam*, pp. 31–32.

75 Cited in F.E. Peters, *A Reader on Classical Islam*, Princeton, NJ: Princeton University Press, 1994, p. 173.

4 Interpretation based on tradition and textualism

1 This is a concept coming from ḥadīth literature. In a ḥadīth there are two parts: the chain of narrators (*isnād*) and the text of the ḥadīth (*matn*).
2 Qaṭṭān, *Mabāḥith fī 'ulūm al-Qur'ān*, p. 350.
3 See, for a detailed discussion, Moḥammad Hashim Kamali, *Principles of Islamic Jurisprudence*, Selangor: Pelanduk Publications, 1995, pp. 109–175.
4 Qaṭṭān, *Mabāḥith*, p. 330.
5 Tabataba'i, *The Qur'ān in Islam*, pp. 130–134.
6 Ibn Taymiyyah, *Majmū'at al-rasā'il wal-masā'il*, Bayrūt: Dār al-Kutub al-'Ilmiyah, 1983, vol. XIII, p. 363; Ibn Taymiyyah, *Muqaddimah fī uṣūl al-tafsīr*, ed. Adnan Zarzour, 2nd edn, Bayrūt, AH 1392, p. 93.
7 Q.16:44.

8 Ibn Ḥajar, *Fatḥ al-bārī sharḥ ṣaḥīḥ al-Bukhārī*, Bayrūt: Dār al-Kutub al-ʿIlmiyyah, 1997, vol. I, p. 123.
9 Ibid.
10 Q.2:187.
11 Ibn Ḥajar, *Fatḥ al-bārī*, vol. IV, p. 629.
12 Ibid., vol. IX, p. 63.
13 Muḥammad ʿAbd al-Aẓīm al-Zurqānī, *Manāhil al-ʿirfān fī ʿulūm al-Qurʾān*, Bayrūt: Dār al-Kutub al-ʿIlmiyyah, 1988, vol. I, p. 16.
14 See, for further details on this, Claude Gilliot, 'Narratives', in Jane Dammen McAuliffe (ed.) *Encyclopaedia of the Qurʾān*, vol. 3, Leiden: Brill, 2001, pp. 516–528.
15 Ibn Ḥajar, *Fatḥ al-bārī*, vol. IX, p. 760.
16 Ṭabarī, *Jāmiʿ al-bayān*, vol. I, pp. 99–100.
17 *Ijtihād* is an exercise of individual judgement to arrive at a solution to a problem in Islamic law.
18 See, for some of the details, Ahmad von Denffer, *ʿUlum al-qurʾan*, Leicester: Islamic Foundation, 1983.
19 Ṭabarī, *Jāmiʿ al-bayān*, vol. I, p. 100.
20 Ibid., p. 58.
21 Ibid.
22 Ibid.
23 Muḥammad al-Khuḍari, *Tārīkh al-tashrīʿ*, Bayrūt: Dār al-Fikr al-ʿArabī, 1992, p. 232.
24 Ibid.
25 Ibn Taymiyyah, *Majmūʿ*, vol. XIII, p. 370; Ibn Taymiyyah, *Muqaddimah fī uṣūl al-tafsīr*, p. 96.
26 Kamali, *Principles of Islamic Jurisprudence*, pp. 109–175.
27 W. Montgomery Watt, *The Formative Period of Islamic Thought*, Oxford: Oneworld, 1998.
28 Imām al-Haramyn al-Juwayni, *A Guide to Conclusive Proofs for the Principles of Belief*, Ithaca, NY: International Specialized Book Service, 2001, pp. 237–240.
29 Ibid.
30 Someone who practises strict adherence to a text, particularly a scripture.
31 Q.5:3.

5 Interpretation based on reason

1 Mannāʿ al-Qaṭṭān, *Mabāḥith fī ʿulūm al-Qurʾān*, p. 323.
2 Ibn Manẓūr, *Lisān al-ʿarab*, Bayrūt: Dār Ṣādir; 1955–1956, vol. V, p. 55.
3 Q.25:33.
4 Qaṭṭān, *Mabāḥith*, p. 324.
5 Ibid.
6 Edward William Lane, *Arabic–English Lexicon*, New York: Ungar Pub. Co., 1955–1956, vol. IV, p. 1370.
7 The Qur'ān appears to use the word *asfār* in relation to *Tawrāt*, which means 'books'.
8 Zarkashī, *Burhān*, vol. I, p. 33.
9 Jalāl al-Dīn al-Suyūṭī, *al-Itqān fī ʿulūm al-Qurʾān*, ed. Muḥammad Abu al-Faḍl Ibrlāhīm, 4 vols in 2, Cairo, 1967, vol. IV, p. 194.
10 Ibn Manẓūr, *Lisān al-ʿarab*.
11 Lane, *Arabic–English Lexicon*, vol. I, p. 126.
12 Q.3:7.
13 Q.12:6.

14 Ibn Sa'd, *al-Ṭabaqāt al-kubrā*, 8 vols, Bayrūt: Dār Ṣādir, 1957–1960, vol. II, p. 365.
15 Zurqānī, *Manāhil al-'irfān fī 'ulūm al-Qur'ān*, vol. II, p. 7.
16 Suyūṭī, *Itqān*, vol. IV, p. 192.
17 Ibid.
18 Ibid., p. 193.
19 Ibid.
20 Ibid., p. 194.
21 An early theological school, whose representatives, such as al-Hasan al-Baṣrī (d. 110/728), advocated the idea of free will to choose actions, as opposed to predestination.
22 Shī'is are generally understood as those who are loyal to 'Alī b. Abī Ṭālib, the cousin and son-in-law of the Prophet Muḥammad and his fourth successor. Shī'ism holds the view that 'Alī is the only rightful successor to the Prophet and does not recognize the legitimacy of the three other caliphs before him.
23 Joseph Schacht, *The Origins of Muhammadan Jurisprudence*, Oxford, 1950, pp. 98–132.
24 Such works include Abū 'Ubaydah Ma'mar b. al-Muthannā, *Majāz al-Qur'ān*, ed. F. Sezgin, 2 vols, Cairo, 1954–1962, which focused on questions of metaphor.
25 Schacht, *The Origins*, pp. 98–132.
26 Cited in Norman Calder, '*Tafsīr* from Ṭabarī to Ibn Kathīr: Problems in the Description of a Genre, Illustrated with References to the Story of Abraham', in G.R. Hawting and Abdul-Kader A. Shareef (eds) *Approaches to the Qur'ān*, London: Routledge, 1993, p. 133.
27 Q.3:7.
28 Ibn Taymiyyah, *Majmū'*, vol. XIII, p. 361.
29 Norman Calder, '*Tafsīr* from Ṭabarī to Ibn Kathīr', pp. 101–134.
30 Q.80:31.
31 Ibn Taymiyyah, *Majmū'*, vol. XIII, p. 372.
32 Ibid., p. 373.
33 Ibid., pp. 373–374.
34 Ibid., p. 374.
35 Ibid., p. 305.
36 Q.20:5.
37 Ibn Taymiyyah, *Majmū'*, vol. XIII, pp. 294–313.
38 Ibid., p. 374.
39 Ibid.
40 Calder '*Tafsīr* from Ṭabarī to Ibn Kathīr', p. 133.
41 Ibid., pp. 131–133. Similar explanation without attribution to Anbarī is given in Zurqānī, *Manāhil*, vol. II, pp. 62–63.
42 Calder, '*Tafsīr* from Ṭabarī to Ibn Kathīr', p. 132.
43 Ibid.
44 The rules and regulations governing the lives of Muslims, derived in principle from the Qur'ān and ḥadīth.
45 Interpretation; often used for mystical interpretation of the Qur'ān dealing basically with the hidden meanings of its terms and concepts.
46 Ibn Rushd, *Faṣl al-maqāl*, Bayrūt: Markaz Dirāsāt al-Wiḥdah al-'Arabiyyah, 1999, pp. 39ff.
47 Coulson, *History of Islamic Law*, p. 12.
48 Majid Khadduri, *Islamic Jurisprudence: Shāfi'i's Risālah*, Baltimore, MD: Johns Hopkins Press, 1961, pp. 111–112.
49 Q.47:24.

50 Q.38:29.
51 Zurqānī, *Manāhil*, vol. II, p. 65.
52 Q.2:195.
53 Ibn Taymiyyah, *Majmū'*, vol. XIII, p. 359.
54 Muḥammad Husayn al-Dhahabī, *al-Tafsīr wa al-mufassirūn*, 3 vols, Cairo: Maktabat Wahbah, 1995, vol. 2, p. 408.

6 Flexibility in reading the text

1 Abū 'Amr al-Dānī, *al-Aḥruf al-sab'ah fi al-Qur'ān*, ed. 'Abd al-Muhaymin Tahan, Jeddah: Dār al-Manārah, 1997.
2 See Lane, *Lexicon*, vol. II, p. 550 for further details.
3 Suyūṭī, *Itqān*, vol. I, pp. 164–176.
4 Those of Abū Bakr, 'Umar, 'Uthmān, 'Alī, Ibn Mas'ūd, Ibn 'Abbās and Ubayy b. Ka'b. See Suyūṭī, *Itqān*, vol. I, p. 175.
5 Ibid., p. 165.
6 Zurqānī, *Manāhil*, vol. I, p. 175.
7 Ibid.
8 Ibid., pp. 156–157.
9 Ibid., p. 159.
10 Suyūṭī, *Itqān*, vol. I, p. 164.
11 Q.2:261.
12 Zurqānī, *Manāhil*, vol. I, p. 181. Some like al-Wāṣiṭī in his *al-Irshad fī al-Qirā'āt al-'Ashr* pointed out that there are 40 dialects. Zurqānī, *Manāhil*, vol. I, p. 182. See also Qaṭṭān, *Mabāḥith*, p. 162.
13 Sijistānī, *Kitāb al-maṣāḥif*, p. 64.
14 Qaṭṭān, *Mabāḥith*, p. 162
15 Bukhārī, *Ṣaḥīḥ al-Bukhārī*, vol. 6, book 61, no. 514, p. 483; Imām Muslim, *Saḥīḥ Muslim*, trans. Abdul Hamid Siddiqī, book 4, no. 1782, Beirut: Dār al-Arabia, 1993; Mālik, *Muwatta' Imām Mālik*, trans. 'A'isha 'Abdarahman at-Tarjumana and Ya'qub Johnson, book 15, no. 15.4.5. See also Zurqānī, *Manāhil*, vol. I, pp. 142–143.
16 Muslim, *Sahiḥ Muslim*, vol. 2, no. 1787, 1993, p. 391; Zurqānī, *Manāhil*, vol. I, p. 143.
17 Bukhārī, *Ṣaḥīḥ al-Bukhārī*, 'Khuṣūmāt, 1; al-Anbiyā', p. 54.
18 Ṭabarī, *Jāmi'*, vol. I, p. 19.
19 Bukhārī, *Ṣaḥīḥ al-Bukhārī*, vol. 6, book 61, no. 513, pp. 481–482; Muslim, *Sahiḥ Muslim*, book 4, no. 1785, p. 390.
20 Cited in Zurqānī, *Manāhil*, vol. I, p. 165.
21 Ibid.
22 E. Lammens and A.J. Wensinck, 'Mecca', in H.A.R. Gibb and J.H. Kramers (eds), *Shorter Encyclopaedia of Islam*, Leiden: E.J. Brill, 1961, p. 370.
23 Ṭabarī, *Jāmi'*.
24 Suyūṭī, *Itqān*, vol. I, p. 208.
25 Ibid.
26 Ibid.
27 Ibid.; Zarkashī, *Burhān*, vol. I, p. 236.
28 Sijistānī, *Kitāb al-masāḥif*, p. 25.
29 Ibid., pp. 20–25.
30 Q.15:9, 'Verily it is We Who have sent down the Dhikr (i.e. the Qur'ān) and surely, We will guard it [from corruption]'.
31 Zurqānī, *Manāhil*, vol. I, p. 170.

7 Abrogation and reinterpretation

1 Scholars of religious sciences; in Sunnī Islam they are regarded as the transmitters and interpreters of religious knowledge, and of Islamic doctrine and law.
2 Lane, *Arabic–English Lexicon*, Part 8, p. 2788.
3 Qaṭṭān, *Mabāḥith*, p. 232.
4 Q.2:106. Other verses adduced in support of abrogation include Q.13:39 and 16:101.
5 The only noted exception to this in the past was Abū Muslim al-Iṣfahānī (d. 1066), who rejected the idea of abrogation. However, in recent times, many Muslims, including Ahmad Khan, Muḥammad Ali, Muḥammad Asad and Ahmad Hasan, have rejected the doctrine of abrogation. For instance, see Ernest Hahn, 'Sir Sayyid Ahmad Khan's "The Controversy over Abrogation (in the Qur'ān)": An Annotated Translation', *The Muslim Word*, vol. 64, 1974, p. 128; Maulana Muḥammad Ali, *Introduction to the Study of the Holy Qur'ān*, Columbus, Ohio: Ahmadiyya Anjuman Isha'at Islam Lahore Inc. (1992), pp. 14–16; Muḥammad Asad, *The Message of the Qur'ān*, Gibraltar: Dār-al-Andalus, 1980, p. 23, fn. 87; Hasan, *Early Development*, pp. 60–79.
6 Hibatullāh, *al-Nāsikh wa al-mansūkh fī al-Qur'ān āl-karīm*, Dimishq: al-Yamāmah, 1407/1987, pp. 21–22.
7 Hasan, *Early Development*, p. 67.
8 David Powers, *Studies in Qur'ān and Hadith: The Formation of Islamic Law of Inheritance*, Berkeley, CA: University of California Press, 1986, p. 143.
9 Shāh Waliullāh, *al-Fawz al-kabīr*, Bayrūt: Dār al-Bashā'ir, 1407/1987, p. 60; Hasan, *Early Development*, pp. 67–68.
10 Qaṭṭān, *Mabāḥith*, p. 236.
11 Ibid., p. 237.
12 A ḥadīth that at every stage of transmission has such a large number of narrators that its authenticity cannot be disputed.
13 Qaṭṭān, *Mabāḥith*, p. 237.
14 Q.53:3–4.
15 Shāfiʿī, *al-Risālah*, pp. 106–108; Qaṭṭān, *Mabāḥith*, p. 237.
16 Qaṭṭān, *Mabāḥith*, p. 237.
17 Ibid.
18 The normative behaviour of the Prophet. It is used sometimes to refer to ḥadīth.
19 Qaṭṭān, *Mabāḥith*, p. 237.
20 Ibid.
21 Ibid.
22 In Islamic law, marriage between those who were breastfed by the same wet-nurse is not allowed.
23 Cited in Muslim, *Ṣaḥīḥ Muslim*.
24 Muslim, *Ṣaḥīḥ*, 'Stoning of a Married Adulterer', no. 4194.
25 But there are problems in using this as an example because 'Umar indicated that the reason for *rajm* is not because the two people who committed *zinā* are an old man and an old woman. Rather the reason for *rajm* is that *zinā* is committed by two people who are considered to be *muhṣan* (one who is or has been married). So it is problematic to use it as an example of the abrogation of recitation while the rule remains in force.
26 Q.4:15.

27 Q.24:2.
28 Hibatullāh, *al-Nāsikh wa al-mansūkh fī al-Qur'ān*, p. 121; Abū ʿUbayd al-Qāsim b. Sallām, *Kitāb al-nāsikh wa al-mansūkh*, pp. 90–91.
29 Q.58:12.
30 Q.58:13.
31 Shāh Waliullāh states that the number of abrogated verses reached 500; and at times it was unlimited (see his *al-Fawz al-kabīr*, p. 53). Suyūṭī brought the number of verses down to 20 (see his *Itqān*, vol. III, p. 77). Shāh Waliullāh reduced this number to five (see his *al-Fawz al-kabīr*, p. 60).
32 Hibatullāh, *al-Nāsikh wa al-mansūkh*, p. 70.
33 Ibid., p. 64.
34 Suyūṭī, *Itqān*, vol. III, pp. 78–79. Hibatullāh also holds the same view. See his *al-Nāsikh wa al-mansūkh*, p. 70.
35 Suyūṭī, *Itqān*, vol. III, p. 78.
36 Ibid., p. 68.
37 Ṣubḥī Ṣālih, *Mabāḥith fī ʿUlūm al-Qur'ān*, pp. 273–274.
38 A.J. Wensinck, *The Muslim Creed*, Cambridge: Cambridge University Press, 1932, p. 187; J.R.T.M. Peters, *God's Created Speech*, Leiden: E.J. Brill, 1976, p. 2.
39 Q.2:19.
40 Q.4:43.
41 Q.5:90.
42 Q.16:126–127.
43 Q.9:5.
44 W. Montgomery Watt, *Muhammad at Medina*, Oxford: Clarendon, 1953, p. 117.
45 Ibid., pp. 174–180.
46 Ibid., pp. 192–220.
47 Ibn Qayyim, *Kitāb al-Iʿlām*, vol. II, p. 11.
48 For example, see Hasan, *Early Development of Islamic Jurisprudence*; Powers, *Studies on Qur'ān and Hadith*; John Wansborough, *Qur'ānic Studies: Sources and Methods of Scriptural Interpretation*, Oxford, 1977; reprint, Amherst, NY, 2004; John Burton, *The Sources of Islamic Law: Islamic Theories of Abrogation*, Edinburgh: University Press, 1990.
49 Q.4:15.
50 Q.24:2.
51 Q.5:41.
52 Ṣubḥī Maḥmassānī's *Turāth al-khulafā'* has gathered a number of decisions of the first four caliphs and the Umayyad caliph ʿUmar b. ʿAbd al-Azīz in which these caliphs sometimes gave rulings different from the texts of the Qur'ān and sunnah. Ṣubḥī Maḥmassānī, *Turāth al-khulafā' al-rāshidīn fī al-fiqh wa al-qaḍā'*, Bayrūt: Dār al-ʿIlm li al-Malāyīn, 1984.
53 Majid Khadduri, *Islamic Jurisprudence*, p. 300.
54 Q.9:60.
55 Ṭabarī, *Jāmiʿ*, vol. X, pp. 161–163; Bayhaqī, *al-Sunan al-kubrā*, Bayrūt: Dār al-Kutub al-ʿIlmiyyah, 1414/1994, vol. XII, p. 20.
56 Maḥmassānī, *Turāth*, p. 341.
57 See Būṭī, especially his response to those who claimed that ʿUmar's jurisprudence included decisions that went against the Qur'ān. Muḥammad Saʿid Ramaḍān al-Būṭī, *Ḍawābiṭ al-maṣlaḥah*, Bayrūt: Mu'assasat al-Risālah, 1986, pp. 140–160.

58 Ibid., p. 142.
59 Wael B. Hallaq, *A History of Islamic Legal Theories*, New York: Cambridge University Press, 1997, pp. 150–153 and pp. 162–206.
60 Muhammad Asad, *Islam at the Crossroads*, Gibraltar: Dār al-Andalus, 1987, pp. 100–101.

8 The meaning of the text as an approximation

1 Ṭabarī, *Jāmiʿ*, vol. I, p. 33.
2 Ibid., p. 34.
3 Q.2:25, 'And convey good news to those who believe and do good deeds, that they shall have gardens in which rivers flow'; Q.18:107, 'Surely (as for) those who believe and do good deeds, their place of entertainment shall be the gardens of paradise.'
4 Q.42:11.
5 Bukhārī, *Ṣaḥīḥ Bukhārī.*
6 Zamakhsharī, *Kashshāf*, vol. II, p. 532; Asad, *Message*, p. 990.
7 Q.16:44.
8 Q.14:4.
9 For instance, Q.2:182, 192, 218, 225–226; 3:31, 89; 4:23, 25, 96, 100, 106, 110.
10 Q.79:21.
11 Q.8:5–12, 41–47.
12 Q.29:36, 'And to Madyan (We sent) their brother Shuʿayb, so he said: "O my people! Serve Allah and fear the Last day and do not act corruptly in the land, making mischief."'
13 Q.7:85–86.
14 Q.29:36–37.
15 Qaṭṭān, *Mabāḥith*, p. 349.
16 Ibn Kathīr, *Tafsīr al-Qur'ān al-ʿaẓīm*, Bayrūt: Dār al-Maʿrifah, 1987.
17 Among the works that specifically deal with Qur'ānic *mathal* is al-Māwardī, *Kitāb amthāl al-Qur'ān.*
18 Suyūṭī, *Itqān*, vol. IV, pp. 44–52.
19 Q.59:21.
20 Q.:27.
21 Q.2:17.
22 Q.2:18.
23 Q.17:29.
24 Suyūṭī, *Itqān*, vol. IV, p. 48.
25 Q.11:81.
26 Q.53:58.
27 Suyūṭī, *Itqān*, vol. IV, pp. 44–45.
28 Q.48:29.
29 Q.49:12.
30 Asad, *Message*, p. 230, fn. 141.
31 Q.7:175–176.
32 Q.2:275.
33 Q.2:261.
34 Q.2:264.

9 Recognition of the complexity of meaning

1 See for instance some of the debates in the twentieth century: Robert Detweiler and Vernon K. Robbins, 'Twentieth-century Hermeneutics', in Stephen Prickett (ed.) *Reading the Text: Biblical Criticism and Literary Theory*, Cambridge, MA: Blackwell, 1991.
2 See how Islamic legal scholars deal with this issue: Kamali, *Principles of Islamic Jurisprudence*, pp. 109–175.
3 Anthony C. Thiselton, 'Meaning', in R.J. Coggins and J.L. Houlden (eds) *A Dictionary of Biblical Interpretation*, London: SCM Press, 1990, pp. 435–438.
4 Esack, *Qur'ān, Liberation and Pluralism*, pp. 73–77.
5 Richard E. Palmer, *Hermeneutics: Interpretation Theory in Schleiermacher, Dilthey, Heidegger, and Gadamer*, Evanston, IL: Northwestern University Press, 1969, p. 51.
6 Ibid.
7 Ibn Taymiyyah, *Majmū'*, p. 370.
8 *Encyclopaedia Britannica*, 'Art: Meaning in Linguistics', MM edition, 1999.
9 Eddy M. Zemach, *The Reality of Meaning and the Meaning of Reality*, Hanover, NH: Brown University Press, 1992, p. 18.
10 Ibid.
11 Ibid., p. 2.
12 This idea is based on the discussion in Tzvetan Todorov, *Symbolism and Interpretation*, Ithaca, NY: Cornell University Press, 1982.
13 Kevin Hart, 'The Poetics of the Negative', in Stephen Prickett (ed.) *Reading the Text: Biblical Criticism and Literary Theory*, Cambridge, MA: Blackwell, 1991, p. 313.
14 Calder, '*Tafsīr* from Ṭabarī to Ibn Kathīr', p. 105.
15 Paul Procter (ed.), *Longman Dictionary of Contemporary English*, Harlow: Longman, 1978, p. 110.
16 Todorov, *Symbolism and Interpretation*, p. 9.
17 This should be signification, not meaning, since there are objections to the term 'meaning'.
18 Q.2:275–279; 3:130; 4:161.
19 Q.3:7.
20 Ṭabarī, *Jāmi'*, vol. III, p. 170.
21 Zamakhsharī, *al-Kashshāf*, vol. I, p. 337.
22 Ṭabarī, *Jāmi'*, vol. III, p. 172.
23 Zamakhsharī, *al-Kashshāf*, vol. I, p. 338.
24 Ṭabarī, *Jāmi'*, vol. III, pp. 172–173.
25 Ibid.
26 Ibid., p. 173.
27 Ibid., pp. 173–174.
28 Ibid., pp. 174–175.
29 Q.3:7.
30 Such as Mujāhid (d. 104/722), a student of Ibn 'Abbās.
31 Ṭabarī, *Jāmi'*, vol. III, p. 183.
32 Q.5:44.
33 Quṭb, *Fī ẓilāl*, vol. II, p. 898; Sa'īd Ḥawwā, *al-Asās fī al-tafsīr*, vol. III, al-Qahirah: Dār al-Salām, 1993, pp. 1391, 1396.
34 Gadamer's concentration on what the text has meant to generations of readers places the interpretative process in the context of history. Such an interpretation could be considered subjective but such subjectivity could be off-set by the critical reading of resultant interpretations by the interpretative community. See Detweiler and Robbins, 'Twentieth-century Hermeneutics', p. 240.

10 Socio-historical context and interpretation

1 Q.38:29.
2 Ghazālī, *Kayfa nataʿāmalu, p.* 28.
3 Ibid.
4 Q.4:11–12.
5 Fakhr al-Dīn al-Rāzī, *al-Ṭafsīr al-kabīr*, VII, p. 113.
6 Shāfiʿī, *Risālah*, pp. 534–535.
7 Ibn Qayyim, *Iʿlām al-muwaqqiʿīn ʿan rabb al-ʿālamīn*, Bayrūt: Dār al-Jīl, n.d., vol. III, pp. 11–38.
8 Ibn Mājah, *Ṣaḥīḥ Sunan ibn Mājah*, vol. 2, Riyadh: Maktab al-Tarbiyah al-ʿArabī, 1988, p. 784.
9 Ṭūfī's 'Risālah', in which he disussed the matter, is in ʿAbd al-Wahhāb Khallāf's *Maṣādir al-tashrīʿ al-islāmī fī mā lā naṣṣa fīhī*, Kuwait: Dār al-Qalam, 1972, pp. 106–138.
10 Q.8:41.
11 Abū Yūsuf, *Kitāb al-kharāj*, al-Qāhirah: al-Maṭbaʿah al-Salafiyyah, 1352/1932, p. 35.

11 Ethico-legal texts and a hierarchy of values

1 ʿAbd al-Salām al-Sulaymānī, *al-Ijtihād fī al-fiqh al-islāmī*, Rabat, Morocco: Wuzārat al-Awqāf, 1996, pp. 132–133.
2 For examples of such rulings, see, for instance: Maḥmassānī, *Turāth al-khulafā' al-rāshidīn fī al-fiqh wa al-qaḍā'*; Syed Sabahuddin Abdur Raḥman, 'Jurisprudence a la Umar – its Contribution and Potential', *Islamic and Comparative Law Quarterly*, vol. 2, no. 4, 1982, pp. 241–249.
3 Ṭūfī, *Risālah*.
4 Muḥammad al-Ṭāhir Ibn ʿAshūr, *Maqāṣid al-sharīʿah al-islāmiyyah*, Tunis: al-Dār al-Tūnisiyyah li al-Nashr, 1978.
5 Ismāʿil al-Hasanī, *Naẓariyyat al-maqāṣid ʿind al-Imām Muḥammad al-Ṭāhir bin ʿAshūr*, Herndon, VA: IIIT, 1995.
6 Q.5:38.
7 Rahman, *Islam and Modernity*, pp. 2–5.
8 Ibid., p. 20.
9 Fazlur Rahman, 'Towards Reformulating the Methodology of Islamic Law: Sheikh Yamani on "Public Interest" in Islamic Law', *New York University Journal of International Law and Politics*, vol. 12, no. 2, 1979, pp. 219–224. 1979, p. 221.
10 Rahman, *Islam and Modernity*, p. 5.
11 Ibid., pp. 13–22.
12 Q.2:256.
13 Q.7:199; 9:71; 22:41; 31:17.
14 Q.9:71.
15 Q.2:129, 231; 4:113; 33:34.
16 The following is recommended: *al-Muʿjam al-Mufahras lī maʿānī al-Qur'ān al-ʿaẓīm*, 2 vols, compiled by Muḥammad Bassām Rushdī al-Zayn, Bayrūt: Dār al-Fikr, 1996. It is a carefully prepared and comprehensive listing of what the author (al-Zayn) calls the 'meanings' of the Qur'ān.
17 The five categories are: obligatory (*wājib*), prohibited (*ḥarām*), reprehensible (*makrūh*), recommended (*mandūb*) and permissible (*mubāḥ*).
18 Q.16:116.
19 Q.10:59.

20 Q.5:90.
21 Q.66:1.
22 Q.5:96.
23 Q.2:187.
24 Q.5:5.
25 Q.5:1.
26 Q.2:173.
27 Q.2:275.
28 Q.4:23.
29 Q.2:228.
30 Q.2:229.
31 Q.4:19.
32 Asad, *Message*, p. 300.
33 Hallaq, *A History of Islamic Legal Theories*, p. 166.
34 Ibid., pp. 88ff.; Ḥasanī, *Naẓariyyat al-maqāṣid*, p. 46.
35 Hallaq, *A History*, p. 166.
36 This process means that a wide variety of pieces of evidence, which, in their totality, support a particular position and lead to certitude, when taken individually, do not rise above the level of probability. Hallaq, *A History*, p. 166.
37 Ibid.
38 Ibid., pp. 166–167.
39 Q.5:41.
40 Q.5:42.
41 Rāzī, *Tafsīr*, vol. XI, p. 230.
42 Muḥammad b. Idrīs al-Shāfiʿī, *Kitāb al-umm*, Bayrūt: Dār al-Fikr, vol. VI, p. 124.
43 Ibn Qudāmah, *al-Mughnī*, vol. X, p. 311.
44 Ibn Qayyim, *Iʿlām*, vol. III, p. 15.
45 Ibid.
46 Q.24:5.
47 Q.2:178.
48 Q.5:36.
49 Q.5:37.
50 Q.4:16.
51 Maḥmassānī, *Turāth al-khulafāʾ al-rāshidīn*, p. 229.
52 Ibid.
53 Muḥammad Saʿīd al-ʿAshmāwī, 'Shariʿa: The Codification of Islamic Law', in Charles Kurzman (ed.), *Liberal Islam*, New York: Oxford University Press, 1998, p. 53.
54 Q.4:2–3.
55 Q.4:34–35.
56 Q.4:36.
57 Q.4:89–90.
58 Q.4:86.
59 See Q.2:177; 4:36; 24:33; 90:12–17.
60 See W. Montgomery Watt, *Muhammad at Mecca*, Oxford: Oxford University Press, 1953; Watt, *Muhammad at Medina*; Rahman, *Islam*; Rahman, *Major Themes of the Qur'ān*.
61 Q.109:1–6.
62 Q.2:256.
63 Q.3:20.
64 Q.10:99.
65 Q.11:28.

66 Q.11:57.
67 Q.16:82.
68 Q.16:82; 18:29; 24:54; 51:54–55; 60:6; 64:12; 74:54–55; 76:29; 80:11–12; 81:27–28.
69 Q.9:29.

12 Epilogue

1 For example Āmidī's (d. 631/1233) *al-Iḥkām fī uṣūl al-aḥkām* was abridged by the author as *Muntahā al-sūl* and by Ibn al-Ḥājib (d. 647/1249) as *Muntaha al-sūl wa al-ʿAmal fī ʿIlm al-uṣūl wa al-jadal*. Ibn al-Ḥājib further abridged his *Muntahā* as *Mukhtaṣar al-Muntahā*.
2 Rahman, *Islam and Modernity*, p. 133.
3 Arkoun, *Rethinking Islam*, p. 43.

Bibliography

Abou El Fadl, Khaled, *Speaking in God's Name: Islamic Law, Authority and Women*, Oxford: Oneworld, 2001.

Abrahamov, Binyamin, *Anthropomorphism and Interpretation of the Qur'ān in the Theology of al-Qasim ibn Ibrahim: Kitab al-Mustarshid*, Leiden: E.J. Brill, 1996.

Abū Yūsuf, *Kitāb al-kharāj*, al-Qāhirah: al-Maṭba'ah al-Salafiyyah, 1352/1932.

Abu Zayd, Nasr Hamid, *Falsafat al-ta'wīl*, Dār al-Bayda': al-Markaz al-Thaqāfī al-'Arabī, 1996.

Abu Zayd, Nasr Hamid, *al-Naṣṣ wa al-ṣulṭah wa al-ḥaqīqah*, Dār al-Bayda': al-Markaz al-Thaqāfī al-'Arabī, 2000.

'Ali, Abdullah Yusuf, *The Meaning of the Holy Qur'ān*, Beltsville, MD: Amana Publications, 1989.

Ali, Maulana Muḥammad, *Introduction to the Study of the Holy Qur'ān*, Columbus, OH: Ahmadiyya Anjuman Isha'at Islam Lahore Inc., 1992.

Arkoun, Mohammed, *Rethinking Islam: Common Questions, Uncommon Answers*, trans. Robert D. Lee, Boulder, CO: Westview Press, 1994.

Arkoun, Mohammed, 'Contemporary Critical Practices and the Qur'ān', in Jane Dammen McAuliffe (ed.) *Encyclopaedia of the Qur'ān*, vol. 1, Leiden: E.J. Brill, 2001, pp. 412–430.

Asad, Muhammad, *The Message of the Quran*, Gibraltar: Dar al-Andalus, 1980.

Asad, Muhammad, *Islam at the Crossroads*, Gibraltar: Dar al-Andalus, 1987.

'Ashmawi, Muhammad Sa'īd al-, '*Sharia*: The Codification of Islamic Law', in Charles Kurzman (ed.) *Liberal Islam*, New York: Oxford University Press, 1998.

Asqalānī, Ibn Ḥajar al-, *Fatḥ al-bārī bi-sharḥ ṣaḥīḥ al-bukhārī*, vol. XIII, Bayrūt: Dār al-Fikr li'l-Ṭibā'ah wa al-Nashr wa al-Tawzī', 1411–1414/1990–1993.

Audi, Robert (ed.), *Cambridge Dictionary of Philosophy*, Cambridge and New York: Cambridge University Press, 1995.

Azad, Mawlana Abul Kalam, *The Opening Chapter of the Qur'ān (Surat-ul-Fatiha)*, trans. Dr. Syed Abdul Latif, Kuala Lumpur: Islamic Book Trust, 1991 [1962].

Baljon, J.M.S., *Modern Muslim Koran Interpretation (1880–1960)*, Leiden: E.J. Brill, 1961.

Baljon, J.M.S., *Religion and Thought of Shah Wali Allah*, Leiden: E.J. Brill, 1986.

Bar-Asher, Meir M., *Scripture and Exegesis in Early Imāmi Shiism*, Leiden: E.J. Brill, 1999.

Barlas, Asma, *'Believing Women' in Islam: Unreading Patriarchal Interpretations of the Qur'ān*, Austin, TX: University of Texas Press, 2002.
Bayhaqī, Aḥmad b. al-Husayn, *al-Sunan al-kubrā*, Bayrūt: Dār al-Kutub al-'Ilmiyyah, 1414/1994.
Boullata, Issa J., 'Literary Structures and the Qur'ān', in Jane Dammen McAuliffe (ed.) *Encyclopaedia of the Qur'ān*, vol. III, Leiden: E.J. Brill, 2001, pp. 192–205.
Brown, Daniel W., *Rethinking Tradition in Modern Islamic Thought*, Cambridge and New York: Cambridge University Press, 1996.
Bukhārī, *Ṣaḥīḥ al-Bukhārī*, trans. Muhammad Muhsin Khan, Riyadh: Dār-us-Salam Publications, 1996.
Burton, John, *The Collection of the Qur'ān*, Cambridge and New York: Cambridge University Press, 1977.
Burton, John, *The Sources of Islamic Law: Islamic Theories of Abrogation*, Edinburgh: Edinburgh University Press, 1990.
Burton, John, 'The Collection of the Qur'ān', in Jane Dammen McAuliffe (ed.) *Encyclopaedia of the Qur'ān*, vol. 1, Leiden: E.J. Brill, 2001, pp. 351–361.
Būṭī, Muḥammad Sa'īd Ramaḍān al-, *Ḍawābiṭ al-maṣlaḥah*, Bayrūt: Mu'assasat al-Risālah, 1986.
Calder, Norman, '*Tafsīr* from Ṭabarī to Ibn Kathīr: Problems in the Description of a Genre, Illustrated with References to the Story of Abraham', in G.R. Hawting and Abdul-Kader A. Shareef (eds) *Approaches to the Qur'ān*, London: Routledge, 1993.
Cason, John, Kamel el-Fadl and Fredrick (Fareed) Walker, *An Exhaustive Concordance of the Meaning of Qur'ān*, Baltimore, MD: Islamic Education and Community Development Foundation of Baltimore, 2000.
Chaudhary, Tahir, 'Tafsīr Literature: Its Origins and Development', in N.K. Singh and A.R. Agwan (eds) *Encyclopaedia of the Holy Qur'ān*, Dehli: Global Vision 5 vols, 2000, pp. 1473–1488.
Coggins, R.J. and J.L. Houlden (eds), *A Dictionary of Biblical Interpretation*, London: SCM Press, 1990.
Coulson, N.J., *History of Islamic Law*, Edinburgh: Edinburgh University Press, 1964.
Cragg, Kenneth, *Readings in the Qur'ān*, Brighton: Sussex University Press, 1988.
Cragg, Kenneth (ed.), *Troubled by Truth*, Edinburgh: The Pentland Press Ltd, 1992.
Dānī, Abū 'Amr al-, *al-Aḥruf al-sab'ah fi al-Qur'ān*, ed. Adby al-Muhaymin Thah, Jeddah: Dār al-Manārah, 1997.
Denffer, Ahmad von, *'Ulūm al-Qur'ān*, Leicester: Islamic Foundation, 1983.
Detweiler, Robert and Vernon K. Robbins, 'Twentieth-century Hermeneutics', in Stephen Prickett (ed.), *Reading the Text: Biblical Criticism and Literary Theory*, Cambridge, MA: Blackwell, 1991, pp. 225–280.
Dhahabī, Muḥammad Husayn al-, *al-tafsīr wa al-mufassirūn*, 3 vols, Cairo: Maktabat Wahbah, 1995.
Draz, M.A., *Introduction to the Qur'ān*, London: I.B. Tauris, 2000.
Esack, Farid, *Qur'ān, Liberation and Pluralism: An Islamic Perspective on Inter-religious Solidarity against Oppression*, Oxford: Oneworld, 1997.
Esack, Farid, *The Qur'ān: An Introduction*, Oxford: Oneworld, 2002.

Faruqi, Ismail R. al-, 'Towards a New Methodology for Qur'ānic Exegesis', *Islamic Studies*, vol. 1, no. 1, 1962, pp. 36–52.
Gätje, Helmut, *The Qur'ān and its Exegesis*, trans. Alford T. Welch, Berkeley, CA: University of California Press, 1976.
Gharnāṭī, Abū Ḥayyan al-, *Tafsīr al-baḥr al-muḥīṭ*, 8 vols, Cairo, 1911. Edited by 'Ādil Aḥmad 'Abd al-Mawjūd and 'Alī Muḥammad Mu'awwaḍ, Bayrūt: Dār al Kutub al-Ilmiyyah, 1993.
Ghazālī, Abu Hamid al-, *Ihya Ulum-id-Din*, trans. Fazul-ul-Karim, Lahore: Islamic Publications Bureau, n.d.
Ghazālī, Abu Hamid al-, *Iḥyā' 'ulūm al-dīn*, Bayrūt: Dār al-Ma'rifah, 1980–1993.
Ghazālī, Muḥammad al-, *Kayfa nata'āmalu ma'a al-Qur'ān*, Herndon: IIIT, 1992.
Ghazālī, Muḥammad al-, *A Thematic Commentary of the Qur'ān, vol.1: Surahs 1–9*, trans. 'Ashur A. Shamis, Herndon: IIIT, 1997.
Gibb, H.A.R., and J.H.Kramers (eds), *Shorter Encyclopaedia of Islam*, Leiden: E.J. Brill, 1961.
Gilliot, Claude, 'Narratives', in Jane Dammen McAuliffe (ed.) *Encyclopaedia of the Qur'ān*, vol. III, Leiden: E.J. Brill, 2001, pp. 516–528.
Gilliot, Claude, 'Exegesis of the Qur'ān: Classical and Medieval', in Jane Dammen McAuliffe (ed.) *Encyclopaedia of the Qur'ān*, Leiden and Boston: E.J. Brill, 2002, vol. II, pp. 99–124.
Gilliot, Claude, 'Exegesis of the Qur'ān: Early Modern and Contemporary', in Jane Dammen McAuliffe (ed.) *Encyclopaedia of the Qur'ān*, Leiden and Boston: E.J. Brill, 2002, vol. II, pp. 124–142.
Goldziher, Ignaz, *Introduction to Islamic Theology and Law*, trans. Andras and Ruth Hamori, Princeton, NJ: Princeton University Press, 1981.
Graham, William A., *Beyond the Written Word*, Cambridge: Cambridge University Press, 1993.
Hahn, Ernest, 'Sir Sayyid Ahmad Khan's "The Controversy over Abrogation (in the Qur'ān)": An Annotated Translation', *The Muslim World*, vol. 64, 1974, pp. 124–133.
Hakim, Khalifa Abdul, *Islamic Ideology, the Fundamental Beliefs and Principles of Islam and their Application to Practical Life*, Lahore: Institute of Islamic Culture, 1993.
Haleem, Muhammad Abdel, *Understanding the Qur'ān: Themes and Style*, London and New York: I.B. Tauris, 1999.
Hallaq, Wael B., *A History of Islamic Legal Theories: An Introduction to Sunnī usul al-fiqh*, New York: Cambridge University Press, 1997.
Hallaq, Wael B., *Authority, Continuity and Change in Islamic Law*, Cambridge: Cambridge University Press, 2001.
Hallaq, Wael B., 'Law and the Qur'ān', in Jane Dammen McAuliffe (ed.) *Encyclopaedia of the Qur'ān*, vol. III, Leiden: E.J. Brill, 2001, pp. 149–172.
Hart, Kevin, 'The Poetics of the Negative', in Stephen Prickett (ed) *Reading the Text: Biblical Criticism and Literary Theory*, Cambridge, MA: B. Blackwell, 1991, pp. 281–340.
Hasan, Ahmad, *Early Development of Islamic Jurisprudence*, Islamabad: Islamic Research Institute, 1970.
Hasanī, Ismā'il al-, *Naẓariyyat al-maqāṣid 'ind al-Imām Muḥammad al-Ṭāhir bin 'Āshūr*, Herndon, VA: IIIT, 1995.

Hawting, G.R. and Abdul-Kader A. Shareef (eds), *Approaches to the Qur'ān*, London: Routledge, 1993.
Ḥawwā, Sa'īd *al-Asās fī al-tafsīr*, vol. III, al-Qāhirah: Dār al-Salām, 1993.
Hibatullāh, *al-Nāsikh wa al-mansūkh fī al-Qur'ān āl-karīm*, Dimishq: al-Yamāmah, 1407/1987.
Hūd b. Muḥakkam (Muḥkim al-Huwwāri), *Tafsīr*, ed. Balḥājj Sa'īd Sharīf, 4 vols, Bayrūt: Dar al-Gharb al-Islāmī, 1990.
Ḥusarī, Aḥmad al-, *Istinbāṭ al-aḥkām min al-nuṣūṣ*, Bayrūt: Dār al-Jīl, 1997.
Ibn 'Āshūr, Muḥammad al-Ṭāhir, *Maqāṣid al-sharī'ah al-islāmiyyah*, Tūnis: al-Dār al-Tūnisiyyah li al-Nashr, 1978.
Ibn Ḥajar, *Fatḥ al-bārī sharḥ ṣaḥīḥ al-bukhārī*, Bayrūt: Dār al-Kutub al-'Ilmiyyah, 1418/1997.
Ibn Kathīr, *Tafsīr al-Qur'ān al-'aẓīm*, Bayrūt: Dār al-Ma'rifah, 1987.
Ibn Khaldūn, 'Abd al-Rahmān, *The Muqaddimah: An Introduction to History*, trans. Franz Rosenthal, 3 vols, New York, 1958; 2nd revised edn, Princeton, NJ: Princeton University Press, 1967.
Ibn Mājah, Muḥammad B. Yazīd, *Ṣaḥīḥ Sunan b. Mājah*, Riyadh: Maktab al-Tarbiyah al-'Arabī, 1988.
Ibn Manẓūr, *Lisān al-'arab*, Bayrūt: Dār Ṣādir; Dār Bayrūt, 1955–1956.
Ibn Qayyim al-Jawziyyah, Muḥammad b. Abī Bakr, *I'lām al-muwaqqi'īn 'an rabb al-'alamīn,* Bayrūt: Dār al-Kutub, 1996.
Ibn Qutaybah, *Ta'wīl mushkil al-Qur'ān*, ed. al-Sayyid Aḥmad Saqr, Cairo, 1954; Cairo, 1973; Medina, 1981.
Ibn Rushd, *Faṣl al-maqāl*, Bayrūt: Markaz Dirāsāt al-Wiḥdah al-'Arabiyyah, 1999.
Ibn Sa'd, *al-Ṭabaqāt al-kubrā*, 8 vols, Bayrūt: Dār Ṣādir, 1957–1960.
Ibn Taymiyyah, *Majmū'at al-rasā'il wal-masā'il*, Bayrūt: Dār al-Kutub al-'Ilmiyyah, 1983.
Ibn Taymiyyah, *Muqaddimah fī uṣūl al-tafsīr*, ed. Adnan Zarzour, 2nd edn, Bayrūt, n.p. 1972.
Iqbal, Muhammad, *The Reconstruction of Religious Thought in Islam*, Lahore: K. Bazar, 1958.
Izutsu, Toshihiko, *God and Man in the Koran*, Tokyo: Keio Institute of Cultural and Linguistic Studies, 1964.
Izutsu, Toshihiko, *The Structure of Ethical Terms in the Qur'ān*, Chicago, IL: ABC International Group, 2000.
Izutsu, Toshihiko, *Ethico-Religious Concepts in the Qur'ān*, Montreal: McGill-Queen's University Press, 2002.
Johns, Anthony H. and Abdullah Saeed, 'Nurcholish Madjid and the Interpretation of the Qur'ān: Religious Pluralism and Tolerance', in Suha Taji-Farouki (ed.) *Modern Muslim Intellectuals and the Qur'ān*, Oxford: Oxford University Press, 2004, pp. 67–96.
Juwayni, al-, *A Guide to Conclusive Proofs*, trans. Paul E.Walker, Ithaca, NY: International Specialized Book Service, 2001.
Kamali, Mohammad Hashim, *Principles of Islamic Jurisprudence*, Selangor: Pelanduk Publications, 1995.
Khadduri, Majid, *Islamic Jurisprudence: Shafi'is Risālah*, Baltimore, MD: Johns Hopkins Press, 1961.

Khuḍari, Muḥammad al-, *Tārīkh al-tashrīʿ*, Bayrūt: Dār al-Fikr al-ʿArabī, 1992.
Kurzman, Charles (ed.), *Liberal Islam: A Source Book*, New York: Oxford University Press, 1998.
Lammens, E. and Wensinck, A.J., 'Mecca', in H.A.R. Gibb and J.H. Kramers (eds), *Shorter Encyclopaedia of Islam*, Leiden: E.J. Brill, 1961.
Lane, Edward William, *Arabic–English Lexicon*, New York: Ungar Pub. Co., 1955–1956.
Luwayḥiq, ʿAbd al-Raḥmān b. Muʿallā, *al-Ghuluww fi al-dīn fī ḥayāt al-muslimīn al-muʿāṣirah*, Bayrūt: Mu'assasat al-Risālah, 1996.
Madigan, Daniel, 'Book', in Jane Dammen McAuliffe (ed.) *Encyclopaedia of the Qurʾān*, vol. I, Leiden: E.J. Brill, 2001, pp. 242–251.
Maḥmassanī, Ṣubḥī, *Turāth al-khulafāʾ al-rāshidīn fī al-fiqh wa al-qaḍāʾ*, Bayrūt: Dār al-ʿIlm li al-Malāyīn, 1984.
Masud, Muhammad Khalid, Brinkey Messick and David Powers (eds), *Islamic Legal Interpretation: Muftis and Their Fatwas*, Cambridge, MA: Harvard University Press, 1996.
Mawdudi, Sayyid Abu'l A'la, *Towards Understanding the Qurʾān*, trans. Zafar Isḥāq Ansari, Leicester: Islamic Foundation, 1995.
Mernissi, Fatima, *Women and Islam: An Historical and Theological Enquiry*, trans. Mary Jo Lakeland, Oxford: Pergamon Press, 1991.
Mernissi, Fatima, 'A Feminist Interpretation of Women's Rights in Islam', in Charles Kurzman (ed.) *Liberal Islam*, New York: Oxford University Press, 1998.
Motzki, Harald, 'Muṣḥaf', in Jane Dammen McAuliffe (ed.) *Encyclopaedia of the Qurʾān*, vol. III, Leiden: E.J. Brill, 2001, pp. 463–466.
Mujāhid b. Jabr, *al-Tafsīr*, ed. Muḥammad ʿAbd al-Salām Abu al-Nīl, Cairo, 1989.
Muslim, *Saḥiḥ Muslim*, trans. Abdul Hamid Siddiqī, Bayrūt: Dār al-Arabia, vol. 2, 1993.
Muthannā, Abū ʿUbaydah Maʿmar b. al-, *Majāz al-Qurʾān*, ed. F. Sezgin, 2 vols, Cairo, 1954–1962.
Nasafī, 'Sea of Discourse', in F.E. Peters, *A Reader on Classical Islam*, Princeton, NJ: Princeton University Press, 1994.
Nasafī, ʿAbd Allah b. Aḥmad b. Maḥmūd al-, *Madārik al-tanzīl wa-ḥaqāʾiq al-taʾwīl*, ed. Zakariyya ʿUmayrat, 2 vols, Bayrūt, 1995.
Naysābūrī, Abū al-Ḥasan ʿAlī b. Aḥmad al-Wāhidī al-, *Asbāb al-nuzūl*, Bayrūt: Dār al-Kutub al-ʿIlmiyyah, 1411/1991.
Palmer, Richard E., *Hermeneutics: Interpretation Theory in Schleiermacher, Dilthey, Heidegger, and Gadamer*, Evanston, IL: Northwestern University Press, 1969.
Peters, F.E., *Judaism, Christianity, and Islam: The Classical Texts and Their Interpretation, Vol. II: The Word and the Law and the People of God*, Princeton, NJ: Princeton University Press, 1990.
Peters, F.E., *A Reader on Classical Islam*, Princeton, NJ: Princeton University Press, 1994.
Peters, J.R.T.M., *God's Created Speech: A Study in the Speculative Theology of the Muʿtazilī Qādi l-gudāt Abūl-Hasan ʿAbd al-Jabbār ibn Ahmad al-Hamadānī*, Leiden: E.J. Brill, 1976.
Poonawala, Ismail K., 'Muhammad Darwaza's Principles of Modern Exegesis', in G.R. Hawting and Abdul-Kader A. Shareef (eds) *Approaches to the Qurʾān*, London: Routledge, 1993, pp. 225–246.

Powers, David, *Studies in Qur'ān and Hadith: The Formation of Islamic Law of Inheritance*, Berkeley, CA: University of California Press, 1986.

Proctor, Paul (ed.), *Longman Dictionary of Contemporary English*, Harlow: Longman, 1978.

Qadhi, Abu Ammaar Yasir, *An Introduction to the Sciences of the Quraan*, Birmingham: al-Hidayah Publishing and Distribution, 1999.

Qaraḍawī, Yūsuf al-, *al-Khaṣā'iṣ al-āmmah li al-Islām*, al-Qahirah: Maktabat Wahbah, 1981.

Qaṭṭān, Mannāʿ al-, *Mabāḥith fī ʿulūm al-Qur'ān*, Bayrūt: Mu'assasat al-Risālah, 1414/1994.

Qummī, Abū al-Ḥasan ʿAlī b. Ibrāhīm al-, *Tafsīr*, ed. Tayyib al-Mūsawī al-Jazā'irī, 2 vols, Najaf, 1967; Bayrūt, 1991.

Qurṭubī, Muḥammad b. Aḥmad al-Anṣārī al-, *al-Jāmiʿ li aḥkām al-Qur'ān*, 10 vols, Bayrūt: Dar al-Kutub al-Ilmiyyah, 1993.

Quṭb, Sayyid, *Fī ẓilāl al-Qur'ān*, Bayrūt: Dār al-Shurūq, 1412/1992.

Quṭb, Sayyid, *In the Shade of the Qur'ān*, trans. Adil Salahi and Ashur Shamis, Leicester: The Islamic Foundation, 2000.

Rahman, Fazlur, *Islam*, Chicago, IL: University of Chicago Press, 1966.

Rahman, Fazlur, 'Towards Reformulating the Methodology of Islamic Law: Sheikh Yamani on "Public Interest" in Islamic Law', *New York University Journal of International Law and Politics*, vol. 12, no. 2, 1979, pp. 219–224.

Rahman, Fazlur, *Islam and Modernity: Transformation of an Intellectual Tradition*, Chicago, IL: University of Chicago Press, 1982.

Rahman, Fazlur, *Major Themes of the Qur'ān*, Minneapolis, MN: Bibliotheca Islamica, 1994.

Rahman, Fazlur, *Revival and Reform in Islam*, ed. Ebrahim Moosa, Oxford: Oneworld, 2000.

Rahman, Syed Sabahuddin Abdur, 'Jurisprudence a la Umar – its Contribution and Potential', *Islamic and Comparative Law Quarterly*, vol. 2, no. 4, 1982, pp. 241–249.

Rāzī, Abu al-Futūḥ Ḥusayn b. ʿAlī, *Rawḥ al-jinān wa-rūh al-janān*, 12 vols, Tehran, 1962–1965.

Razī, Fakhr, *al-Tafsīr al-kabīr*, Bayrūt: Dār Iḥyā' al-Turāth al-ʿArabī, n.d.

Rice, Philip and Patricia Waugh (eds), *Modern Literary Theory*, London and New York: E. Arnold, 1992.

Riḍā, Muḥammad Rashīd and Muḥammad ʿAbduh, *Tafsīr al-Qur'ān al-hakīm al-shahīr bi-tafsīr al-Manār*, 12 vols, Bayrūt: Dār al-Maʿrifah, n.d.

Rippin, Andrew, 'Tafsir', in Mircea Eliade (ed.) *The Encyclopedia of Religion*, New York: Macmillan, 1987, pp. 236–244.

Rippin, Andrew, 'Occasions of Revelation', in Jane Dammen McAuliffe (ed.) *Encyclopaedia of the Qur'ān*, vol. III, Leiden: E.J. Brill, 2001, pp. 569–572.

Rubin, Uri, *Between Bible and Qur'ān: The Children of Israel and the Islamic Self-Image*, Princeton, NJ: The Darwin Press, 1999.

Saeed, Abdullah, *Islamic Banking and Interest: A Study of the Prohibition of Riba in Islam and its Contemporary Interpretation*, Leiden: E.J. Brill, 1996.

Saeed, Abdullah, 'Rethinking "Revelation" as a Precondition for Reinterpreting the Qur'ān: A Qur'ānic Perspective', *Journal of Qur'ānic Studies*, vol. 1, no. 1, 1999, pp. 93–114.

Saeed, Abdullah, 'The Charge of Distortion of Jewish and Christian Scriptures', *The Muslim World*, vol. 92, Fall, 2002, pp. 419–436.
Saeed, Abdullah, 'Fazlur Rahman: A Framework for Interpreting the Ethico-legal Content of the Qur'ān', in Suha Taji-Farouki (ed.) *Modern Muslim Intellectuals and the Qur'ān*, Oxford: Oxford University Press, 2004, pp. 37–66.
Saeed, Abdullah, 'Qur'ān: Tradition of Scholarship and Interpretation', in Lindsay Jones (ed.) *Encyclopedia of Religion*, 2nd edn, New York: Thompson, 2005, vol. 11, 7561–7569.
Saeed, Abdullah and Hassan Saeed, *Freedom of Religion, Apostasy and Islam*, Aldershot: Ashgate Publishing, 2004.
Schacht, Joseph, *The Origins of Muhammadan Jurisprudence*, Oxford: Clarendon Press, 1950.
Schacht, Joseph, *An Introduction to Islamic Law*, Oxford: Clarendon Press, 1964.
Schick, Robert, 'Archaeology and the Qur'ān', in Jane Dammen McAuliffe (ed.) *Encyclopaedia of the Qur'ān*, vol. I, Leiden: E.J. Brill, 2001, pp. 148–156.
Sells, Michael, *Approaching the Qur'ān: The Early Revelations*, Ashland, OR: White Cloud Press, 1999.
Shāfiʿī, Muḥammad b. Idrīs al-, *Kitab al-umm*, Bayrūt: Dār al-Fikr, 1993.
Shāfiʿī, Muḥammad b. Idrīs al-, *al-Risālah*, ed. Aḥmad Muḥammad Shakir, Bayrūt: al-Maktabah al-ʿIlmiyyah, 1980–1999.
Shawkānī, Muḥammad b. ʿAlī al-, *Fatḥ al-qadīr al-jāmiʿ bayna fannay al-riwāyah wa al-dirāyah fī ʿilm al-tafsīr*, 5 vols, Cairo, 1930; reprint, Bayrūt: Dār al-Maʿrifah, 1973.
Sijistānī, Abī Bakr ʿAbd Allah b. Abī Dāwūd Sulaymān b. al-Ashʿath al-, *Kitāb al-maṣāḥif*, Bayrūt: Dār al-Kutub al-ʿIlmiyyah, 1405/1985.
Sulamī, Abū ʿAbd al-Raḥmān Muḥammad b. al-Ḥusayn al-, *Ziyādāt ḥaqā'iq al-tafsīr*, ed. Gerhard Böwering, Bayrūt: Dar al- Mashriq, 1995.
Sulaymānī, ʿAbd al-Salām al-, *al-Ijtihād fī al-fiqh al-islāmī*, Rabat, Morocco: Wuzārat al-Awqāf, 1996.
Suyūṭī, Jalāl al-Dīn al-, *al-Itqān fī ʿulūm al-Qur'ān*, ed. Muḥammad Abu-l-Fadl Ibrāhīm, 4 vols in 2, Cairo: Al-Hay'ah al-Misriyyah al-'Āmmah li al-Kitāb, 1974–1975.
Suyūṭī, Jalāl al-Dīn al-, *al-Durr al-manthūr fī l-tafsīr bi-l-ma'thūr*, Bayrūt: Dār al-Kutub al-ʿIlmiyyāh, 1990.
Ṭabarī, Abū Jaʿfar Muḥammad b. Jarīr al-, *Jāmiʿ al-bayān ʿan ta'wīl āy al-Qur'ān*, Bayrūt: Dār al-Fikr, 1988.
Ṭabarī, al-, *The Commentary on the Qur'ān*, trans. J. Cooper, Oxford: Oxford University Press, 1987.
Tabataba'ī, Allamah Sayyid M.H., *The Qur'ān in Islam*, London: Zahra Publications, 1987.
Taji-Farouki, Suha (ed.), *Modern Muslim Intellectuals and the Qur'ān*, Oxford: Oxford University Press, 2004.
Todorov, Tzvetan, *Symbolism and Interpretation*, Ithaca, NY: Cornell University Press, 1982.
Troll, Christian, *Sayyid Ahmad Khan: A Reinterpretation of Muslim Theology*, New Delhi: Vikas Publ. House, 1978.
Ṭūfī, Najm al-Dīn al-, 'Risālah al-Ṭūfī fī riʿāyat al-maṣlaḥah', in ʿAbd al-Wahhāb Khallāf, *Maṣādir al-tashrīʿ al-islāmī fi mā lā naṣṣa fīhī*, Kuwait: Dār al-Qalam, 1972.

Wadud-Muhsin, Amina, *Qur'ān and Woman*, Kuala Lumpur: Fajar Bakti, 1992.
Wadud-Muhsin, Amina, 'Qur'ān and Woman', in Charles Kurzman (ed.) *Liberal Islam*, New York: Oxford University Press, 1998, pp. 127–138.
Waliullāh, Shāh, *al-Fawz al-kabīr fi uṣūl al-tafsīr*, Bayrūt: Dār al-Bashā'ir, 1407/1987.
Waliullāh, Shāh, *The Conclusive Argument from God*, trans. Marcia K. Hermansen, Leiden: E.J. Brill, 1996.
Wansborough, John, *Qur'ānic Studies: Sources and Methods of Scriptural Interpretation*, Oxford: Oxford University Press, 1977; reprint, Amherst, NY, 2004.
Watt, W. Montgomery, *The Faith and Practice of al-Ghazālī*, London: Oxford University Press, 1953.
Watt, W. Montgomery, *Muhammad at Mecca*, Oxford: Oxford University Press, 1953.
Watt, W. Montgomery, *Muhammad at Medina*, Oxford: Clarendon University Press, 1953.
Watt, W. Montgomery, *Bell's Introduction to the Qur'ān*, Edinburgh: Edinburgh University Press, 1970.
Watt, W. Montgomery, *Islamic Creeds: A Selection*, Edinburgh: Edinburgh University Press, 1994.
Watt, W. Montgomery, *The Formative Period of Islamic Thought*, Oxford: Oneworld, 1998.
Wensinck, A.J., *The Muslim Creed*, Cambridge: Cambridge University Press, 1932.
Wild, Stefan (ed.), *The Qur'ān as Text*, Leiden: E.J. Brill, 1996.
Zamakhsharī, Maḥmūd b. 'Umar al-, *al-Kashshāf 'an ḥaqā'iq ghawāmiḍ al-tanzīl wa-'uyūn al-aqāwīl fī wujūh al-ta'wīl*, ed. Muḥammad 'Abd al-Salām Shāhīn, 4 vols, Bayrūt, 1947/1995.
Zarkashī, Badr al-Dīn Muḥammad b. 'Abd Allah al-, *al-Burhān fī 'ulūm al-Qur'ān*, Bayrūt: Dār al-Jīl, 1408/1988.
Zayn, Muḥammad Bassām Rushdī al- (compiler), *al-Mu'jam al-mufahras li ma'ānī al-Qur'ān al-'aẓīm*, 2 vols, Bayrūt: Dār al-Fikr, 1996.
Zemach, Eddy M., *The Reality of Meaning and the Meaning of Reality*, Hanover, NH: University Press of New England.
Zurqānī, Muḥammad Abd al-Aẓīm al-, *Manāhil al-'irfān fī 'ulūm al-Qur'ān*, 3 vols, Bayrūt: Dār al-Kutub al-'Ilmiyyah, 1988.

Index

socio-historical context 1, 4, 26, 27, 107, 125; sunnah 78; towards alternative understanding of 38–41
Riḍā, Muḥammad Rashīd 11
right action 129; values related to 129–43

Saʿd b. Abī Waqqāṣ 74
Sabians 14
sacred: notion of 146
sacrifice 119
Saeed, Abdullah x
Saʿīd b. al-Musayyab 49
Salafīs x, 3
al-Ṣālih, Ṣubḥī 82
Sassanid empire 121
Saudi Arabia 2
Schacht, Joseph 13, 60
scholastic disciplines 105
scripture: conception of Qurʾān as 35–6, 53–4, 110–11, 113; and guidance 96; importance of socio-historical context 124; reconciling modern attitudes to ix
semi-Textualists 3, 82
seven *aḥruf*: interpretations and debates 69–74, 75–6
al-Shaʿbī 49
al-Shāfiʿī, Muḥammad b. Idrīs 123, 135; jurisprudential theory 16, 54, 85, 87, 88, 145, 146; work on ḥadīth 60, 65–6, 78
Shāh Waliullāh 10–11, 78
Shaltūt, Maḥmūd 13
sharīʿah 77, 88, 89, 133; disciplines 61, 64, 94, 96–7, 145; Textualist view of 123, 124; *see also maqāṣid al-sharīʿah*
Shāṭibī 88, 124, 127, 133, 145
al-Shaybānī 53
Shīʿah 59; *tafsīr* 10, 67, 68
Shuʿayb 95–6
six pillars of faith (*īmān*) 130
slavery 119
social changes: and abrogation 85, 89; and concerns of Muslims today 5
socio-historical context 1–2, 3–4, 7, 116, 118–20, 124–5, 152, 153; cultural language 122–3; laws of inheritance 120–2; and mutability/immutability issues 123–4; neglect of 149; in Rahman's methodology 4, 128; recognition of 117–18; revelation of Qurʾān 26, 27, 39, 41, 107, 108, 151
soothsayer texts (*sajʿ al-kuhhān*) 28, 29
speech of God: revelation of Qurʾān 29–34, 38, 82–3; three methods 31–2
'spirit of the Qurʾān' approach 67; Rahman 4, 6
spiritual development 85
spoken word 30, 35, 105
stoning to death verse 80–1
structuralist approaches 23
Successors 4, 48, 52, 62, 65; interpretation of Qurʾān by 6, 9, 10–11, 22, 42, 43, 48–9, 52, 103, 111, 126
Sufyān al-Thawrī 49
sunnah 2, 19, 20, 21, 38, 43, 65, 129; and abrogation 78–9, 85, 87, 88; idea of immutability of 82, 123, 132; reinterpretation and change in 124
Sunnī Islam 24, 56; hierarchy of authoritative sources 43, 50; meaning of *taʾwīl* 59; *tafsīr* 10, 68, 115
supernatural *see* mythological/ supernatural elements
Suyūṭī 69, 78, 85, 97, 98–9, 107
Syria 48, 52, 75

al-Ṭabarī 47, 49, 58, 72, 75, 90, 103, 107, 109, 111
Ṭabaṭabāʾī, Allamah Sayyid M.H. 34
tafsīr (exegesis) 1, 5, 154; based on reason 57, 59–60; classical tradition 4, 5, 8–10, 21–2, 27, 50, 128, 143, 149, 152–3; contemporary scholars seeking new approaches 147; diversity of approaches and methods 146; inclusive view 63, 64, 68; interpretation of historical events 94,

[illegible] subscription packages